REACHING THE AUTISTIC CHILD

Reaching the Autistic Child

A Parent Training Program

Revised Edition

Martin A. Kozloff

Brookline Books

ISBN 1-57129-056-7

Library of Congress Cataloging-In-Publication Data
Kozloff, Martin A.
    Reaching the autistic child : a parent training program / Martin
A. Kozloff. -- Rev. ed.
      p.   cm.
    Includes bibliographical references and index.
    ISBN 1-57129-056-7 (pbk.)
    1. Autism in children--Treatment.   2. Operant conditioning.
   3. Parenting--Study and teaching.   4. Autistic children--Education.
   I. Title.
RJ506.A9K69   1998
618.92'8982--dc21   98-14158
                                                  CIP

Cover design, interior design and typography by Erica L. Schultz.

Printed in USA by Data Reproductions Corporation, Auburn Hills, Michigan.
10 9 8 7 6 5 4 3 2 1

Published by
BROOKLINE BOOKS
P.O. Box 1047
Cambridge, Massachusetts 02238
Order toll-free: 1-800-666-BOOK

... we stand apart for a brief space, like spectators who are permitted to be witnesses of these tremendous struggles and transitions. Alas! It is the magic effect of these struggles that he who beholds them must also participate in them.

— FRIEDRICH NIETZSCHE

For Karen, Julian, and Anthony

Contents

Preface

For most major occupations, careers, and roles in this society there is an initial period of training from which the novice learns required skills. This is not so with parenthood. Perhaps to no other major role in our lives do we bring so litttle explicit knowledge. Most of us, like pioneers following a wind-blown trail, rely on trial and error, the "common sense" of elders and friends, or popular magazines.

A basic cultural assumption is that parents will be able to socialize a child so that he or she will function responsibly in society. While fads and trends in child-rearing have come and gone, the basic prescription has remained the same: A child who is well-loved and properly disciplined will turn out well enough. *How* one is supposed to love a child well and discipline him properly is another story. Fortunately, most of us "luck out," and our children learn to relate to their environments in personally satisfying and socially acceptable ways. Others are not so fortunate.

When developmental irregularities appear, parents are seldom prepared. They are confused about what is wrong, anxious about the future, strained by the extraordinary demands of caregiving, and sometimes burdened by the nagging question of whether they are to blame (Featherstone, 1980; Kozloff, 1979, 1994a; Weiss, 1991; Wilton & Renaut, 1986). When parents finally receive a diagnosis for their child, "autism," they may feel less confused—"At last we know what it is."—and relieved of self-blame—"It's a neurological problem." However, in the absence of early and extensive assistance, parents are unlikely to provide their child with the sort of family environment that their child's learning needs and capacities require. Parents may not know how to foster their child's attention and participation in activities, what to teach their child, or how to teach. Moreover, parents inadvertently may reinforce "behaviors" (e.g., screaming, making messes) they find hard to bear—for when their child gets what he or she wants, or is allowed to escape or avoid tasks and settings that the child's whining and tantrums "say" she does not like, the child is calmer and less of a problem. The reader can see a vicious cycle taking shape. The more a child's "condition" worsens, the more parents may doubt that their child can learn (change). If a child's problem behaviors and impairments finally exhaust a family's and school's coping resources, the child may be "placed" in a residential facility.

No matter what explanations of autism and forms of education and treatment are offered, the objective is teaching new behavior patterns. A child must learn to participate competently in mutually rewarding, instructive exchanges (turn-taking interactions) with others during conversation, meals, play, lessons and other social activities. However, for a child to learn and reliably use competencies that are functional in everyday environments, parents must know how to initiate and sustain productive exchanges with their child. This book presents in detail methods for fostering psychosocial development in autistic children and their families. The parent training program described here was developed and tested in a laboratory-school and in the home, and was designed to change the social environments of autistic children so that new and valued competencies, roles and identities were fostered, elaborated and sustained.

A few words about the tone of this book are in order. For some individuals, including myself, helping other persons to handle the sufferings conjoined with life ("The heart-ache and the thousand natural shocks that flesh is heir to...") is more than a vocation. However, progress is hampered by difficulties acquiring and organizing knowledge. We observe individuals and groups from different perspectives, on different levels of analysis, within different schools and paradigms. We dissect human activity into pieces easier to grasp. We never get the whole picture. Consequently, current theories offer partial explanations and generate incomplete remedies for human problems.

For those working to help autistic children and their families, criticism of theories and therapies is hard to take, perhaps because criticism implies that we are wasting not merely our time, but others' lives. To me, and certainly to other researchers and practitioners, the suffering involved in autism far outweighs the sting of criticism. Moreover, the urgent need for more effective prevention and treatment demands that we lower our defenses enough to see that no one has the complete solution and that we must continue working together to find one.

I would like to thank a number of people whose ideas, assistance, and encouragement made this book possible. I would like, first, to thank Dr. Robert L. Hamblin, former Director of the Instructional Systems Program for the Central Midwestern Regional Educational Laboratory (CEMREL), St. Ann, Missouri. Time has not weakened my debt to him for the opportunity to work in the Laboratory-school with autistic children and for his help designing and analyzing data from several experiments. Of greatest importance to me was Dr. Hamblin's conceptualization of direct learning and primary socialization as part of systems of social exchange. Through him, principles of respondent and operant learning, set in the broader context of social exchange, became relevant to the understanding and remediation of developmental disorders.

I remain indebted to Lois J. Blackwell, former Assistant Director of the Instructional Systems Program and head teacher of the Laboratory-school; currently Executive Director of the Judevine Center for Autistic Children, St. Louis, Missouri. Through Ms. Blackwell I received much of my training in the application of applied behavior analysis to the education of autistic children. Her ideas, encouragement, and help were invaluable.

I am deeply grateful to Robert E. Tyndall, Dean of the Watson School of Education; Roy E. Harkin, Professor of Education; Provost Martin K. Moss; and Chancellor James R. Leutze for appointing me to the faculty of the University of North Carolina at Wilmington, and for providing me with the time to prepare this book.

Many thanks to Erica Schultz, whose fine artistic sense and editing skills transformed a difficult manuscript into a fluent whole.

I gratefully acknowledge the help of CEMREL and Washington University for allowing me to use their facilities, which were funded by Contract No. OEC 3-7-062875-3056 awarded by the Office of Education and co-sponsored by CEMREL and the Social Science Institute of Washington University, St. Louis, Missouri.

My thanks to the parents who participated in the training programs are of a special nature. I hope they know that the work we put in together has been of benefit to other families of children with autism.

—Martin A. Kozloff

Donald R. Watson Distinguished Professor of Education
Department of Specialty Studies
Watson School of Education
University of North Carolina at Wilmington
Wilmington, North Carolina

1 Autism: Theories, Therapies, and New Directions

The Autistic Child

Leo Kanner's 1943 paper, "Autistic disturbances of affective contact," made autism a medical entity. It took twenty more years for autism to become a cultural entity—an intriguing (to outsiders) and devastating (to families) aberration of child development whose incidence, causes, and treatment were mysteries demanding solutions. According to an estimate made by the National Association for Mental Health in the early 1960s, over one half-million children in the United States suffered from "severe emotional disturbance," sometimes diagnosed with autism, childhood psychosis, or schizophrenia. These children were said to be confused as to their identities and unable to relate normally to persons, objects, and situations (Arnstein, 1965). With respect to children diagnosed with autism, prevalence estimates have ranged from the earlier figure of approximately 4 or 5 per 10,000 children (Rutter, 1965; Lotter, 1966, 1967) to more recent findings of about 1 per 1,000 children (Bryson, 1996), with a ratio of 3 or 4 males to each female. Differences in rates over time may reflect expansion of the list of criteria that define autism, increased reporting (Coleman & Gillberg, 1985; Wing & Gould, 1979), environmental pollution, and iatrogenic (illness-producing) effects of antibiotics (Rimland, 1997).

Severe behavioral excesses (too much problematic behavior) and behavioral deficits (too little socially desirable, personally functional and developmentally typical behavior) characterize the childhoods of many persons with autism. However, three characteristics have emerged as essential for diagnosis. These include: (1) difficulties forming and sustaining social relationships; (2) deficits in social communication via language; and (3) repetitive, stereotypical behaviors (Folstein & Rutter, 1987). As suggested by this list, the "symptoms" of autism are similar to symptoms of schizophrenia. However, unlike persons with schizophrenia, individuals with autism do not have a prolonged period of generally typical development. Moreover, the latest onset of autism is at least five years earlier than the earliest onset of adult-type schizophrenia (Folstein & Rutter, 1987, p. 84). Following is a composite picture of the behavioral repertoires, symptomatology, and psychosocial development seen in many individuals with autism. However, the reader should understand that there is no typical individual with autism and no universal course of autism. Therefore, what follows cannot be used to predict a child's future, but only to suggest what to look for.

The onset of autism (the beginning of a child's deviant trajectory of psychosocial development) often occurs in the first months of the child's life (Coleman & Gillberg, 1985). Early abnormalities of development crystallize into "autism" around the age of two and a half (Rutter, 1978; Folstein & Rutter, 1987). As indicated by the name itself, the most striking and pervasive feature of autism is a child's difficulty participating in the social world. Even with his or her parents, an autistic child may seem alone; in social relationships generally, he or she may be unattached or have a difficult time sustaining attachment (Mundy & Sigman, 1989). In particular, a child may: (1) pay little attention to other persons; (2) avoid physical contact and even the gaze of other persons (Lord, 1993; Lovaas, 1967; Hutt & Ounsted, 1966; Mirenda et al., 1983); (3) fail to initiate interaction with others, or initiate interaction in ritualized ways (Hauck, Fein, Waterhouse, & Feinstein, 1995; Kennedy & Shulka, 1995); (4) fail to imitate simple routine actions, e.g., waving bye-bye (Coleman &

Gillberg, 1985); (5) fail to follow simple instructions (Coleman & Gillberg, 1985); and (6) have much difficulty taking the role or standpoint of the other person (Baron-Cohen, 1990; Schopler & Mesibov, 1995), as indicated by not sharing attention with others to the same task at hand, not displaying empathy, and seemingly not understanding emotions displayed by other persons (Lord, 1993). In summary,

> The autistic baby is not able to benefit from his environment and often is unable to send feedback messages through meaningful glances and smiles to his parents to further parent/child interaction. The nurturing environmental stimuli, just as essential for the organizational growth of a human brain as food is for the physical growth of the human body, are improperly processed by these children, thereby depriving them of much of the emotional and cognitive nutrients that they need in the first years of life. (Coleman & Gillberg, 1985, p. 10)

Compare this with interaction between a typical two-month-old infant and his mother.

> The infant produces two long bursts of animated behaviour and one short one which is abruptly terminated by a shift of gaze away from the mother. In between these "displays" the infant looks attentively at the face of the mother who, at these moments, is calling or speaking to the baby. (Trevarthen, 1977, p. 239)

In other words, although there is no linguistic content, mother and child express (communicate) excitement about their interaction; the interaction has structure (turn-taking) which the infant partly understands; and each person engages in turn behavior that seems contingent upon (is cued by) and that reinforces (strengthens) the other person's behavior. This suggests that infants typically are geared into elementary forms of social interaction soon after birth. These interactions (exchanges) are the vehicle that *brings* infants into the already organized world of social activities. Similar to scripts (Martens & Hiralall, 1997), the exchanges teach children *how* to take part in social life.

A second feature of autism is "overselectivity" and "overreactivity" in attention and attachment. For example, a child with autism may: (1) pay attention to stimuli that are irrelevant to a task (e.g., a shiny bolt on a refrigerator door, rather than the handle); (2) stare fixedly and for long periods at spinning objects and flapping hands; (3) have "bizarre attachments to certain objects, such as stones, curls of hair, pins, pieces of plastic toys, or metals," apparently on the basis of color or texture (Coleman & Gillberg, 1985, p. 21); and (4) pay little attention and underreact to relevant events (e.g., verbal, facial, and postural cues signifying intentions, expectations and feelings of other persons) (Dawson & Lewy, 1989a; Green, Fein, Joy, & Waterhouse, 1995; Ornitz, 1989). It had been thought that overreactivity or "overactivation" was a chronic condition in autism (Hutt, Hutt, Lee, & Ounsted, 1964). This "stimulus overload" would help explain disorganized thinking, anxiety, social withdrawal, stereotypical behavior, and the narrow range of cues to which a child responds. However, recent researchers suspect that overarousal is variable—more and less intense over time. This, too, could help explain variability and unpredictability in mood, social behavior, and task performance (Kinsbourne, 1987).

Third, individuals with autism show uneven levels of competence across "functional domains" (Dawson, 1996; Dawson & Lewy, 1989b; Rutter, 1983). It is estimated that approximately 75 percent of autistic children are mentally retarded (Rutter, 1983). For example, autistic children may have much skill with spatial relations and memory along with severe impairments in the following areas.

1. Language. Autistic children generally acquire speech sounds in typical fashion and learn to form words, but are impaired with respect to comprehension and language use, e.g., sharing or requesting information and initiating or reciprocating in conversa-

tion (Green, Fein, Joy, & Waterhouse, 1995; Prizant, 1996; Rimland, 1964; Tager-Flusberg, 1989). For example, a child with autism may repeat over and over something another person just said or something he or she heard at some time—a behavior known as "echolalia" (Lovaas & Kassorla, 1966; Myklebust, 1995).

2. Social skills, e.g., greetings and goodbyes, understanding and following requests, jointly working at tasks, taking the role of another person.

3. Abstract reasoning, e.g., figuring out sequences and abstracting general principles from specific events; imagination.

4. Typical or appropriate play, e.g., imaginative and cooperative play (Hudson & DeMyer, 1968; Lewis & Boucher, 1995; Lord, 1993; Stahmer, 1995; Tilton & Ottinger, 1964). A child with autism may sit for hours rocking back and forth, staring intently at his or her fingers or at shiny objects. A child may make hundreds of ritualistic gestures during the day, moving his or her hands and fingers in a fixed pattern, pulling at his or her hair, twisting his or her face into strange expressions. When not physically or socially withdrawn, a child may wander aimlessly or run through the house, throwing things off tables, playing with water in sinks, pulling and pushing parents and siblings to turn on music, to get food, or anything he or she happens to want at the time. When frustrated, destructive behavior may increase (Lovaas, 1967); the child may bite himself or throw himself against the wall or onto the floor kicking and screaming.

Fourth, a child with autism may engage in self-injury or even self-mutilation, especially if he or she is nonverbal (Shodell & Reiter, 1968). Examples include pinching, scratching, biting or striking himself, raising callouses and welts and sometimes tearing his or her flesh (Lovaas et al., 1965; Schopler, 1995).

Finally, there is substantial evidence of neurological abnormalities or differences in individuals with autism (Dawson, 1996). For example, Reichler and Lee (1987) comment that autism is generally seen as "the expression of some underlying brain dysfunction" that is "associated with multiple etiologies, any one of which could potentially cause central nervous system dysfunction" (p. 15). Pathogenic agents range from genetic to infectious processes during prenatal (e.g., rubella and possibly cytomegalovirus), perinatal, early postnatal (e.g., herpes simplex infection), and later occurring conditions (Coleman, 1987; Reichler & Lee, 1987).

Early genetic explanations of autism and schizophrenia (represented by the work of Franz Kallmann, 1946; Kallmann & Roth, 1956; Bender, 1953; Bender & Grugett, 1956; Kringlen, 1970; Slater, 1953), usually proposed that hereditary factors predispose some individuals to respond to certain stimuli with a schizophrenic type of reaction. However, genetic theories did not rule out environmental effects; they proposed that environmental factors precipitated schizophrenia only in persons already genetically predisposed.

Today, there is rather strong evidence of a genetic component in autism (Bailey, Phillips, & Rutter, 1996). For example, one-egg (identical) twins have a higher probability than two-egg twins of both being diagnosed with autism. In addition, the probability of autism in siblings is 50 times higher than in the general population (Silliman, Campbell, & Mitchell, 1989). However, if genetic factors play a role in autism, it is not yet clear what that role is (Folstein & Rutter, 1987).

A number of early biogenic theories also focused on the structure and functioning of the central nervous system. For example, an interesting theory by C.F. Carlson (1967; more fully developed in DesLauriers & Carlson, 1969) proposed that autism is the result of arrested development in the two *neurological* systems responsible for drive energy and for affective contact and the experience of reward. The arrest in the development of the latter system results in a state of high activity in the child, but an inability of the child to "feel" the consequences of his activity, and hence, an inability to learn.

Ritvo et al. (1968) and Ornitz and Ritvo (1968, 1969) suggested that many symptoms of autism (language deficits, inconsistent or nonexistent imitative behavior, disturbances of relating, heightened sensitivities, etc.) could be seen as manifestations of "perceptual inconstancy," meaning that "identical percepts from the environment are not experienced as the same each time" (Ornitz & Ritvo, 1969, p. 431). Ornitz and Ritvo further traced perceptual inconstancy to an underlying failure of homeostatic regulation within the central nervous system. The autistic child, they proposed, experiences random sensory overloading and underloading, which accounts for alternating periods of extreme excitation and inhibition, frenzy and withdrawal.

Another earlier biogenic theory was Rimland's (1964) theory of "cognitive dysfunction." Rimland argued that the basis of the autism syndrome is the child's impaired ability to relate new stimuli to remembered experience. Hence, the child does not use speech to communicate because he cannot symbolize or abstract from concrete particulars. And he is unresponsive to his parents because he does not associate them with previous pleasurable experiences. Rimland proposed that the "cause" of the child's cognitive dysfunction is an impairment in the brain's reticular formation—the part of the brain which is felt by many to link sensory input and prior content. Such impairment, he hypothesizes, may be the consequence of an excess of oxygen given in infancy, which destroyed the not-yet-developed reticular tissue. The autistic child, he argues, may be predisposed to oversensitivity to oxygen.

A third group within the early biogenic approach focused on biochemical and metabolic abnormalities. Earlier studies by Kety (1959), for instance, pointed to faulty metabolism of epinephrine. Later, Goodwin et al. (1971), in a study of 15 autistic children, found abnormal responses in the children's TCDC (Transcephalic Direct Current) system to gliadin and variations in cortisol levels, suggesting a correlation between autism and malabsorption or sensitivities to food. Bouillin et al. (1971), moreover, found rather consistent differences between autistic, nonautistic psychotic, and normal children on the efflux of 5-hydroxytryptamine from blood platelets.

Finally, several early physiological theories suggested that autism is *not* the direct result of a specific biochemical imbalance or neurological defect, but rather, is a secondary reaction to such defects. Bender, for example, saw autism as not itself an inborn impairment of the nervous system, but a *defensive reaction* to one. Bender felt that by withdrawing, the child protects himself from the anxiety and disorganization arising from the more basic genetic or structural pathology (Bender, 1960). Similarly, Goldstein viewed autism as a defense against the child's inability to engage in abstract thinking. Again, autism was seen as a protective mechanism safeguarding the child from unbearable anxiety (Goldstein, 1959).

Recent medical research has found additional factors that may start a trajectory towards the diagnosis of autism and may help explain certain behavioral excesses and developmental deficits identified earlier. For example, some researchers have found:

1. Elevated levels of serotonin and dopamine in the blood, immature patterns of circadian rhythms for corticosteroids, and abnormalities in brain-stem auditory evoked responses (Campbell, Perry, Small, & Green, 1987; Coleman & Gillberg, 1985; Volkmar & Anderson, 1989).
2. Abnormalities (e.g., reduced size, or hypoplasia) of the brain's cerebellar vermis, which may help explain difficulties in arousal, attention, speech and motor output (Courchesne, 1989; Hashimoto et al., 1995).
3. Possible overactivation of the right hemisphere of the brain, which may help explain "chronic high levels of arousal" and therefore overselectivity to novelty and underattention to speech and social cues (e.g., facial expressions) (Dawson & Lewy, 1989b).

A variety of medications, vitamins, dietary changes, and psychiatric treatments have been used over the years—not as remedies for autism per se, but for specific symptoms and associated problems, such as seizures, destructive behavior, and stimulus overreactivity (Gualtieri, Evans, & Patterson, 1987). These include vitamin B6, Deanol, chlorpromazine, clozapine, imipramine, gluten free diets, lithium, haloperidol, fenfluramine, L-dopa, D-amphetamine, Naltrexone, electroconvulsive therapy, insulin coma therapy, opiate antagonists, and leucotomy (Campbell, Perry, Small, & Green, 1987; Coleman & Gillberg, 1985; Goodwin et al., 1971; Hammock, Schroeder, & Levine, 1995; Hittner, 1994; Lewis, 1996; Pfeiffer, Norton, Nelson, & Shott, 1995; Quintana et al., 1995; Rimland, 1964, 1968; Rutter, Greenfield, & Lockyer, 1967; Tobias, 1959). Results have ranged from poor to good. The current situation with respect to medical explanations and treatments is perhaps best summarized by Waterhouse, Wing, and Fein (1989):

> Despite clinical impressions of a unity among typically autistic children, investigations of the group, regardless of which set of diagnostic criteria has been used, have found no shared etiology, no shared uniquely pathognomic neural deficit, no shared cognitive deficit, no distinct shared behavioral pattern, no shared specific life course, and no shared response to drug treatment.

The lives of many individuals with autism are characterized by *marginality* with respect to ordinary adolescent and adult activities (DeMyer et al., 1973; Eisenberg, 1956; Lotter, 1974). Several decades ago, for example, Rutter et al. (1967) stated that a minority of persons with autism reached a good level of social adjustment by adolescence, and even fewer entered paid employment. Recent research is more encouraging. As an autistic child grows through adolescence and adulthood, there is a decrease in activity level, greater ease at managing undesirable behavior, and improvement in language, sociability, and activities of daily living (Mesibov, 1983). Indeed, good outcomes (e.g., social relatedness and independent living) appear to be predicted by reactions to sound, less problem behavior at earlier ages, language, schooling, and higher IQ in early childhood (Coleman & Gillberg, 1985). Still, the likelihood that persons with autism will more competently participate in the social world depends very much on: (1) continuing education programs; (2) living and working opportunities that are congruent with the learning needs and preferences of persons with autism, and that can manage and reduce difficult behaviors without stifling psychosocial development; and (3) skills and continued involvement of families (Schroeder & LeBlanc, 1996). This last is the subject to which we now turn.

The research reported in this book rests on several assumptions and hypotheses. First, a curriculum for autistic children ought to synthesize contributions of *many* (even typically opposed) bodies of knowledge to our understanding of psychosocial development. Contributors include:

1. *Respondent learning*—on how movements are assembled into reflexive emotional and attention responses.
2. *Operant learning*—on how contingencies of reinforcement teach individuals to perform actions with more or less skill, frequency, fluency, intensity, generality and duration.
3. *Applied behavior analysis*—on using principles of respondent and operant learning to assess an individual's behavioral repertoire and environments, and suggest how to foster beneficial change.
4. *Social exchange theory*—on how individuals teach and learn from each other during interaction.
5. *Cognitive developmental psychology and ecological psychology*— on how routine tasks and activities in a person's round of daily life (akin to scripts, frames, templates, or scaffolds) help a person organize actions into larger classes and sequences (Barker, 1963, 1968; Bronfenbrenner, 1979; Bruner, 1983; Connolly & Dalgleish, 1989; Fogel, 1992; Piaget, 1954; Valsiner, 1987; Vygotsky, 1978).
6. The *personalization process*—by which valued vs. degraded social positions, roles, and identities are bestowed on children (Henry, 1966; Kozloff, 1994a).

Second, since this research entailed extensive observation of parents and children in natural and experimental conditions, I expected to identify exchange patterns that "control" (foster, shape) children's desirable and undesirable behaviors. Third, the research tests the propositions that parents can be taught to: (1) modify long-standing interaction patterns or exchanges with their children; (2) effectively teach their children in a laboratory-school; (3) generalize productive interaction and effective instruction to the home; and therefore (4) substantially improve their children's competencies, problem behaviors, and participation in family life.

Finally, it was hoped that this study of family exchanges would yield important findings on psychosocial development in general.

To the extent the research was successful, it contributes to the assessment and treatment of children with autism. It also demonstrates how a curriculum for children and training for families can be made available to the only persons upon whom children with autism can really depend.

Training Parents as Teacher-Therapists: An Overview

The professional healer or therapist is relatively new. Before the medical doctor, psychotherapist, or applied behavior analyst, individuals with serious problems received help from persons in other social institutions—priest, shaman (Frank, 1961), and of course family and friends. Until the 1960s, parents of children with autism were considered either detrimental or incidental to the treatment or socialization of their children, perhaps as a result of theories that implicated parents in the causation of severe childhood disorders. At present, systematic efforts are made to teach parents to be teacher-therapists in programs for educating, treating, or socializing their children. Recognition of several facts accounts for this trend.

First, early, skillful and sustained involvement of families in the education and treatment of children with autism is *necessary* for the children's psychosocial development, that is, for substantial growth in their competence, roles, and identities (Bricker & Casuso, 1979; Bromwich, 1976; Cutler, 1991; Jones, 1980; Kogan, Tylor, & Turner, 1974). For example, parents have extensive and detailed *practical* knowledge of their children's strengths, impairments, capacities, learning needs and preferences (e.g., reinforcers and effective prompts). This knowledge vastly improves assessments, program plans, and instruction. In addition, parent training and involvement increase children's *rates of learning* (Kaufman, 1977; Kaufman, Prinz, Bakalor, Tyson, & Paradise, 1978) and make it possible to plan and employ ways to help children generalize and adapt skills learned in school or at home (e.g., making requests, playing) to different environments. Yet, parents seldom have sufficient knowledge and skill to navigate the complex and often fragmented service delivery systems, to collaborate with educators and other service providers, and to satisfy their children's special needs in the home (Brewer & Kakalik, 1979; Canter & Canter, 1991; Turnbull & Turnbull, 1990).

Second, in the absence of timely and adequate parent training and support, autistic children's developmental deficits and behavioral excesses may worsen; children's social place and identity may become more deviant and disvalued (e.g., "our sweet child" and "our child no matter how challenging" may become "our burden" and even "our adversary"); and parents' desperation and social isolation may increase (DeMyer, 1979; Wilton & Renault, 1986), sometimes leading to depression, marital conflict, or removal of the child from the classroom, school, or family (Brotherson & Goldstein, 1992; Cutler, 1991; Cutler & Kozloff, 1987; Darling, 1979; Fogon & Schor, 1993; Kozloff, 1979, 1988, 1994a; Weiss, 1991). However, timely and adequate assistance helps maintain the integrity of family systems strained by parents' grief, overwork, and experience of social rejection (Jennings, 1990).

A third factor is the supply of professional resources. As long ago as the late 1960s, it was argued that there were too few professionals to aid the number of children with severe disorders. For example, Mosher et al. (1970) noted an 88% increase between 1957 and 1967 in the number of hospitalized persons under the age of 15. Trachtenberg and Goldblatt (1968) estimated that there were over 2,000 autistic-like children in the Philadelphia area alone. More dramatically, Lindsley (1966), using the statistics of 1961, calculated that in the allocation of professional resources, there were 3,600 children between the ages of 5 and 17 for each psychiatrist, approximately 2,500 for each psychologist, and 1,500 for each social worker. Behavior change is impossible, argued Lindsley, with these ratios of children to professionals.

Fourth, parent training was fostered by serious shortcomings in existing approaches. This is the subject to which we now turn.

Challenging The Early Psychogenic Approach

Until the mid-1960s, the psychodynamic or psychogenic approach provided a predominant explanation and treatment of autism. For reviews of early treatment approaches, the reader should see Rimland (1964, 1969); Laufer and Gair (1969), Wing (1966), Rutter (1969, 1996), Rutter and Bartak (1971), and Kanner (1948).

The psychogenic approach was characterized by two assumptions. First, a child's disordered behavior and atypical development were understood as signs of an emotional disturbance, a disorder of the self, or a disturbance of the child's perception or conception of reality. These alleged internal disturbances were said to be caused by the child's environment, especially child–caregiver interaction. Homeopathy was a hallmark assumption underlying treatment; that is, therapy was to be derived from and consistent with notions of causation. One could not treat a child's behavior alone (the alleged symptoms); one had to treat the "underlying" pathologies of emotion or self. In treating obvious illnesses (say, pneumonia), homeopathy makes sense. One uses medication to kill infection that is causing symptoms (e.g., fever and coughing). However, in the case of autism, the psychogenic practitioner saw *only* the alleged symptoms (disordered behavior and atypical development). Therefore, in treating an alleged (underlying and unobservable) "real" disorder of the mind or self, the psychogenic therapist was treating a fiction.

For example, Goldfarb (1955) and others such as Spitz (1945) cited "maternal deprivation" as a cause of "hospitalism," a syndrome much like autism. Similarly, Eisenberg and Kanner saw autism as a reaction to parental mistreatment. The child, they argued, may be responding to the cold, obsessive, mechanical care he receives from his parents (Eisenberg & Kanner, 1956).

The centrality of parent-child interactions was consistent, too, with the psychogenic approach to studying the family. Both Bateson et al. (1956) and Haley (1959) used the paradigm of the "double bind" to investigate family communication. The emphasis in their research was on the inability of a child to develop a coherent conception of himself and the world in the face of incongruent messages. Wynne's investigations, on the other hand, focused on role structures. He proposed that the family life of the young schizophrenic was conducted on the basis of "pseudo-mutuality," when in fact roles were either too rigid or too ambiguous, communication was disjointed, and there were pressures to maintain a facade of mutuality, which resulted in the child's conforming to a sham system (Mischler & Waxler, 1970).

By far the most popular psychogenic explanation of autism was the psychoanalytic one of Bettelheim's. According to Bettelheim, autism is "basically a disturbance of the ability to reach out to the world" (Bettelheim, 1967). The cause of the disturbance is the relationship between parent and child. For the child to feel secure enough to "reach out" to the world, to enter it as an active participant, the child must develop self-confidence—i.e., a feeling that the self is potent, that efforts of the self can be realized in the world. Bettelheim believed that the parents of autistic children prevented this feeling from developing. They either stifled their children's attempts to interact with their environments or forced their children to attempt too much, resulting in failure. Therefore, the children *reject* the world. The world is a hostile and frightening place for them, and they are not potent enough to survive in it. Thus, they withdraw, and occupy their time and energy in the repetitive manipulation of familiar objects. Even if they have speech, they are unable or unwilling to refer to themselves as "I" since they have no "self."

Therapy, for Bettelheim, required that a child have positive experiences with others, and that his own actions have an influence on the environment. In this way, the child would see the world as safe and himself as potent. He would therefore relinquish the autistic defenses, repetitive gestures, and apathy which enable him to block out the world. Such therapy would require many years in intimate relationships with a very few persons who were to become parent surrogates in a permissive environment.

The psychogenic approach to autism was criticized in terms of both the logic and verification of psychogenic theories and the effectiveness of psychogenically-oriented therapy. The major proposition in most psychogenic theories was that the child had withdrawn into himself as a defense against threatening, cold, or traumatic relationships with his parents. To verify this proposition, the theorist-researcher would have had to be present before and during the development of the child's disorder. He would have had to observe the parents behaving in a cold, hostile, or threatening manner toward the child, and the child then beginning to exhibit autistic behavior. However, researchers using the psychogenic approach typically observed relationships between parents and child *after* the child had become autistic or was diagnosed with autism. Thus, they were unable to eliminate, either logically or empirically, the strong possibility that any "coldness" or "rejection" of the child by the parents was due to the earlier unresponsiveness of the child to the attention of the parents. The obvious alternative proposition is that the parents feel rejected by their child.

Additionally, most psychogenic theories posited a cause (e.g., early patterns of parent-child interaction) which was temporally distant from the present autistic behavior of the child. Such a causal factor might or might not have been relevant to the onset of the disorder, but it is not necessarily relevant to the *persistence* of the disorder. An important theoretical and practical question is what factors control the autistic behavior now.

Second, many writers argued that psychogenic theories of autism were unsupported by the data. In particular, various researchers and practitioners sharply criticized the hypothesis that parents caused their child's disorder, on the basis that there was little confirming and more disconfirming evidence (Creak & Ini, 1960; Frank, 1965; Rimland, 1964; Peck et al., 1949; Rutter & Bartak, 1971; Rutter,

Bartak, & Newman, 1971; Schopler & Loftin, 1969; Schopler & Reichler, 1971). The double-bind hypothesis was also criticized on the basis that there was no evidence that the double-bind phenomenon is exclusive to pathological communication processes or has an etiological connection with schizophrenia (Schuham, 1967). Frank (1965), finally, argued against the assumption of an overwhelming influence of family life on the development of psychotic disorders, asserting that characteristics of the families of schizophrenics are also found in the families of controls.

Third, the psychogenic approach was criticized for lack of evidence that psychotherapeutic treatment helped children with severe developmental disorders (Eisenberg, 1956; Leff, 1968). Rimland, for instance, cited Kanner's data to the effect that children who received the most adequate psychotherapy showed poorer records of improvement than those provided little or no treatment. Similarly, Levitt (1957, 1963), after reviewing a large number of studies of the results of psychotherapy with children, found that the percentage of cases rated "improved" was approximately the same for both treated and control groups, and Wenar et al. (1967) found no differences in children's progress in communication skills between state institutions and a small, psychoanalytically-oriented clinic.

In summary, one negative implication of the psychogenic approach was that the parents were generally blamed for the child's disorder *despite the lack of evidence, either logical or empirical, for the contention* (Schopler, 1969). The parents, it would seem to me, had enough difficulty trying to rear an unresponsive, destructive, screaming child without the added burden of feeling that they were to blame, especially since there was little proof that this was the case.

It should be pointed out that even today, I am not arguing that the variables central to psychogenic explanations of autism are irrelevant. Indeed, variables such as parental punitiveness and unresponsiveness to the child are included in both the operant conditioning and social exchange approaches to autism, as will be seen later. What I do argue is that the above variables, in the hands of many psychogenic theorists, served as pejorative labels. The parents became "types" of people who were punitive or unresponsive toward their child; punitiveness and unresponsiveness became stable "traits" of the parents. The child was thus viewed as being at the mercy of parents having such traits.

My position, on the other hand, is that both "punitiveness" and "unresponsiveness" are *behaviors,* as are the "symptoms" of autism. Moreover, the behavior of the parents and the behavior of the child may well be under the control of the *same* kinds of variables. Consequently, the task becomes one of analyzing the home environment as a social system to see (1) whether and how parental unresponsiveness, for instance, influences the behavior of the child and (2) whether parental unresponsiveness is itself a function of other features of the home environment, e.g., certain behaviors of the child.

Conclusion

This chapter examined the psychosocial development of persons with autism and historical efforts to explain and treat autism. We are able to suggest the following tentative conclusions. Satisfactory psychosocial development requires that a child's body (brain, sense organs, muscles) be in continual contact with, finely attuned to, and able to learn quickly from important features of the world—e.g., the speech and gestures of other persons, qualities of objects, cause-effect relationships, consequences of actions. For some reason or reasons, the nervous systems of autistic children are not sufficiently in contact with, attuned to, and able to learn quickly from important features of the world.

Although significant progress is being made, there are no sure psychotherapeutic, biochemical or surgical means to undo the predisposing influence of genetic factors, repair a damaged nervous system, or restart a brain that is developing too slowly. Therefore, at the same time that we look for biochemical explanations and treatments, we must continue to concentrate on the environment. We must make important environmental features (e.g., the organization of tasks, oc-

casions to participate, signals, prompts, and performance feedback)
salient, frequent, dependable, and tailored to the needs, preferences
and capacities of autistic children—to help them organize and reor-
ganize their behavior in ways their own bodies do not do very well
under ordinary circumstances. In summary, autistic children need
powerful educational environments. This is the subject of Chapter
Two.

2

The Behavioral Approach To Autism

The behavioral approach to developmental disorders rests on about seventy-five years of behavioral science research—in particular, social learning and the experimental analysis of behavior. (See Ullmann & Krasner, 1965, for examples of important early studies.) For practitioners of the behavioral approach, a child's maladaptive behavior and development are the most pressing problem. Moreover, the most verifiable and reliable remedies to date are "environmental operations," "events of instruction," and patterns of communication in the child's environments, as described by Engelmann and Carnine (1991), Mattaini (1996), Kunzelmann (1970), Schlinger and Blakely (1994), and Gagné, Briggs, and Wager (1992), and discussed in this chapter.

A sample of reportedly effective behavioral-educational programs for children with autism includes those described by Anderson, Avery, DiPietro, Edwards, and Christian (1987); Fenske, Zalenski, Krantz, and McClannahan (1985); Fox, Dunlap, and Philbrick (1997); Hamblin et al. (1971); Harris, Handleman, Kristoff, Bass, and Gordon (1990); Harris, Handleman, Gordon, Kristoff, and Fuentes (1991); Holmes (1998); Howlin and Rutter (1987); Hoyson, Jamieson, and Strain (1984); Koegel and Johnson (1989); Koegel and Koegel (1996); Koegel, Rincover, and Egel (1982); Kozloff (1974, 1988, 1994a, 1994b); Lord, Bristol, and Schopler (1993); Lovaas (1977, 1987); Maurice, Green, and Luce (1996); McEachlin, Smith, and Lovaas (1993); Prizant and Wetherby (1989, 1993); Rogers (1996); Rogers and DiLalla (1991); Rogers and

Lewis (1989); Schopler, Lansing, and Waters (1983); Smith, Eikeseth, and Lovaas (1997); and Watson, Lord, Schaffer, and Schopler (1989).

Perhaps the most important contribution of the behavioral approach to educating autistic children and training their parents is its assumption concerning change. In contrast to the homeopathic therapy of the psychogenic model, in which treatment is derived from and consistent with notions of causation, the behavioral model is: (1) concerned more with *present* determinants of the child's behavior and development; and (2) consistent not with theories of causation but with theories of the nature of education. Whatever the reasons why an autistic child did not learn to play, speak, or cooperate, the fact remains that he or she does not know how to play, speak, and cooperate *now*. Treatment within behavioral approaches is designed to teach a child skills which are necessary for participation in the natural community, and also for the realization of his or her intellectual and emotional potentials.

This chapter provides important concepts, principles, and methods of instruction from two bodies of research that contribute most to the behavioral approach: respondent and operant learning (or "conditioning"), and social exchange theory.

Respondent and Operant Learning

Concepts, principles, and methods of instruction from the fields of respondent and operant learning cannot alone provide adequate assessments, program plans, curricula, and instruction. However, no assessment, program plan, curriculum, or instruction for children with autism is adequate *without* a serious consideration and inclusion of respondent and operant learning.

Respondent Learning

Respondent behavior includes *attention* (a child turns her head in response to a car horn), *feelings* (pains and pleasures), and activities of *smooth muscles* (e.g., walls of blood vessels and intestines) and *glands* (e.g., salivary, lachrymal, and adrenal). Respondent behavior is often considered involuntary—i.e., *reflexive* responses to antecedent events (stimuli). However, one can learn to elicit or to inhibit "involuntary" responses; e.g., a person can use relaxation to inhibit fear responses. Following are major concepts and principles of respondent learning.

1. *Certain events (stimuli) have the capacity to elicit specific respondent behaviors (responses) without a person's having prior experience with these events.* For example, loud noises elicit startle responses (shaking and perhaps crying) in young children; warm milk (to hungry infants) elicits attention, pleasure, salivation, and relaxation. Loud noise and milk are "unconditioned (i.e., unlearned) stimuli"; responses to them are "unconditioned (unlearned) responses"; and the relationship between stimulus and response is an "unconditioned reflex" (Pavlov, 1927).

2. *Background events that do not have the capacity to elicit responses (i.e., "neutral stimuli") can acquire the capacity to elicit responses.* This is called "respondent conditioning." It happens through repeated *associations* between neutral stimuli and unconditioned stimuli. For example, over and over an infant experiences her mother's smell, voice, body temperature, and touch (neutral stimuli) at the same time or shortly before the infant receives food (unconditioned stimuli that elicit attention, pleasure and relaxation). After enough associations ("respondent conditioning trials"), the previously neutral stimuli (e.g., mother's voice and smile) become *meaningful;* they *signify* that food is coming. At this point, the previously neutral stimuli elicit the same responses from the infant that were elicited only by food. The previously neutral stimuli are now "conditioned (learned) stimuli"; the infant's responses are "conditioned (learned) responses"; and the relationship between the new conditioned stimuli and the infant's conditioned response is a "conditioned reflex."

    Furthermore, *when previously neutral events become conditioned stimuli, they can condition still more previously neutral events*. For instance, when the mother's smile is a conditioned stimulus that elicits her infant's attention and pleasure, other facial expressions of the mother (e.g., wide-opened eyes) that happen at the same time or that precede the mother's smiling also come to elicit the infant's attention and pleasure (Dawson, Catania, Schell, & Grings, 1979).

3. *Stimuli (events) that resemble conditioned and unconditioned stimuli will also elicit similar responses*. For example, voices that sound like the mother's voice will elicit the infant's attention and pleasure. This is "respondent stimulus generalization." It helps to explain why a child reacts with fear or with pleasure when entering places he or she has never been.

4. *The presence of conditioned stimuli* (for example, music, task materials, and persons associated with a child's having been reinforced at a high rate for a behavior) *may sustain the child's behavior* (i.e., impart "behavioral momentum") even when the child is otherwise being distracted (Plaud & Gaither, 1996).

5. *If the same stimulus is presented over and over* (e.g., a mother smiles at her infant again and again in a short period of time), *the child may "habituate" to the stimulus, and cease responding to it* until there is a lengthy break (Bornstein & Ludemann, 1989). This helps to explain how overusing praise, food, music and other "reinforcers" results in their losing effectiveness.

6. *If a conditioned stimulus is no longer followed by an unconditioned stimulus (or another conditioned stimulus), a person is likely to stop responding to it*. This is called "respondent extinction." For example, a caregiver's tone of voice (conditioned stimulus) may elicit fear in a child (conditioned response) because the tone of voice has been followed many times by spanking (an unconditioned stimulus). However, if the tone of voice is no longer followed by spanking or by anything else (e.g., angry looks) that elicits fear, then the tone of voice will gradually lose its meaning (threat), and the child will stop responding with fear. Still, if the tone of voice is *occasionally* followed by spanking, then the meaning of the tone of voice will be reinforced (maintained),

and so will the conditioned reflex—hear tone of voice and become afraid.

Principles of respondent conditioning are essential in conducting assessments and planning instruction for children with autism. For example, they help to determine why some events are powerful conditioned stimuli and why other events are not; they suggest how the strength of fear-eliciting or pain-eliciting events can be weakened (by extinction) and how neutral events (e.g., praise and activities) may be transformed into conditioned stimuli by associating them with other unconditioned and conditioned stimuli, as when praise is quickly followed by food or when less enjoyable activities (lessons) are followed by more enjoyable activities (free play). We turn now to *operant* learning.

Operant Learning

In contrast to respondent behavior (e.g., attention and feelings elicited by stimuli), operant behavior (e.g., talking) consists of voluntary, purposeful *actions* whose future strength (e.g., rate, skill, intensity) is affected by the *consequences* of the actions (e.g., the reactions of other persons). The following discussion of operant learning focuses on: (1) ways operant behaviors (actions) can change; (2) phases of learning and instruction; (3) consequences and contingencies of reinforcement; (4) signals or cues; (5) prompts and prompting strategies; (6) chaining; and (7) methods for reducing or replacing problem behaviors.

Ways Operant Behavior Can Change. *Operant behavior (action) can change in a number of ways.* For example, a person may learn to perform actions:

1. At higher or lower *rates*—e.g., fewer disruptive episodes and more self-calming episodes per day.
2. For longer or shorter *durations*—e.g., staying with hard prob-

lems for longer periods and being upset for shorter periods.

3. At greater or lesser *intensities*—e.g., the average episode of anger is less intense, or a student speaks louder when answering.

4. With greater *skill*—e.g., a child performs all the component actions, makes fewer errors, takes less time between steps of a task, and completes the task.

5. In more *settings*—e.g., a student uses problem solving skills learned in math class in other classes as well (*stimulus generalization*)—or in fewer settings: e.g., a student performs tantrums in fewer places, only where they are reinforced (*stimulus discrimination*).

6. In longer *chains* or sequences—e.g., a child learns to do all of the steps in making a bed.

7. More *quickly* or more *slowly* following cues—e.g., solving problems more quickly, or thinking instead of blurting out answers.

Two things must be addressed in order to understand how these changes come about and how to foster them: (1) *phases* of instruction, and (2) *functional relationships* in the learning environment.

Phases of Learning. There are five phases of instruction or learning. (For more information, see Haring,1988; Haring, White, & Liberty, 1978; White & Haring, 1980; Wolery, Bailey, & Sugai, 1988).

1. *Acquisition* is the early phase, when a person learns *how* to accomplish a task, e.g., drying dishes. Acquisition includes learning: (a) *what* is to be accomplished (e.g., a stack of dry dishes); and (b) to perform correct or effective *actions* (task components, such as reaching, grasping, lifting) at the right *spots* in a sequence in response to relevant *signals* (e.g., the sight of a wet dish as a signal for reaching and the feel of a dry dish as a signal for setting it down). The extent of acquisition can be measured by the percentage of correct responses to signals or the number of completed steps in a task.

2. *Fluency-building* is the phase when a person learns to perform a

behavior or task: (a) smoothly (i.e., eliminating extraneous behavior and reducing gaps between steps); and (b) at high, effective and/or culturally desirable speeds, durations, and intensities. In speaking, this means a child pronounces words clearly, quickly moves from one sound or word to the next, and modulates pitch and loudness in relation to the understanding and attention of the audience.

Much research reveals the benefits of working on both fluency (rapid and smooth performance) and acquisition (correct or accurate performance). Fluent performances tend to be more enjoyable; they can be sustained for extended periods and in the face of distractions ("endurance"); they remain strong after the passage of time between performances (e.g., "retention" of bike-riding skill after years without riding); and they facilitate *response adduction:* combining task elements into newer or longer sequences (Binder, 1996; Binder & Watkins, 1990; Binder, Haughton, & Van Eyk, 1990; Jordon & Robbins, 1971; Lindsley, 1990). For example, if a child is fluent in the separate component actions (or "tool skills") of reaching, grasping, lifting and rotating objects, the child will more easily (and more independently) assemble these actions into the composite task sequences of working puzzles or brushing teeth.

Fluency is fostered by (a) teaching with great attention to how well and how fast a child performs the component actions or tool skills (reaching, grasping, and fitting objects; math facts; vowel and consonant sounds) found in composite tasks (chores, arithmetic problems, speaking); (b) providing regular practice sessions on tool skills or components and on assembling components into relevant composite sequences, with sessions very short at first, but increasingly longer to build endurance; and (c) encouraging a child to achieve higher and higher rates of accurate activity (Dougherty & Johnston, 1996; Haughton, 1980; Johnson & Layng, 1992, 1996; Lindsley, 1964, 1996).

3. *Generalization* (sometimes called "application") means a person learns to *transfer* (use) skills acquired in one environment

to other environments. For example, generalization of reading skill would involve reading at home and in class; reading newspapers, posters, graffiti, TV screens, and computers as well as school books; reading different typefaces; and reading for various purposes, e.g., for pleasure, to follow a recipe, and to cross a street (Mundschenk & Sasso, 1995). Note that a person may generalize *all* or *portions* of a sequence or skill. For example, when working a new and somewhat different candy machine, a child might generalize the "insert coin" step but not the "select candy" step.

4. *Adaptation,* not to be confused with generalization, involves *altering* (not simply transferring) a behavior or task to *suit* the circumstances. This could mean using different movements, tools, or sequences, or even adding a side-sequence. For example, if there is no knife, a child might spread mustard with a spoon, a finger, or a Frito; or if a child's cup is leaking, the child might add a side sequence—holding a finger over the hole—to the main sequence.

5. *Maintenance* means that a person performs competently in the absence of instruction or assistance. Maintenance is fostered by: (a) prior instruction to a high degree of skill and fluency; (b) slowly fading instruction and assistance; and (c) teaching children to self-evaluate their performance and follow a problem solving sequence, e.g., a guideline such as "Try another way."

The changes described above do not happen by magic or mere maturation. They happen as persons *interact* with and learn from their environments. We can say that behavior change is *functionally related* to features of the environment. These features (shown in the figure on the next page) include contingencies of reinforcement, cues or signals, prompts, and chaining methods. Let us examine in more detail the *functional relationships* shown by the arrows.

Contingencies of Reinforcement. These are *regular (i.e., reliable) arrangements between actions and their consequences.* There are five contingencies of reinforcement, as follows.

Functional Relation of Behavior Change
to Features of the Environment

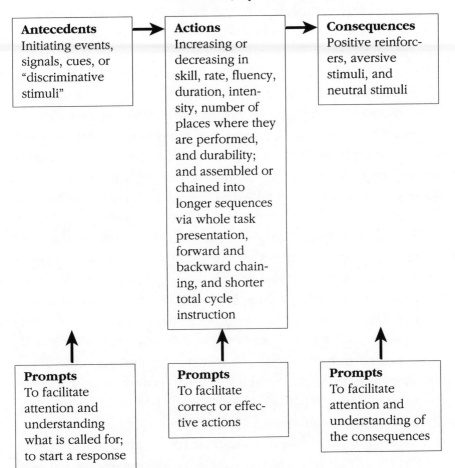

[**Contingencies of reinforcement**: Positive and Negative Reinforcement; Type 1 and Type 2 Punishment; Operant Extinction]

Antecedents
Initiating events, signals, cues, or "discriminative stimuli"

Actions
Increasing or decreasing in skill, rate, fluency, duration, intensity, number of places where they are performed, and durability; and assembled or chained into longer sequences via whole task presentation, forward and backward chaining, and shorter total cycle instruction

Consequences
Positive reinforcers, aversive stimuli, and neutral stimuli

Prompts
To facilitate attention and understanding what is called for; to start a response

Prompts
To facilitate correct or effective actions

Prompts
To facilitate attention and understanding of the consequences

Prompting methods: stimulus accentuation, gestures, instructions, models, manual, templates, other devices.

Prompting strategies: stimulus manipulation, graduated guidance, most-to-least, least-to-most, time delay (constant interval and changing interval)

1. *Positive reinforcement.* A contingency (the relationship between an action and its usual consequence) is called "positive reinforcement" if an action *produces* (is followed by) an event and the action is thereby *strengthened*, i.e., performed more often, with more skill, for longer durations, and/or at higher intensity. For example, a child finds that as soon as she puts on her coat she can go outside (positive reinforcement); in the future she puts on her coat (action) more readily when she is near the door (cue).

2. *Type 1 punishment.* In this contingency, action *produces* (is followed by) an event, and the action is *weakened*, i.e., decreases in rate (happens less often), intensity, duration, and/or skill. The consequent event is called an *aversive stimulus, punisher,* or *negative reinforcer.* For instance, a child throws a tantrum and bumps his head on the hard floor. This happens several times. If the child now throws fewer, milder, or more cautious tantrums (e.g., makes sure he is on a rug), we say that a head bump is an aversive stimulus and that tantrums have been receiving Type 1 punishment. Note, however, that such "punishment" may *not* teach a child not to throw tantrums, but simply to throw them in a way or in a place that makes the punishment less likely or milder. Also, if a child is spanked when she throws tantrums, and her tantrums *increase* in strength (e.g., happen more often), then spanking is not Type 1 punishment; it is positive reinforcement. In other words, the name of a contingency and the name of the stimulus function of a consequent event (positive reinforcer, neutral stimulus, aversive stimulus) depend on how the contingency *affects* the strength of an action.

3. *Negative reinforcement.* A contingency is called negative reinforcement if an action *removes* (allows a person to escape), avoids, delays, reduces the intensity, or reduces the duration of an event, and the action is *strengthened*—i.e., increases in rate, intensity, duration, and/or skill. For example, if whining enables a student to avoid, delay, lower the difficulty, or decrease the duration of tasks, the student may whine more often. And if hitting enables a student to escape from a task, the student may hit more often.

The event (e.g., task) would be called an aversive stimulus, punisher, or negative reinforcer; and we would say that hitting is negatively reinforced by escape from tasks.

4. *Type 2 punishment.* In this contingency, an action *removes,* avoids, delays, reduces the intensity, reduces the duration, or reduces the quality of an event, and the action is *weakened*—i.e., decreases in rate, intensity, duration, and/or skill. For example, a child pushes another child and has to wait 10 minutes before she can use the computer; in the future she is less likely to push. Or a child behaves competently; her parents see her as more independent and spend less time with her; and the child begins acting *less* competently. In this case, time with the computer and time with parents would be considered *positive reinforcers;* and the delay or decrease in these reinforcers has punished the behaviors (hitting, behaving competently) that resulted in their delay or decrease.

5. *Operant extinction.* In operant extinction, an action produces no change in the environment (or the change is a *neutral event*) and the action is *weakened*—i.e., decreases in rate, duration, intensity, and/or skill (Ducharme & Van Houten, 1994). For example, a student who is used to whining and then being excused from tasks, now finds that she cannot have more enjoyable tasks *until* she does a little work on assigned tasks (with or without whining); her whining to get out of tasks decreases. Note that extinction (no longer reinforcing an action) often produces escalation in the action; e.g., its intensity, rate, and/or duration increase. This is called an "extinction burst." For example, a child whose whining no longer gets her out of tasks might whine louder and longer at first, as though trying to coerce persons into giving the usual reinforcement for whining. Therefore, the wise caregiver *never* "gives in to" (reinforces) an escalated problem behavior.

Positive reinforcement is probably the most important contingency in educating children with autism. The guidelines below will help the reader to use it well.

1. Know that there are different *kinds* of positive reinforcers.
   a. *Primary* reinforcers are events that reinforce behavior without prior experience with the events. Examples include food and water, if one is hungry or thirsty.
   b. *Social* reinforcers include praise, being noticed, and being allocated a valuable social place; e.g., being respected, invited, included, protected, honored, celebrated, and given opportunities to perform valued tasks and roles.
   c. *Activity* reinforcers might include working on a computer, listening to music, having a conversation, or playing games.
   d. *Efficacy* can be a powerful reinforcer because it signifies the power of the self. Examples include solving problems, successfully asking another child to play, successfully controlling one's feelings, and in general finding that one's actions produce reliable or rapid results.
   e. *Generalized* reinforcers. Some events have little reinforcement value in themselves, but acquire reinforcement value because they can be *used* to obtain other (e.g., the above) reinforcers, or because they reliably precede or *predict* other reinforcers (Ferster & Perrott, 1968). Examples include money, tokens, stars, grades, graphs or charts that depict progress, and praise (e.g., when praise is often followed by play and hugs).
2. It is important to have *assessment information* regarding which events are reinforcers and which are not reinforcers for children. Information may come from several sources. These include:
   a. *Direct observations*, e.g., observing which events a child talks about, asks for, or tries to obtain, and (more importantly) which events actually increase the child's behavior.
   b. *Interviews* with a child, family, and other teachers.
   c. A child's use of *reinforcer menus*, e.g., a list of words or pictures of events that a child points to or checkmarks to indicate preferences.
3. Use known reinforcers to strengthen desirable behaviors.
4. Temporarily stop using events that do not strengthen behavior.

5. Positively reinforce desirable behaviors quickly, frequently, and enthusiastically.
6. Make clear which behavior is reinforced. "That was excellent the way you relaxed yourself! Feel better now?"
7. Increase and sustain the strength of reinforcers by:
    a. *Rotating* them and/or by giving children the chance to rotate them *before* they are satiated.
    b. Changing the *delivery* of praise.
    c. Decreasing background *access* to reinforcers; e.g., *saving* music as a reinforcer for selected behaviors.
    d. Teaching children to *choose* some reinforcers.
    e. *Ending* instruction before children are overly fatigued or satiated.
8. Positively reinforce behaviors that change in a desirable direction—i.e., use *shaping*. What is shaping? Certainly one would not wait until a child speaks in full sentences before reinforcing the child's speaking. Shaping means *reinforcing successively closer approximations to a desired performance.* Almost any feature of a performance can be selectively reinforced—increased skill, increased generalization, increased adaptation, requiring less prompting, increased or decreased speed, increased or decreased intensity, increased or decreased duration. Following are guidelines for shaping behavior.
    a. Analyze a behavioral objective (e.g., regarding accuracy, fluency, frequency, duration, intensity) into successively *closer approximations* to the desired performance. *Write* the list of approximations on a teaching program plan.
    b. Determine a child's or a group's *current* step or level of approximation: e.g., the child works attentively on most tasks for an average of three minutes. Begin teaching at the current level. For example, reinforce episodes of attentive working that are at least three minutes long. Also reinforce performances done with less prompting and more skill, effort, and enjoyment.
    c. As a child's performance at the first level of approximation

stabilizes (e.g., a child consistently pays attention for three minutes), move to the next level or step, and only reinforce *improved* performances. For example, reinforce episodes of attentive working that are four or more minutes long.

   d. If a child has trouble on a harder step, *return* to the last easier step for awhile, build fluency, and try again. Or, if a step is a "composite" that consists of several component skills, carefully observe the child's performance to identify weak components (sometimes called "tool skills" or input-output "learning channels"; e.g., see a model [input] and then imitate the model [output]; hear the name of an object and then point to the object; see an array of objects and then count the objects); give the child extra practice on the tool skills or learning channels to build accuracy and fluency; and then return to the harder composite step (Haughton, 1980; Johnson & Layng, 1992; Lindsley, 1992).

9. Reinforce on a *continuous* (every time) schedule during the phase of acquisition (when a child is acquiring the initial skill) and at the start of a new phase (e.g., helping a child to generalize skillful performance). As a behavior improves (e.g., happens more often, for longer durations, with greater skill or effort, with less prompting, or in new places), gradually reinforce the behavior on an *intermittent* (once in a while) schedule. Also, gradually *delay* reinforcement, but bridge the time between the performance and the expected reinforcer with a conditioned reinforcer (e.g., praise and/or charting the number or rate of correct responses).

10. Return to a schedule of more frequent reinforcement if a child's performance or participation (e.g., attention, cooperation, enjoyment, effort) weaken under intermittent reinforcement. When performance and participation again improve, slowly return to more intermittent schedules.

11. Condition new reinforcers. For example, pair neutral or even mildly aversive events with events that are stronger positive reinforcers. For example, follow short math lessons with time on the computer.

12. Reinforce current target behaviors and other desirable behav-

iors—both behaviors worked on earlier and behaviors that appear spontaneously, such as displays of enjoyment or unusually strong effort.

13. Teach children contingency management. For example, one might teach a child to:

   a. Set behavioral *objectives* for periods of time (e.g., a week, a lesson, a practice session) and to *select* contingent reinforcers. "I do 10 problems and then play with the Gameboy."

   b. *Keep track* of her own behavior (participation and achievement) by *counting*, for instance, minutes of attentive work, questions asked during an activity, problems worked on without being disruptive, correct responses, or task completions.

   c. *Record* behavior counts on a form that clearly displays a number of time periods in a row, e.g., days, lessons, 15-minute blocks.

   d. *Graph* or chart the behavior counts.

   e. *Evaluate* her performance in relation to objectives, and reinforce herself (Lindsley, 1990).

Signals, Cues or Occasions. We now examine *signals or cues— antecedents that initiate actions.* The purpose of a signal is to initiate action, and to provide a clear and understood opportunity— e.g., to earn reinforcers by engaging in a specified activity. Examples of signals include the following.

1. *Requests*—"Fred, remember to use calming breaths when you feel tense."

2. *Questions*—"Bill, what is 5 plus 2?"

3. *Instructions*—"Ron, first pick up the plate." Or, written instructions.

4. *Models*—"Now watch this." Teacher shows Ron how to pick up a plate.

5. *Contracts*—"As soon as you do five problems, you can get on the Internet. Okay? Good. How many problems ... ?" (This technique is known to some as "Grandma's law.")

6. *Devices* of many kinds—e.g., bell timers to start tasks, dimming lights to help students shift from high to low activity levels.

In general, signals ought to: (1) get attention; (2) foster interest; (3) dispel boredom; (4) mean business; (5) coax courage; (6) communicate what is expected in the task; and (7) teach students to signal themselves—e.g., with lists of steps to follow, guidelines, mottos, or visual imagery.

In selecting signals and providing opportunities to learn, one must consider "recipient design"—tailoring instruction (signals, prompts, consequences) to the learner in accordance with the following guidelines.

1. Use signals that maximize understanding, e.g., simple words, few words, stress on important words, tones of voice that get and sustain attention but do not elicit fear, words that say unambiguously what a child is to do (Becker & Carnine, 1981).
2. Be mindful of your speaking tone, rate, volume and modulation (vibrant and changing vs. steady droning).
3. Use gestures of your head, hands and arms to supplement speaking.
4. Use lighting, pointers, and electronic devices to gain attention and clarify the message (but be careful not to muddy the situation with the extra cues).
5. Gain the child's attention before giving signals.
6. Avoid excessive background talk and gestures, or your words will lose salience.
7. Determine whether a child learns and performs best (a) with a clean break of a few seconds between learning trials or problems (a "discrete trials format"); or (b) when allowed to respond in an uninterrupted (self-paced) fashion to a series of task events (Binder, 1996; Lindsley, 1996).
8. Periodically change your tone of voice, words and gestures used, and room decorations to sustain attention and promote generalization.

Prompts and Prompting Strategies. Prompts are another feature of the learning environment. As shown in the diagram on p. 27, prompts facilitate three things.

1. A person's attention and understanding of signals. For example, some students' understanding is increased if a *second* modality (a prompt) is added to the first, e.g., pictured instructions plus written instructions.
2. A person's performance in response to signals, e.g., helping a child to perform correct responses at the right spot in a sequence, or preventing errors.
3. A person's understanding of the consequences (as feedback) that he or she has just received or will receive shortly.

There are at least seven kinds of prompts that can be added to signals, ongoing performances, and consequent performance feedback:

1. *Stimulus accentuation.* Examples include spotlights and laser pointers on relevant objects or portions of a visual display; highlighting important words or lines in a text with a different color or font (e.g., in a set of instructions); and exaggerating gestures and voice ("Yes, CAT!").
2. *Gestures.* Examples include pointing to the correct picture choice or accentuating certain steps in a modeled performance (e.g., pulling up the cover in making a bed).
3. *Instructions.* For example:
   a. "Pay attention to this next point."
   b. "Pour the soup INTO the water." (Note the stimulus accentuation.)
4. *Models.* For example, demonstrating how to solve an arithmetic problem, work a puzzle, or relax.
5. *Manual.* This means hands-on help; e.g., moving a child through a task with your hand placed over the child's hand.
6. *Templates.* These include physical *formats* that guide behavior (e.g., a placemat with pictures of dishes and utensils in the proper

place) and *flow diagrams* or *picture sequences* of how to accomplish tasks.

7. *Other devices.* These include: (a) tape recorded instructions, hints and reminders; (b) electronic feedback (e.g., an anxious child wears a device that signals the rate of respiration or the galvanic skin response, and therefore helps the child to control anxiety and tension); (c) a metronome set to run slowly, to help a child work calmly and steadily; and (d) music (e.g., Bach for solo violin vs. Handel's "Music for the Royal Fireworks") to decrease or increase arousal, attention, or the pace of work.

Seven different kinds of prompts were identified above. There are also *five strategies for introducing and fading out these prompts* (Demchak, 1989; Gast, Ault, Wolery, Doyle, & Belanger, 1988; Miller & Test, 1989; Wolery, Bailey, & Sugai, 1988; Wolery, Ault, Gast, Doyle, & Griffin, 1990), as follows.

1. *Stimulus manipulation.* This strategy involves *accentuating and then fading out extra cues.* For example, the prompt called "stimulus accentuation" might be more intense at first. As a child learns to pay attention to cues and becomes more skillful, extra highlighting is faded out. For instance, as a child learns to read large print, the size is gradually reduced.

2. *Graduated guidance.* This strategy involves providing *as much or as little prompting* as needed at any step in a task. For example, during a language lesson, the teacher reinforces good approximations and correct responses, but does *not* use instructions ("A bit faster, please"), models ("Say it like this ..."), or gestures (e.g., to signify "slow down"), *unless* a child is making errors or would benefit from the teacher preventing errors.

3. *Most-to-least prompting.* This strategy is used to *prevent errors—* which may be important when a child has a history of low achievement and/or high rates of errors, has low tolerance of frustration/errors, and is not yet competent at anticipating errors and self-correcting. In this strategy, the teacher *begins* with *more* in-

tense, controlling, and/or more complete prompts, and then fades these as a child becomes more competent.

4. *Least-to-most prompting.* This strategy is useful when children do not take well to prompting. The teacher *begins* with the *least* intense, controlling, or complete prompt, and increases these levels if children make the same errors or have the same difficulties over and over.

5. *Time delay.* This method helps to prevent errors and also helps children learn to *prompt themselves* by imitating the teacher's prompts (Schoen & Ogden, 1995; Touchette & Howard, 1984). The method involves *waiting a longer and longer time* (in seconds) after a signal and before giving the prompt. For example, in a lesson on math facts the teacher gives an initiating cue ("What is 2 plus 2?") *along with* the answer/prompt ("Four."). The student *repeats* the prompted answer. Next the teacher asks the *same* question, but waits *one second* before giving the answer prompt. Next the teacher waits *two* seconds, then three seconds, etc., before prompting. The point is for the child to *anticipate* the prompt and answer on his or her own. If the delay interval gets above five seconds, it suggests that the child is having difficulty paying attention, understanding the question, or answering. If so, then these difficulties should be worked on.

Chaining. Another aspect of respondent and operant learning to examine is *chaining.* Virtually every behavior or performance is a *sequence of smaller behaviors* (components, "tool skills," or "learning channels"; Binder, 1996). To brush one's teeth, for example, consider the "links" or steps in the chain and the alternative sequences in which the steps could be assembled to complete the task. There are at least four chaining methods for helping children assemble (link) components into longer sequences.

1. *Whole-task or total-cycle instruction.* In this method, the teacher helps a child through *all* of the steps in a task during a lesson. Naturally, the teacher provides signals, prompts and reinforce-

ment at each step depending on a child's skill or fluency.

2. *Forward chaining.* In forward chaining, the teacher begins instruction with the first step in a chain. This step is repeated until the child performs it fluently, without extra signals and prompts. Then the teacher helps the child perform the first (learned) step followed by the second (new) step. When the child performs the two-step chain skillfully, the teacher adds the third (new) step to the first two (learned) steps. The process is completed until the child skillfully performs the whole chain.

3. *Backward chaining.* In backward or back-chaining, the teacher usually demonstrates the whole sequence, and then teaches a child to perform the *last* step. When the child performs the last step skillfully, the teacher helps the child to perform the second to last (new) step followed by the last (learned) step. Gradually, the teacher adds earlier steps to the chain until the child can skillfully perform the chain from the beginning.

4. *Shorter total-cycle instruction* (Gaylord-Ross & Holvoet, 1985; McWilliams, Nietupski, & Hamre-Nietupski, 1990; Naylor & Briggs, 1963). In this method, the teacher analyzes a long or complex task or problem (e.g., clearing a meal table) into segments (i.e., shorter sequences of links, such as clearing the plates, clearing the utensils, putting the food back in the refrigerator, and wiping the table). Then the teacher teaches the child to perform the actions *within* the first segment. The teacher might use forward chaining to teach the child to assemble the segments into the whole sequence.

Problem Behavior. A final aspect of operant learning principles and methods concerns *reducing or replacing problem behaviors.* Following is a summary of common methods.

1. *Operant extinction.* Here, reinforcement that strengthens or sustains a problem behavior is *discontinued* (Ayllon, 1965b; Carlson et al., 1968; Hart et al., 1965; Williams, 1965). For example, instead of trying to stop a child's tantrums by "talking or joking him

out of it" or by promising a favorite activity if the child will stop, teachers go about their business as if the tantrum were not happening. Extinction is usually coupled with some form of reinforcement for desirable alternative behavior, as shown below.

2. *Differential reinforcement of other behavior, or DRO* (Didden, de Moor, & Bruyns, 1997; LaVigna & Donnellan, 1986). Here, a child who throws tantrums when told that she cannot do something, is reinforced whenever she performs *any* other desirable behavior in this situation. For example, the child is praised if she is silent or walks away or begins to play in her room when told that she cannot go outside yet.

3. *Differential reinforcement of alternative behavior, or DRA* (Donnellan, Mirenda, Mesaros, & Fassbender, 1984; Durand & Carr, 1992; LaVigna & Donnellan, 1986; Ringdahl, Vollmer, Marcus, & Roane, 1997; Sigafoos & Meikle, 1996; Vollmer, Northup, Ringdahl, LeBlanc, & Chauvin, 1996). Here, instead of reinforcing any other behavior besides the problem behavior (as in DRO), a behavior that is a *functional alternative* (a more desirable way of communicating, for example) is reinforced. For instance, a child is reinforced for raising her hand or for asking, rather than slapping herself or screaming, when she wants something.

4. *Differential reinforcement of incompatible behavior, or DRI* (Ayllon & Michael, 1959; Hamblin et al., 1968; Hamblin et al., 1971; LaVigna & Donnellan, 1986; Patterson & Brodsky, 1966; Wahler et al., 1965). In this method, the class or set of behaviors to reinforce is even narrower than in DRA. The behaviors to reinforce are not merely functional alternatives, but are incompatible (e.g., physically incompatible) with the problem behavior. For example, a child is reinforced for remaining calm or for trying again when he makes errors, instead of yelling or throwing materials as he usually does.

5. *Differential reinforcement of lower rates, or DRL* (LaVigna & Donnellan, 1986). Imagine a child who engages in self-stimulation at a high rate (e.g., about three episodes per minute). Caregivers might divide a recording sheet into consecutive one-

minute intervals. The child is reinforced at the end of every interval (if the child is *not* engaging in self-stimulation at that time) that the child performs *fewer* than three episodes of self-stimulation. Gradually, the child is reinforced only at the end of one-minute (or longer) intervals with fewer episodes of self-stimulation.

6. *Shaping.* Earlier, we described shaping desirable behavior in the direction of greater skill, longer duration, or higher rate. We can also *shape undesirable behavior in a desirable direction.* For example, a child may throw a dozen tantrums each day. Observation reveals that some tantrums are shorter and/or less intense and/or performed in a more appropriate place, such as the child's room. Therefore, we *differentially reinforce* the form of tantrum (e.g., the intensity) we want to see more of. For instance, tantrums full of "sound and fury" are ignored (are on extinction); all milder tantrums are reinforced. "GOOD! You kept your hands and feet to yourself. You are learning to CONTROL yourself. Now we can PLAY!"

7. *Stimulus control.* Desirable behaviors are often "under stimulus control"—that is, they are performed in the presence of or following specific signals, or discriminative stimuli. For example, a physician's examination table, white coat, and diplomas on the wall evoke (in some patients) a high probability of talking about important personal matters and cooperating with "doctor's orders." Controlling signals may be quite obvious (as in the above example), or they may be subtle and hardly noticed. Some problem behaviors may be improved by "getting them under stimulus control"; that is, happening only where they are less of a problem. For example, a child could be *redirected* repeatedly to spin objects at her play table, to rock in a rocking chair, or throw tantrums in her room, and then *reinforced* for cooperating, and later reinforced for performing these behaviors without special signals or prompts (Pace, Iwata, Edwards, & McCosh, 1986; Jones, McDonnell, & Houlihan, 1994).

8. *Satiation.* The point of this method is to decrease either the value

of the behavior or the value of reinforcers that sustain the behavior. For example, a child is given (a) so much opportunity to perform problematic activities (e.g., water play in the sink) that she becomes "full" (disinterested) and performs the activity less often; or (b) so much *noncontingent* (free) reinforcement that motivation to engage in problem behavior to obtain the reinforcers is reduced (Ayllon, 1965a; Ayllon & Michael, 1959; Fischer, Iwata, & Mazaleski, 1997; Hanley, Piazza, & Fisher, 1997; Wilder, Draper, Williams, & Higbee, 1997). In either case, reducing the frequency of the problem behavior increases opportunities to teach alternative behavior (Rast, Johnson, Drum, & Cronin, 1981).

9. *Errorless learning.* Some problem behaviors (e.g., yelling, hitting, or breaking things) result from a child making too many errors during instruction (e.g., trial and error learning). Decreasing the likelihood of errors (e.g., by using easier tasks and shorter sessions at first, and using time delay, graduated guidance, or most-to-least prompting) should reduce the rate of errors and therefore increase cooperation and decrease the rate of problem behaviors (Ducharme, 1996; Hamblin, Buckholdt, Ferritor, Kozloff, & Blackwell, 1971).

10. *Self-control.* Many problem behaviors can be reduced or replaced by teaching children to relax (e.g., as an alternative to anger), to prompt themselves ("Try again"), and to count desirable behaviors and reinforce themselves when they reach objectives (Gelfand & Hartman, 1984; Koegel, Koegel, Hurley, & Frae, 1992; Newman, Buffington, O'Grady, McDonald, Poulson, & Hemmes, 1995; Stahmer & Schreibman, 1992).

11. *Time out.* Time out is a form of Type 2 punishment—the removal of positive reinforcers as a consequence of a behavior (Wahler et al., 1965; Wolf et al., 1966). Examples of time out include having a child sit quietly in a special chair for a certain period of time; stopping a lesson for a certain period of time (assuming that losing the chance to earn reinforcers is aversive for a child); or walking away from the child. When time out involves isolating a child (e.g., in a time out chair), the correct use

of time out is *every time* and *immediately* after a problem behavior happens. The time out period is not ended until the child is calm. When the time out is over, the child must finish a task that had been assigned. If the child again refuses, the child might be warned ("Do it NOW!"), and if the child still does not cooperate, time out is repeated.

12. *Cooperation (or "compliance") training.* Here, a program is instituted to increase the chances that a child will cooperate with requests—one type of "pivotal response" (Koegel, Schreibman, Good, Cerniglia, Murphy, & Koegel, 1989; Laski, Charlop, & Schreibman, 1988; Stahmer, 1995). Improved cooperation in general may decrease the chances that a child engages in undesirable behavior to escape requested tasks. In addition, if a child is taught to cooperate with directions to stop a problem behavior before it is out of hand, the child can then be given requests to engage in an alternative behavior that would be reinforced (Ducharme, 1996; Englemann & Colvin, 1983; Piazza, Fisher, Hanley, Remick, Contrucci, & Aitken, 1997).

13. *Negative practice.* Negative practice involves having a child repeat an undesirable behavior (e.g., throwing books off a table) so often that further repetition is aversive (Dunlap, 1932; Yates, 1958).

14. *Aversive methods.* These generally involve Type 1 punishment, or the delivery of aversive events as a consequence of a behavior (e.g., self-injury). Examples include: (a) painful electric shock; (b) mild electrical stimulation; (c) spanking; (d) physical restraint; and (e) water mist sprayed in the face (Axelrod & Apsche, 1983; Lichstein & Schreibman, 1976; Lerman, Iwata, Shore, & DeLeon, 1997; Linscheid, Iwata, Ricketts, Williams, & Griffin, 1990; Lovaas et al., 1965; Luiselli, Suskin, & Slocumb, 1984; Risley, 1968; Singh, Watson, & Winton, 1986).

The use of aversive methods is hotly debated. The reader will find alternate sides of the issue presented by Guess, Helmstetter, Turnbull, and Knowlton (1986); Hill and Bruininks (1984); LaVigna and Donnellan (1986); Paisey, Whitney, and Hysop (1990); Repp and Singh (1990); and Rolider and Van Houten (1990).

The above principles and methods of respondent and operant learning form the basis of behavior modification, or applied behavior analysis, exemplified by the pioneering work of Ayllon and Azrin (1968), Ayllon and Michael (1959), Baer and Wolf (1967), Davison (1964), Ferster (1958, 1968), Ferster and DeMyer (1961, 1966), Fuller (1949), and Lindsley (1956). Programs for autistic children based on principles of respondent and operant learning are generally designed as educational environments whose aim is to foster competencies in children that will enable them to participate in family, peer group, church, school, and other "natural" environments. In general, the educational environment is engineered so that inappropriate behaviors are weakened (usually with combinations of extinction, time out, and procedures identified earlier for strengthening alternative behavior) while developmentally feasible and socially functional behaviors (attention, cooperation, imitation, play, speech, activities of daily living) are improved via the systematic use of methods for signaling, prompting, reinforcing, and chaining.

Learning appropriate behavior (e.g., speech) as a substitute for inappropriate behavior (e.g., pulling and pushing) is a slow process consisting of numerous steps. The teacher might first reinforce a mute child for making any sounds. Then when the child's rate of vocalizing has increased and she is emitting many different sounds, the teacher will reinforce the child only when the child repeats a particular sound after the teacher, i.e., when she imitates him. In this way, words, sentences, and conversation are "shaped up" as closer and closer approximations to functional speech are prompted and reinforced. The same shaping process is used to teach a child to name objects, to read and write, to play, and to cooperate. In other words, the teacher attempts to build up the child's repertoire of appropriate behavior as a substitute for autistic behavior.

A number of early practitioners noted the many differences between a controlled laboratory-school and the home, and cautioned that beneficial changes produced in school might not be maintained if parents are not trained to promote desirable behavior and decelerate undesirable behavior. To meet the problem of generalization and maintenance of positive behavioral change, a number of applied researchers trained parents to use principles of learning theory in the home. Their work, indeed, contributed much to this program. The following are examples of some of the excellent studies that have been done.

Williams (1965) instructed parents in how to eliminate their child's nightly tantrums by putting the child to bed, leaving the room, and then ignoring the child's tantrum. Within nine days there were no more tantrums. Similarly, Wolf et al. (1966) and Risley and Wolf (1966) taught the parents of an autistic child how to teach their child to work puzzles and name objects, and how to eliminate the child's shrieking and crying. Wahler et al. (1965) and Hawkins et al. (1966) trained parents to eliminate their child's commanding, oppositional, and dependent behavior and, simultaneously, to strengthen cooperation and independent behavior. Straughan (1964) and Russo (1964) taught parents to handle anxiety and disruptive behavior, while Reid et al. (1967) worked with the parents of a selectively mute child, and Allen and Harris (1966) focused upon the elimination of excessive scratching. More comprehensive training programs were conducted by Engeln et al. (1968), Howard (1970), Lindsley (1966), Mira (1970), Patterson et al. (1967), Peine (1971), Zeilberger et al. (1968), Schell and Adams (1968), and Walder et al. (1966, 1967).

More recent programs for families of children with autism include those reported by Anderson, Avery, DiPietro, Edwards, and Christian (1987); Hemsley, Howlin, Berger, Hersov, Holbrook, Rutter, and Yule (1978); Holmes (1998); Huynen, Lutzker, Bigelow, Touchette, and Campbell (1996); Kaufman (1976, 1977); Kaufman, Prinz, Bakalor, Tyson, and Paradise (1978); Koegel, Bimbela, and Schreibman (1996); Kozloff, Helm, Cutler, Douglas-Steele, Wells, and Scampini (1988); Kozloff (1979, 1988, 1994a); Laski, Charlop, and Schreibman (1988); Marcus and Schopler (1989); and Schreibman, Koegel, Mills, and Burke (1984).

Evaluation of the Early Respondent and Operant Learning Programs. Early educational programs for autistic children based on principles of respondent and operant learning principles were remarkably successful (cf. Ulrich, Stachnik, & Mabry, 1966; Sloane & MacAulay, 1968; Ullmann & Krasner, 1965). However, the approach had several limitations. First, with the exception of Patterson and Reid (1970), many applied researchers and educators focused so closely on how children's behaviors were shaped by contingencies of reinforcement that they overlooked the way caregivers and children *reciprocally* signal, prompt, reinforce and punish (and therefore teach) each other during their interactions. As we shall see, the autistic child is engaged in *structured exchanges* with his parents in which the behavior of *each* person is powerfully influenced by the behavior of the other. This concept of exchanges (reciprocal contingencies of reinforcement) is essential not only to understanding socialization but also to explaining long-term changes in families where the parents have been trained.

Second, there were deficiencies in the parent training programs developed within the operant learning approach. For instance, in most programs, parents were trained to handle isolated behavior problems, rather than a large portion of the behavior in the autism syndrome—the tantrums, absence of normal speech, inability to play or work, difficulty cooperating with others, self-stimulation. In addition, in most reported studies, parents received limited instruction in observation, assessment, program planning, and behavior change techniques. Many complex and long-range problems which parents must handle (boredom, satiation, shaping complex behaviors) were neglected. Last, there were no systematic and standard ways of (1) analyzing patterns of interaction in the home, (2) training parents as teachers, and (3) restructuring exchanges in the home to promote the child's socialization.

The program reported in this book attempted to overcome the above-mentioned shortcomings in parent training. Before we discuss the program itself, let us take a few pages for an introduction to social exchange theory—the second of the behavioral approaches, upon which the program was based.

Social Exchange Theory

From the sociological perspective of exchange theory, autism is more than a set of behavioral-developmental excesses and impairments. It is also (1) *social positions* that are allocated to and occupied by individuals said to have autism; (2) *social roles* that these individuals play in family, school, and community environments (e.g., "member in good standing" vs. "outsider"); and (3) *identities* (e.g., inferred intelligence, sensitivities, capabilities, value, and personality traits) that other persons bestow upon individuals with autism, as well as the self-perceptions and self-feelings that individuals with autism acquire through social interaction (Bart, 1984; Goffman, 1963; Goode, 1984; Oliver, 1996; Schwartz, 1992). Below is a brief look at some contributions of exchange theory to an understanding and treatment of autism. Notice that respondent and operant learning are embedded in processes of social exchange (Homans, 1961; Kozloff, 1988, 1994a).

Society is the coordination of members' actions into script-like forms. These forms range from passersby swapping greetings to elaborate interactions among nations. The simplest form of social organization is an exchange (Blau, 1964; Homans, 1961; Kozloff, 1988; Patterson & Reid, 1984; Simmel, 1971). Examples of exchanges include mutual compliments; question and answer; invitation and acceptance; request and cooperation; request and refusal; threat and placation; punishment and counterpunishment. Soon after birth, children participate in exchanges (back and forth turn-taking) with caregivers. These exchanges, which occur hundreds of times each day, are embedded in social activities such as feeding, diapering, soothing, and playing. In fact, social activities are *sequences* of exchanges. Exchanges are the immediate environment in which children's psychosocial development is fostered or hindered. This is because the *structure* of exchanges (e.g., how each person responds to the other person) organizes and shapes the feelings, attention, and actions of the participants, as described by the principles of respondent and operant learning.

Exchanges between infants and parents (or more generally between newcomers and established members) are at first irregular, variable, and "out of sync"; that is, persons respond somewhat unpredictably to initiating signals (e.g., requests); fail to take their turns; or take their turns too early or too late. This is because newcomers may not know (and infants certainly do not know) what an adult's words, facial expressions, postures, and hand gestures signify about the adult's feelings or next actions, or what the newcomer is expected to do in response. In addition, parents at first may not tailor initiations (signals), prompts, and reciprocating consequences to their young child's competencies, capacities, and communicative intentions. However, with repeated interaction (practice), parents and children usually learn what each person's actions signify or mean (Jones, 1977), and each person becomes more skilled at taking his or her turns (Brazelton, Kozlowski, & Main, 1974; Cohn & Tronick, 1987; Schaffer, Collis, & Parsons, 1977).

When interaction is characterized by *congruity* (i.e., each person does pretty much what the other person expected and receives responses from the other person that are fairly consistent with what he or she was trying to communicate), and when interaction involves *mutual reward* (i.e., each person's actions are positive reinforcers for the other person), then the child becomes attentive to social activities, and learns to organize affect (e.g., pleasure), the expression of affect (e.g., laughter), vegetative functions (eating, sleeping, toileting), and purposive actions (vocalizing, reaching, grasping, lifting, etc.) into complex routines such as conversation and everyday tasks (Field, 1989; Fogel, 1992; Trevarthen, 1977). Simultaneously, caregivers learn how to further the child's development—to initiate, prompt, and reinforce the child's actions in ways that are congruent with his or her competencies, capacities, needs, and preferences. In summary, interaction becomes increasingly smooth and cooperative. Furthermore, as the child learns to collaborate in social activities, other persons may come to see and treat the child as increasingly competent, and provide resources (e.g., toys and affection), protection, more mature ways to contribute, and personhood (i.e., they see the child as a member with rights, responsibilities, and personality traits) (Abidin, Jenkins, & McGaughy, 1992; Brazelton, Tronick, Adamson, Als, & Wise, 1975; Henry, 1966; Schaffer, 1984; Valsiner, 1987).

However, this is not ordinarily the case when children have autism. Children with autism lack the motivation and skills for paying attention, figuring out what parents' behaviors mean and what the children are supposed to do during exchanges, or performing the right actions at the right spots. Therefore, *many children with autism begin life with deficits in the very "tool skills" required for participating in the exchanges that ordinarily foster psychosocial development.* The children are literally outside the existing vehicle (exchanges) for bringing them into society as competent participants. Tragically, it is easy to become competent at performing destructive exchanges; e.g., a child screams and a parent accidentally reinforces it. This is why productive exchanges with autistic children must be made so salient, frequent, consistent, and powerful that children are successfully enticed into the environment of social interaction where their socialization can begin. We turn now to the question of how exchanges work.

The behavior of each person in an exchange—e.g., the autistic child's behavior in an exchange with his parents—is influenced by the consequences he or she receives for his or her actions (reinforcement, neutral stimuli, and punishment). By definition, a person will repeat actions which result in his being reinforced or rewarded, e.g., obtaining something he likes, wants or needs (a positive reinforcer), or avoiding or escaping something he dislikes (a negative reinforcer). On the other hand, a person will tend *not* to repeat actions which have aversive consequences, or those which have neutral consequences (this phenomenon, extinction, may occur because the physical cost of making an unrewarded response outweighs the reward).

The above relationships between the consequences of an action and the future strength of that action apply to both the parent and the child. If an autistic child begins to bang her head and the parent, finding the child's behavior disturbing, *inadvertently rewards* the child with attention by trying to make her stop banging her head, then (1) the child may in the future repeat head-banging in order to produce attention, and (2) the parent will repeat giving the child inadvertent attention because giving the child attention is rewarded by allowing the parent to escape, for a time, the disturbing head-banging.

This state of affairs will not develop all at once (for reasons we will discuss later). For the present, let us simply note that what we have above is an *exchange*. Each person emits a response, and each person's response is *reciprocated* by the response of the other person. Moreover, the reciprocation from the other is what constitutes the rewarding or costly consequence for the first person of the response he directed at the other. When the autistic child engages in head-banging, her parents' attention is the reciprocation, and it is often a rewarding consequence. And when the parent gives the child attention, the fact that the child temporarily *stops* banging her head is the reciprocation, and it is likewise rewarding—in the short run at least—to the parent.

Since a person will repeat responses which are reinforced (the principles of positive and negative reinforcement), whenever the responses of *each* person in an exchange are rewarded by the responses of the other, the *exchange itself* will tend to be repeated. This statement is central to the explanation of the maintenance and worsening of many autistic behaviors. What is meant by an exchange being repeated is that the responses of each person, and the *rewards* each person receives as a consequence of his responses, become fixed in a sequence or pattern; this pattern is what is repeated. Thus, over and over again, the autistic child will engage in head-banging, and over and over again the parent gives the child attention and/or another reinforcing consequence—and over and over again, the responses of child and parent receive their respective rewards. In sum, what might have once been an accidental sequence of events becomes a *structured exchange* which child and parent frequently and fluently reenact. The structure or pattern of the exchange is like a rule. It is as if the child were saying, "I will stop banging my head if you give me attention," and the parent were saying, "I will give you attention if you will stop banging your head shortly after you get my attention."

The contribution of sociology is that it enables us to view exchanges as components of social systems. When an exchange is no longer adventitious but occurs over and over, it is part of the social structure of the system (Blau, 1964; Emerson, 1969; Homans, 1961; Jones & Gerard, 1967; Weingarten & Mechner, 1966). Many, if not all, social systems—be they families, classrooms, or business organizations—consist of structured exchanges which influence the behavior and feelings of their participants. Social systems, by virtue of the direct influence of social exchanges on behavior and feelings, are essentially socializing systems or learning environments. Depending upon the exchanges in the system, the system can encourage and strengthen healthy, adaptive, and personally satisfying behavior, or pathological, maladaptive, and personally painful behavior for the participants—teachers, parents, and children.

The long-term destructive effects of counterproductive exchanges are dramatically and painfully evident in families and many classes of autistic children. Hundreds of hours of observation reveal that many exchanges between autistic children and their caregivers involve the negative reinforcement of a caregiver as he or she attempts to escape a child's disruptive behavior. There are several long-term consequences of these kinds of exchanges.

For example, the caregiver may realize that he or she is "giving in" to the child, and resolve henceforth not to do so. Thus, when the child throws a tantrum in order to get music, the caregiver may ignore the child. In this event, it is likely that the child's tantrums will "escalate," i.e., become more intense and prolonged. If and when the caregiver can no longer tolerate the tantrums at their new level and gives in by allowing the child to hear music, the caregiver will have, in effect, put the child's tantrums on what is known as an intermittent reinforcement schedule—making the tantrums *more* resistant to extinction. Moreover, the caregiver will have reinforced an even more intense tantrum, thereby shaping tantrums in a worse direction.

Over time, the caregiver may adopt a strategy of *avoidance* instead of escape. Rather than wait for the child to tantrum, the caregiver begins to anticipate the child's demands, giving the child music, food (at all hours), or water to play in. In this way, the caregiver avoids having to suffer through so many episodes of disruptive behavior. But he or she is also inadvertently wasting reinforcers which could be used to strengthen appropriate behavior.

The reasons why a caregiver (say, a parent) might continue to reinforce an autistic child's inappropriate behavior offer only a partial explanation of the child's behavioral excesses and deficits. What would account for a parent's nonreinforcement of appropriate behavior, and why would a parent not *require* the child to engage in appropriate behavior in exchange for various reinforcers, as he would his typically developing children? Several possibilities present themselves.

- In the first place, the parent may be so preoccupied with, or so overwhelmed by, the child's disruptive behavior that he or she does not notice the few instances in which the child engages in appropriate behavior, e.g., fitting one piece into a puzzle or putting one of his toys away.
- Second, the child's approximations to a class of appropriate behavior may be so weak that the parent does not even recognize them as approximations, or realize that those approximations should be reinforced.
- Third, the disruptiveness and unresponsiveness of a child may have respectively punished and extinguished the parents' efforts to teach the child to play, speak, and perform simple chore and self-care routines.
- It is possible, finally, that the definition of a child as "damaged" (a definition which may have been ascribed by friends and professionals whose help the parents sought, or acquired after years of trying to teach the child) makes it difficult for the parents to

"put pressure" on their child. They may no longer see him as capable of further learning, so they stop trying as hard.

It must be made quite clear, however, that although the behavior of the parents in part maintains the autistic behavior of the child, the parents, from a social exchange perspective, cannot be *blamed*, because (in the absence of social support and instruction) the behavior of the parents is itself a function of (strongly controlled by) the behavior of the child. As already mentioned, giving the child attention for inappropriate behavior, for instance, constitutes an "escape" response: the parents are attempting to stop their child from engaging in behavior (screaming, tantrums) which is aversive to them and may be injurious to the child. And since the parents' attention often does produce a temporary termination of the child's aversive behavior, the parents' attention-giving behavior is strengthened. On the other hand, the parents' attempts to teach the child and to interact with him are extinguished by the unresponsiveness of their child. Thus, the parents try less and less often to teach their child, may make fewer demands upon the child, and may become quite solicitous to him.

In sum, both parents and child are trapped in a vicious circle. The more parents try to terminate their child's inappropriate behavior, the stronger the inappropriate behavior becomes. And the less often parents attempt to teach the child and the more solicitous they become, the fewer opportunities the child has for learning appropriate behavior.

The education of an autistic child does not involve searching out the initial cause, e.g., why a child *first* banged his head. Rather, it involves *restructuring* exchanges with the child. First, the old structure is broken. No longer is the child reinforced for autistic behavior. Second, a new and equally attractive set of exchanges is instituted which *requires* and hence promotes appropriate behavior. For instance, in order to obtain food, a child must sit quietly at the table. After a period of testing the new structure, the child learns what the structure is and how to *use it* in order to obtain what he wants, e.g., food. Little by little, a series of exchanges is created between the child and the parent or teacher, each of which promotes a new form of behavior—*appropriate* behavior. Just as he had engaged in destructive exchanges, so the child, having learned that the old exchanges no longer exist, now engages in productive (mutually rewarding) exchanges because he is rewarded only for appropriate behavior. In fact, the new structures are often less costly for the child. It is, for instance, physically easier to get food by asking for it than it is to bang one's head a dozen times.

At the time the first edition of this book was written, the effectiveness of an educational system based on social exchange theory and applied behavior analysis was remarkable. Virtually all of the younger children who had been attending the Social Exchange Laboratory at Washington University for one year were learning to talk, value other people, and relate to and cooperate with others (Hamblin et al., 1971). Several had even entered a kindergarten situation where they were learning to read and write with children their own age; others were attending public school.

However, the same theory which explained why the children improved could explain how they might worsen. If exchanges in the home between parents and child remained the same, then autistic behavior might return to the same strength as it was prior to the child's education. Indeed, there are several reasons why the child's behavior might worsen at home. First, the child's undesirable behavior would not be eliminated all at once in school; it would decelerate gradually. In the meantime, disruptive behavior would continue at home. The parents, however, had been negatively reinforced for years in using counterproductive techniques for temporarily terminating disruptive behavior, and would likely continue to use those techniques when disruptive behavior occurred at home. Second, the child had been reinforced for years for engaging in undesirable behavior and had not learned that the acceptable behaviors he had been acquiring in the school would be reinforced at home. Hence, he would continue to "try" undesirable behaviors in the home.

It is imperative, then, that parents learn to manage desirable and undesirable behaviors in the home in the same ways they are managed in the better classes and schools for children with autism. Specifically, parents must learn:

1. which responses to require of their child and which to regard as unacceptable;
2. how to *initiate* exchanges with the child so that new, productive, structured exchanges will develop;
3. how to *teach* the child new kinds of behavior, e.g., speech, play, and cooperation;
4. how to reward appropriate behavior and how to handle inappropriate behavior; and
5. how to *maintain* exchanges that are rewarding both to the parents and to the child.

The goals of the applied research described in the following chapters were:

1. To isolate the variables in the exchanges between parents and their autistic children which were most important in *controlling* the behavior of the children.
2. To demonstrate that a curriculum for children based on principles of social exchange theory and applied behavior analysis offers a promising approach for socializing autistic children.
3. To develop a program by which parents (and siblings) of autistic children could be taught to apply principles of social exchange and applied behavior analysis such that the home will promote and maintain appropriate, constructive behavior in the child.

3 The Parent Training Program

The Training Program and research were adapted to the needs and strengths of each family. However, I envisioned several phases common to all families. These were:

1. Pre-Experimental Phase
2. Experimental or Parent Training Phase
   a. First baseline (A_1, before training)
   b. Training in the Laboratory
   c. Description of the system of exchanges in the home after initial training (B)
   d. Observing and coaching at home to restructure the system of exchanges (C_1)
   e. Experimental reversal of new, orthogenic system of exchanges (A_2)
   f. Reinstatement of orthogenic system of exchanges (C_2)
3. Follow-Up Phase

Social Exchange Theory and the Parent Training Program

Social exchange theory, the Parent Training Program, and the experimental research were tightly integrated. Exchange theory contributed to an account of learning and socialization. The Parent Training Program focused on socializing or educating autistic children and changing behaviors of the parents which had direct implications for their child's socialization. Finally, in order to evaluate the results of the Parent Training Program and to test the principles of social exchange theory, the phases of the experimental research were made to coincide with the stages of the Parent Training Program. In other words, experiments were designed and observation periods were scheduled so as to test the effectiveness of the various stages and techniques used in the Training Program.

The main hypotheses in the applied research were:

1. that the system of exchanges between parents and children can foster or impede primary socialization;
2. that training parents will promote positive changes in the system of exchanges in the home; and
3. that, as a consequence, there will be changes in the behavior of the children—in effect at least partially socializing or educating them.

One problem in the research was, of course, to demonstrate the proposed causal sequence. It was felt that the problem could be solved in the following manner.

First, whether the Training Program modified the exchange behavior of parents toward their child could be tested by comparing data on the parents both at home and in the Laboratory before (A_1) and during training. Since exchange theory proposes that the behavior of parents is controlled to some extent by the behavior of their children, this comparison was extremely important. It enabled the researcher to observe the effects of training on parents *independent* of the behavior of the children—for, during their initial training, parents responded directly to coaching by the researcher.

Second, whether changes in the behavior of parents (i.e., changes in the exchanges parents managed) changed the behavior of their children could be determined by comparing observations of the children in the A_1 (pre-training) with the B and C (post-training) periods. In other words, if the behavior of children at home (during B and C) differed from what it had been before their parents were trained (A_1), then the behavior of the parents could be said to have an effect on the behavior of their children. Progress after the training was determined by comparing the C_1 or C_2 periods with the Follow-up period.

Several steps were taken to avoid the confounding influence that the researcher—often a child's teacher in the Laboratory-school—might have on the behavior of the child at home. First, parents in the home and teachers in the school usually addressed different classes of behavior. For instance, some parents had sole responsibility for teaching their child to play, imitate, or speak certain words. Second, parents conducted reversal experiments, which constituted intra-subject replications, to see if change in their child's behavior was a function of change in the parents' behavior (which itself was a function of the Training Program). Parents, for example, conducted smaller ABAB experiments on speech, play, cooperation, and disruptive behavior.

Variables

A set of variables was needed to make comparisons across experimental-training phases, to test the hypotheses that the Training Program would help parents change exchanges with their children and that these changes would foster substantial improvements in their children's behavior. In developing a set of variables, the family was examined as a *system of structured exchanges*. By "structured" it is meant that exchange relationships are relatively stable or recurrent. The word "system" indicates that exchanges do not exist in isolation, but influence one another. The introduction of an exchange involving punishment for a child may influence other exchanges between the parents and the child. Parents and child may speak to each other less often or play together less often. On the other hand, a new and mutually pleasant exchange may increase the frequency of other exchanges between parents and child.

Although there are structured exchanges between all family members, only those exchanges between children and their parents and older siblings were studied. Certainly, exchanges between the mother and father influence exchanges each has with their child. However, a study of mother/father exchanges was beyond the scope of the research. At any rate, exchanges in which the autistic children were participants were the ones which, theoretically, had the strongest and most direct influence on their behavior.

The exchange was the basic unit of analysis. All exchanges were seen as involving two main classes of responses: *exchange initiations* and *reciprocations.* When a parent initiated an exchange, the exchange had three steps. The parent initiated the exchange with an *exchange signal,* the child participated in the exchange by engaging in some class of response, and the parent completed the exchange with a *reciprocation.* When the child initiated an exchange, the exchange had two steps. The child initiated, and the parent completed the exchange with a reciprocation.

Parental exchange signals. Parents could signal, initiate, or structure exchanges with the following types of exchange signals: *directives, questions,* and *contracts. A directive* involved requesting, telling, or demanding that the child perform a specific response. Examples include "Pick up your clothes" or "Let's get to work" or "Please put this in the trash can." *Questions* involved inquiring whether the child was willing to perform a particular response. Unlike directives, questions—such as "Will you pick up your clothes?" or "Can you say 'Mama'?"—actually give the child the choice of *not* complying with the implicit request. *Contracts,* finally, informed the child that a certain reciprocation was contingent upon his performance of a particular response, e.g., "As soon as you pick up your clothes you may listen to records," or "If you finish this puzzle you may have a cookie." Contracts were statements based upon the Premack principle of making a high-probability behavior contingent upon a low-probability behavior (Premack, 1965).

Parental reciprocations. Each response from a child could be followed by a reciprocation (consequence) from the parents (or siblings).

- The parent could *reward* the child, presenting him with a material reinforcer (food, music, or toys) or with a social reinforcer, that is, attention: either positive (praise, hugs, kisses) or negative (yelling, threatening, or chasing after him).
- The parent could *ignore* the child, i.e., act as if she were unaware of the child's behavior.
- The parent could *time out* the child. Time out involved isolating the child from the rest of the family for a short time by putting him in his room or making him sit in a chair in the corner. In effect, time out temporarily stopped the child's opportunity to engage in rewarding exchanges.
- The parent could *remove* an object from the child or remove the child from the situation, without giving the child much attention in the process. Removal was an ineffective method parents sometimes used to handle disruptive behavior. If the child were spinning a plate, the parent might take the plate away. Or if the child were playing in the bathroom water, the parent might remove him from the bathroom.
- And finally, the parent could *punish* the child either by presenting an aversive stimulus (e.g., a spanking) or by taking away something the child valued (withdrawal of a reinforcer). This latter is not to be confused with removal. When removal is used, the object that is removed is not necessarily valued by the child; it is the activity (usually disruptive) that the child enjoys. Removing the object simply makes the activity impossible. Furthermore, removal does not decrease the probability of the response as punishment does; the child still spins the plate when it is available.

The stimulus functions (or values) to a child of the various types of consequences (or reciprocations) were determined prior to *baseline* observations in the home. This was done through observations of the child and discussions with the parents about their child's reactions to the reciprocations. If, for instance, a child continued to engage in a behavior that produced negative attention, then negative attention was tentatively defined as a reinforcer for that child.

For purposes of later analysis, all reciprocations were categorized as either *reward* or *nonreward*. Nonreward included, of course, ignoring, time out, removal, and punishment.

The child's responses. A child could perform many possible exchange responses. Most of those relevant to the research had been specified beforehand. One class of behavior was *bizarre-disruptive* behavior, which included breaking objects, hitting, spinning plates, and self-mutilation. Included too were behaviors that were generally disruptive: tantrums, screaming, excessive water play, getting into food, etc. Another category was *cooperative* behavior. Cooperation was defined as the child's compliance with a parental exchange signal. Noncooperative responses were also measured.

Speech was a third form of behavior studied. The words and sentences the child said, and the number of instances, were recorded. A final variable under study was the child's *constructive activity,* a category which included chores and playing.

Just as parental reciprocations were classified as reward and nonreward, so the behavior of the child was categorized as *appropriate* (speech, cooperation, and constructive activity) or *inappropriate* (bizarre-disruptive behavior, noncooperation). "Appropriate" behavior was behavior recognized by the researcher and the child's parents as part of the repertoire of any "typical" child, or which would facilitate the acquisition of such behavior. "Inappropriate" behavior either was generally accepted in the literature as indicating pathology (Kanner, 1943; Rimland, 1964) or would impede the acquisition of appropriate behavior. For instance, most children enjoy playing in water, but when a child played in water to the extent that it inhibited cooperative play with other children, it was considered inappropriate.

Systemic behavior change. Much of the data consisted of event recordings and measures of duration. Therefore, changes in individual behavior were easily determined by noting changes in the frequencies and/or duration of the variables in question. Change in parent-child exchanges was determined by noting *covariation* between child and parental variables. For instance, change in the system of exchanges could be seen by computing the percent of the child's *appropriate* versus *inappropriate* responses which produced *reward* vs. *nonreward* before and after training. Similarly, change in speech, play, or cooperation exchanges could be determined by computing the percentage of speech, play, and cooperative responses which produced *reward* vs. *nonreward* before and after training.

As the basic variables for describing and analyzing exchanges in the family have now been described, let us turn to the stages in the Parent Training Program.

Phase 1: Pre-Experimental Phase

The purpose of the Pre-Experimental Phase was to help the researcher design training programs for the parents, curricula for their children, and protocols for observations during the later first baseline period. The Pre-Experimental Phase consisted of gathering data which gave a general description of the child and his or her family prior to the Training Program. The following data were gathered: (1) general home observations, (2) daily "logs" kept by the parent(s), (3) Rimland's "Diagnostic Check List for Behavior-Disturbed Children" (Form E-2), and (4) notes from informal discussions with the parents.

In the general home observations, made a few days prior to the first baseline period, the researcher spent several hours in the home for two days, at different times of the day. Having asked family members to try to go about their business, and locating himself in an inconspicuous place (e.g., in an adjacent room), the researcher recorded onto a portable tape recorder as complete a description as possible of the ongoing interaction (narrative recording). The purpose of the general home observations was to help the researcher identify behavior for further study and to accustom the family members to his presence.

Parents were also asked to keep "logs" which described the day's events. These sensitized the researcher to variables requiring future study, e.g., a child's disruptive behavior and especially the parents' reactions (behavioral and emotional) to the child. In addition, the logs helped the researcher to understand the parents' attitudes and values (for example, their statements concerning the nature of their child's problem, what he or she could and could not learn, and what they felt *they* could and could not learn) which might have required changing if progress were to be made.

Third, the Rimland "Check List" is a questionnaire concerning the development of the child. Designed by Bernard Rimland for a factor analytic study of autism, it yielded information on developmental and behavioral variables. With it, the writer learned how a child had related to others, how he or she had developed physically, how much speech he or she used, and what kinds of bizarre behavior he or she performed. It also yielded information about the parents, such as their occupations and level of education.

And finally, through informal discussions with the parents, the researcher learned, again, problems the child had (or the parents felt he or she had), goals the parents had in mind for their child's education, and, perhaps most important, the child's behavioral, familial, and *medical* history, i.e., if and when the child had been on medication or been to psychiatrists, and with what results.

In sum, the Pre-Experimental Phase enabled the researcher to (1) develop a picture of a child's psychosocial development; (2) specify instructional variables to be studied, i.e., the behavior of the child and his parents to replace, modify, or promote during the child's education and the parents' training; (3) accustom family members to the researcher's presence; and (4) determine a time of day for home observations during the experimental phases.

Phase 2: Experimental Phase

First Baseline (A₁)

The first baseline period consisted of *structured* observation of interaction between the parent(s) and child in the home and (when possible) in the Laboratory-school. Baseline observation provided a reference point from which to evaluate the training program. For instance, during two-hour sessions in the home, the researcher measured the frequency and duration of the child's bizarre behavior, self-destructive and aggressive behavior, playing and working at constructive activities, production of words and sentences, and cooperation with the parents' exchange signals. The researcher also measured the frequency with which the parents attempted to initiate exchanges with their child, the frequency of the different types of signals (directives, questions, and contract statements), and the frequency with which they reinforced, timed out, punished, or ignored appropriate versus inappropriate behavior.

During the Laboratory (classroom) baseline, parents were asked to engage their child in some form of constructive activity, e.g., looking at picture books or working puzzles. Patterns of interaction between parent and child were recorded. These data enabled the researcher to evaluate the parents' progress in applying principles of exchange management and applied behavior analysis. The home baseline, on the other hand, was of broader import, for it was the goal of the Training Program to produce changes in the family setting. By comparing observations made before, during, and after the Training Program, the investigator was able to assess the effects of the Training Program on parents and children and to confirm, modify, or disconfirm the research hypotheses.

Home baseline observations were similar to the general home observations. Family members were asked to "act just as you normally do"; observers located themselves in as inconspicuous a place as possible, and refrained from interacting with family members. In contrast to the general home observations, however, the variables to record had been specified and defined in advance. This was done on the basis of discussions with the parents, analysis of parents' logs, and general home observations. Naturally, when new and relevant events were observed, they were incorporated into the baseline.

To serve as a criterion for judging the effects of experimental conditions (i.e., phases of the Training Program), baseline behavior rates and durations must be in a "steady state," i.e., fluctuate little from session to session (Sidman, 1960). Generally, steady states were obtained in five days of baseline observation.

Training in the Laboratory

Each family's training in the Laboratory was a sequence of instructional units. What was taught and how it was taught were guided by the investigator. The training involved conceptual and practical aspects of applied behavior analysis and exchange management.

Stage 1: Learning exchange theory. It was important that parents learn applied behavior analysis techniques and the principles on which the techniques are based. This conceptual understanding fosters creative use of techniques and application to novel situations. Since the parents would eventually take over much of their child's education, creativity in handling new problems and teaching new skills was imperative.

Parents were taught principles of social exchange theory and behavior analysis and the relevance of the principles to their child's education through reading, discussion, and observation. First, parents read short papers on exchange theory and operant learning. One paper was an exchange-oriented "Parents' Introduction to Behavior Therapy," which I had written. Parents were also given the highly readable *Child Management: A Program for Parents* (Smith & Smith, 1966) and *Living With Children* (Patterson & Gullion, 1968). Later, they were given articles illustrating the techniques (e.g., Williams, 1965; Wolf, Risley, & Mees, 1966). These were discussed with the parents, in order to answer any questions they had, and to make sure they understood the principles of learning and the relevance of family interaction to learning and to their child's future. The researcher also discussed with the parents his analysis of their logs, the general home observations, and the home baseline observations, pointing out how the parents might have been rewarding disruptive behavior and missing opportunities to promote or strengthen constructive behavior.

Special care was taken to help parents understand that they were not to blame for their child's condition, that indeed, the behavior of each was partly determined by the other. They were, however, told that their child's progress depended on their learning how to be teacher-therapists.

Next, parents observed sessions between a teacher and their child from behind a one-way mirror. Parents were coached to: (1) punctuate the stream of interaction into exchange initiations and reciprocations; (2) notice the difference between directives and contract statements (initiations), and ignoring, positive reinforcement, and time out (reciprocations) by the teacher; (3) notice the difference between a child's attending and disattending, and between cooperating and not cooperating with the teacher's initiations; and (4) identify ways that the teacher prompted the child.

To strengthen skill at observing, identifying, and analyzing exchanges, parents were next taught to *record* their observations of sessions on a dictaphone. Again, they were coached by the researcher, who prepared them to notice certain events ("Watch how she rewards him for that") and prompted them when they had difficulty remembering appropriate terms ("Say, 'He imitates correctly and she rewards him with approval and food'."). Proficiency at recording sessions was necessary, too, because the parents would be periodically asked to take data (e.g., the frequency of the child's tantrums or the duration of play) at home when the researcher was not there. The coach heaped approval on the parent(s) for achieving an understanding of theoretical principles and for increased skill in observing and recording.

Stage 2: Learning basic techniques of exchange management.
When a parent was able to discuss his or her child's problems, the
teaching sessions, and the family situation in exchange-theory and
behavior analysis terms and to record sessions accurately and fluently without coaching, he or she was taught *how* to apply the behavioral principles in practical techniques.

As with the child, the parent's training was made as easy as possible at first. A parent's first practical experience using applied behavior analysis consisted of working with either his own or another
child on a task with which the child was already fairly competent.
Thus, the parent merely had to learn how to *maintain* ongoing exchanges.

Having already seen a teacher doing what he or she was to learn,
the parent was asked before the session to work on a specified task
and to behave just as he or she had observed the teacher behaving.
However, the parent was coached by the researcher from behind the
one-way mirror via a wireless intercom system—a modified Zenith
"Award" hearing aid worn by the parent, a Bogen model MTA-10
amplifier, and a Shure model 450 microphone into which the researcher talked. The researcher might, for instance, give the parent a
suggestion on how to initiate the session: "Tell him, 'Okay, Michael,
let's put the puzzle together.'"

As long as exchanges proceeded smoothly, the parent was left
on his or her own. However, the coach gave suggestions when problems arose (e.g., the child's attention decreased) or when the parent's
technique was dysfluent: "Perhaps you ought to reward him faster"
or "Just ignore that." The coach praised the parent as the parent
worked with the child, and the coach identified what the parent had
done properly, e.g., "Good, that was a *quick reciprocation.*" As the
parent became more proficient, the coach faded himself out as a
prompt (i.e., said less and less) until the parent was teaching without
any coaching, except in extreme or novel situations.

Data were taken on the parent's behavior while the parent worked
with the child. These data were later compared with Pre-Training
Laboratory Baseline data to assess the effects of training on the par-

ent. Furthermore, data on the child were taken. Improvement in the child's performance when the parent was no longer being coached could be attributed to the behavior of the parent—i.e., the new structured exchanges the parent was managing.

Specific techniques parents were learning at this time were as follows: (1) to reward correct responses, and to do so immediately; (2) to praise and/or cuddle the child when the child made correct responses, and to present this social reinforcement just before presenting a small amount of the food reinforcer; (3) to ignore irrelevant behavior; (4) to time out the child for disruptive behavior; (5) to shift gradually from continuous to intermittent reinforcement; (6) to initiate exchanges with directives or contract statements, never with questions; and (7) to alternate reinforcers and tasks so the child would not become either satiated or bored.

Once a parent was proficient with the application of the above techniques—so basic to maintaining the child's participation in the learning situation—the parent was taught more difficult techniques for teaching the child *new* behavior, e.g., complicated puzzles or stacking blocks and boxes. Later, parents would use these new skills to teach even more complex competencies, such as play, speech, and cooperation. For example, the parent now learned: (1) *shaping*—rewarding successive approximations to the desired responses; (2) *prompting* and *fading*—verbally and/or manually helping the child to perform the correct response, but gradually withdrawing the prompt as the child learned the response; (3) backing up, or lowering the level of skill required, should the child show signs of stress or fatigue; (4) *differential reinforcement*—immediately rewarding correct responses and ignoring incorrect ones, so as to strengthen the former and weaken the latter; and (5) *chaining* component actions and tasks into larger sequences. Again, the parent was initially coached by the researcher from behind the one-way mirror.

Once a parent was skillful at teaching his or her child new skills, as indicated by the data, and could do so with little uneasiness or fear, he or she was given additional training to help develop creativity and to extend that knowledge to other members of the family.

For instance, a mother learned how to train other persons, such as the child's siblings or father, or the parent of another child. Here, the parent-coach was coached in *how* to coach, via the wireless intercom, by the researcher who was in a third room listening to the interactions both between the new trainee and the child and between the mother-coach and the trainee. The researcher reminded the mother-coach to praise the new trainee for correct behavior and to give suggestions when necessary.

After parents received initial training in the Laboratory, the Training Program moved to the homes. The period of home training and observing was the longest and most crucial phase, for it tested whether the parents' training in the Laboratory was effective. It was also the period when efforts were made to restructure exchanges in the home to promote constructive behavior in the child and replace inappropriate behavior. In general, work with the family at home proceeded through the following stages.

Description of the System of Exchanges in the Home After Initial Training (B)

After parents' initial training in the Laboratory, observations (each session for the same duration and at the same time of day as the home baseline) were made to see if parents had generalized the principles and techniques from the Laboratory to the home, to identify any changes in the child's behavior, and to note remaining problems. Without coaching the parents, the observer recorded the same variables as during the home baseline.

Observing and Coaching at Home to Restructure the System of Exchanges (C$_1$)

The second stage consisted of (1) coaching parents to modify their own undesirable responses (e.g., attending to bizarre behavior) and teaching complex techniques for educating their child; and (2) subsequently *observing* the effects of the changes in the parents' behavior on the behavior of the child. Parents were first coached on techniques they had not successfully generalized to the home. Then other problems in the family, such as the child's deficiencies in speech and play, were addressed.

Specifically, a list of current problems was drawn up with the parents, based on the earlier home observations, logs, and discussions. The list included *counterproductive exchanges* to be replaced and *learning deficits* of the child to be overcome. Concurrently, "prescriptions" in written form were discussed and given to the parents. The prescriptions instructed the parents, in terms they had learned from the Laboratory training, how to decelerate the child's inappropriate behavior and how to teach new, constructive behavior. The specific techniques for decelerating inappropriate behavior and teaching and strengthening constructive behavior will be discussed later in this chapter.

Next, the researcher coached the parents at home in following the prescriptions, i.e., applying behavior modification procedures to the targets selected from the list. Data were taken each session at home on the progress of parents and child. Of course, only a few targets were worked on at any one time. The researcher then faded out coaching and took note of the parents' success at changing the child's behavior by themselves. As each target improved, the cycle of coaching and observing was repeated with more difficult patterns of behavior. Periodically, the parents were re-coached in the Laboratory on complex instructional techniques, such as teaching their child to talk.

Experimental Reversal (A_2) and Reinstatement of Orthogenic System of Exchanges (C_2)

Replication is one of the most direct ways to assess the reliability and generality of findings. Two kinds of replication were made: "intersubject" replication and "intrasubject" replication (Sidman, 1960). The former was accomplished by using several different families in the Training Program. Intersubject replication enables us to determine

whether "uncontrolled and/or unknown variables might be powerful enough to prevent replication" (Sidman, 1960). Thus, intersubject
replication indicated the *adequacy* of the experimental training techniques and the *generality* of findings from one family to another.

Intrasubject replication by reversal, on the other hand, took place
in the A_2 and C_2 periods. The intrasubject replication was essential.
Even if observations during B or C_1 at home showed that the behavior of parents and child had changed, there would be no basis for
attributing change to the Training Program (the independent variable). As Baer (1968) pointed out, "Even if the second stage has
apparently succeeded, only an anecdote has been gained, and the
possibility of coincidence is readily entertained" (p. 8). Change, in
other words, might have resulted not from the Training Program but
from maturation of the child, the additional attention the parents
gave the child, or other extraneous variables. If it could be demonstrated, however, that the child's behavior changed in a consistent
and reliable manner as a function of changes in his or her environment, the phenomenon of change could be considered *real;* such a
demonstration would constitute evidence that the investigator had
control of (and that the Training Program incorporated) the *relevant*
variables.

Procedurally, during A_2, parents were asked and/or coached to
behave as they had during A_1 (prior to training), and during C_2 they
were asked to behave as they were taught during the Training Program. If the behavior of the child changed concomitantly with that of
the parents' reversal, such change demonstrated that the child's behavior was not a function of extraneous variables, but under the
control of the parents and the exchanges they managed (Mill, 1949).

Experimental reversals have been conducted by many investiga-
tors who have trained parents of children with disabilities. It was not
considered feasible or ethical, however, to attempt *total* reversals
with severely impaired children, even if the parents agreed to it.
Since a total reversal of the exchange structure was not done, substitute variations were employed. Although less desirable than complete reversal, such procedures as changing the schedule of recipro-

cation or reversing the exchange structure for a limited aspect of the target behavior could be used to demonstrate behavioral control (Gelfand & Hartmann, 1968).

It should be pointed out that experimental reversals served purposes beyond that of weakening rival explanations of progress. After a concrete demonstration that their child's behavior changed concomitantly with their own, parents gained confidence in the techniques and in themselves as parents and educators. Secondly, reversals often intensified desirable behavioral changes. A child might, for instance, play longer and be less disruptive after a reversal.

Phase 3: Follow-Up Phase

The final phase consisted of follow-up home observations, a month or more after the previous phase, to determine how well the parents retained their training, how well they maintained their child's appropriate behavior, and what additional progress the child had made. Again, each observation session took place for the same length of time and at the same time of day as the other home observations.

Instructional Techniques in the Home

The children's education in the Social Exchange Laboratory and in the home proceeded through a number of stages. At each stage, parents were taught how to teach their child the relevant skills. The parents were not, however, trained in all of the areas or stages in the curriculum at the Social Exchange Laboratory, since (1) some were developed during the research, and (2) some of the children had already completed several stages prior to the Parent Training Program. The specific skill areas or stages and instructional techniques used by parents will be presented below, with notation of where examples can be found in later chapters. A discussion of the stages is also found in Hamblin et al. (1971) and in Kozloff (1974, 1994a).

Creating a Teaching-Learning Environment

Most of the skills acquired by the children and procedures used by the parents had general application in the home. For instance, parents were to ignore disruptive behavior and encourage appropriate behavior in a variety of settings. However, the parents were taught to introduce new stages of education or to work on certain skills within a special instructional setting. Each time a parent worked with the child was considered a session. Parents were taught to design and run their home sessions along the following lines.

Place. At first, sessions were to be held in a smaller room that had minimal distracting stimuli. Parents avoided conducting sessions in a room where other people were likely to be or to enter, or where music or other noises could be heard. Objects which might have attracted the child's attention (such as any toys or room decorations) were removed or placed far out of the child's reach. Sessions were held in the same place each day, at least initially. Once a child acquired reliable working and learning skills (primarily paying attention to the parents' directives and working steadily at tasks), the parents began to introduce ordinary home stimuli into the sessions by holding sessions in the presence of others and in rooms where other activities were taking place.

Time. Most sessions were run at the same time of day. Parents conducted sessions when the child was likely to be motivated. Thus, they chose meal and snack periods, usually between 10:00 A.M. and 4:00 P.M. Since, at first, food was often used as a reinforcer, it was extremely important that the child not have anything to eat for at least two hours before a session. However, parents did not deprive the child of meals so that he would be hungry by the next session; they merely prevented their child from snitching food between meals.

Managing the reinforcer. When food was used as a reinforcer, care was taken to insure that it was food the child liked. In fact, parents generally used the child's favorite foods during sessions. To facilitate immediate reinforcement, parents placed the food within easy access (e.g., on their laps); to prevent the child from becoming satiated, they used small bites of food for each reinforcement.

Seating arrangements. Parents usually conducted sessions at a table, sitting close enough to the child that they could physically prompt when necessary.

Eye Contact

The first stage of the children's education focused on eye contact. Autistic children spend much of their time staring at walls and ceilings, shiny objects, or their hands; they often avoid looking at, or avert their gaze from, other people. By teaching a child to make eye contact and to observe the behavior of other people, the parent or teacher: (1) substituted appropriate social behavior for inappropriate behavior (e.g., the child could use eye contact to invite interaction or to reciprocate the initiations—greetings, requests—of other people); and (2) facilitated (in fact, made possible) the child's learning more complex behaviors that involve visual inspection (e.g., motor imitation). For some children, learning to make eye contact during back-and-forth exchanges with their parents and classroom teachers literally brought them into the social world. Indeed, once eye contact was strengthened, other positive changes occurred. For example, the child approached, smiled, and vocalized more often.

Two steps were used to strengthen eye contact. In the first step, the parent or teacher simply reinforced the child *whenever* he made eye contact. The parent held up to her eye a bite of the child's meal and *waited* for him to make eye contact. She then immediately praised, patted, or hugged him and presented the food. If the data taken during sessions indicated that the child's rate of eye contact was not increasing, the parent began to *prompt* the child by slowly moving the food by her eyes. As the child's eye contact improved, the parent faded the prompt. Parents were instructed not to prompt

eye contact by forcibly moving the child's head, as this usually results in a fight. Of course, the parents also reinforced the child for
eye contact at other times of the day that were not sessions.

In the second step, the parent taught the child to make eye contact *on request*. The parent held up a bite of the child's meal, said,
"Look at me," prompted the child if necessary, and reinforced the
child if he made eye contact within approximately five seconds. As
the child's eye contact improved, the parent faded the prompts, for
instance, the food she was holding up.

Constructive Behavior

Many children with autism alternate between self-stimulation and
periods of aimless staring and wandering. At times a child appears to
be trying to pass the time with the only behavior he knows. At other
times, his behavior appears aimed at producing attention from others, perhaps also as a way to increase the level of stimulation. The
goal of this second stage was to provide the child with a repertoire
of play and chore skills. Specifically, the aim was to: (1) increase the
child's attentiveness to a task; (2) further strengthen eye contact; (3)
help the child learn color, shape, and size discriminations; (4) improve hand-eye coordination; and (5) teach socially appropriate and
personally satisfying means of spending time and relating to others,
as alternatives to undesirable forms of self-stimulatory and attention-
getting behavior.

When teaching simple manipulative (play) skills or chores, the
parents had to do more than *manage* an ongoing exchange using
such procedures as differential reinforcement, extinction, or time out.
The parents also had to institute and manage a *counter exchange*—
i.e., to motivate, prompt, and sustain the child's engaging in behavior incompatible with self-stimulatory, disruptive, attention-getting
behavior. To help parents structure counter exchanges to strengthen
constructive behavior at home, the researcher provided a behavioral
prescription listing specific steps to follow:

1. Specify the behavior that you want—speech, play, helping you, working at tasks.
2. Next break the desired behavior into small steps. A child does not learn how to speak in sentences at first—he learns sounds. And before he learns how to complete a puzzle, he learns how to put in one piece.
3. Now take the first small step as your goal. This is the behavior that you want your child to learn.
4. Next, locate all the things your child likes and likes to do—food, music, going for a ride, anything you know he likes.
5. Now state to yourself what the new rule is going to be—what the new *exchange* is. For instance, "Michael must ____ before he gets ____." Remember, make the first behavior he must perform to get what he wants something simple—just the first step of something more difficult. Decide that only when he does what you have specified in the rule, will he get the reward.
6. Next, and most difficult, start to put the new rule into effect. There are several ways to do this.
   a. You can wait until he spontaneously does the task you have selected—but this is not likely.
   b. You can ask or direct him to perform it.
   c. You can *wait* until he indicates that *he* wants something. Then *you* tell him what the rule is: e.g., "As soon as you put in the puzzle piece, you can hear a record."
   d. You can set aside a certain period of the day when he is to have the opportunity to work for what he wants, e.g., the record. You tell him, "Now it's time to work for records." You bring him over to the work area and prompt him to start working. If he refuses, you just ignore him, and he will find out that he will miss his chance to hear music. Eventually, he will start working, and you must reward him with praise as he works. When he has finished, reward him with whatever it was that he was working for. Do not require him to work for too long at first before you reward him. Only gradually should you increase the time he must work.

7. The last step is to apply all of the techniques you learned in the Laboratory. Ignore irrelevant behavior. Time out for intolerable behavior. Immediately reinforce correct responses. Prompt him through the task physically if necessary, or act as a model for him to imitate.

Parents used the above instructions to institute and manage counter exchanges for simple tasks and chores.

Simple manipulative tasks. Immediately following the stage of eye contact, parents began working on simple tasks, such as puzzles, stacking blocks, shape boxes, or peg boards. During sessions, the parent presented a well-defined task (e.g., completing a puzzle or fitting shapes into a shape-box). The parent first waited for the child to make eye contact (or, if necessary, requested eye contact); handed the child a puzzle piece or shape; prompted the child to properly place the object (using less restrictive prompts at first, such as gestures); and reinforced the child for accomplishing each step of the task. At first, a child was rewarded for *every* correct task response with hugs, praise, and a bite of lunch. As the child acquired skill, the parent faded the prompts; that is, she helped the child less and less, and gradually thinned the ratio of reinforcement until the child was reinforced intermittently for the completion of, on the average, three or four puzzles.

This stage was extremely important. It was the first time the child engaged in complex, new, and often difficult activities in exchange for reinforcers. It was necessary, then, that the child enjoy and succeed at the tasks and exchanges; his cooperation in later stages would depend on it. Consequently, parents were careful to: (1) allow the child to progress at his own rate and not require responses he was incapable of performing; (2) keep bites of food small to prevent satiation; (3) rotate tasks to prevent boredom; (4) gradually increase the difficulty of tasks to promote adaptation and response chaining (see Chapter Two); and (5) talk to the child about the task and praise him highly for completing it, but refrain from a steady stream of talk, to prevent the parent's voice from becoming a meaningless background noise.

Parents also used this stage to further strengthen their child's eye contact, and to teach the child to use eye contact to sustain exchanges with the parent. They did this by requiring the child to make eye contact in order to receive each puzzle piece or block. Since eye contact had already been strengthened, it was not necessary to reinforce eye contact itself on a schedule of continuous reinforcement. Instead, eye contact was chained to other responses (puzzle working) which were reinforced. Procedurally, the parent held up a puzzle piece (much as she had held up food in the previous stage), gave it to the child only after he made eye contact, and then reinforced him with attention and food for putting in the piece.

Chores. Teaching simple chores was also begun in this stage and continued throughout the child's education. Using the above prescription, parents set aside certain times of the day when the child had the opportunity to earn a reinforcer in return for performing one of his chores (e.g., helping wash the dishes, cleaning the kitchen table). Examples of parents teaching their children chores and simple manipulative tasks are found in Chapters 4, 5, 6, and 7.

Motor Imitation

The third stage in a child's education was motor imitation, which was considered essential for success in the later stage of speech training. See Chapter 4 for a behavioral prescription for motor imitation.

Speech Training

Speech training was the fourth major stage in the child's education and one of the most crucial concerns in the Training Program. Speech has the obvious function of enabling people to engage in concerted action and to learn things from others indirectly (i.e., symbolically). It also enables people to direct their own behavior (Luria & Yudovich,

1968). In addition, it was expected that once an autistic child learned to communicate with speech, other problems, such as bizarre-disruptive behavior, would be lessened.

The program of speech training borrowed much from the work of Lovaas (1966b), Lovaas and Kassorla (1966), Risley and Wolf (1966, 1967), and Ferritor (1969). Like them, we utilized the techniques of *presenting* a verbal stimulus (a sound to imitate, a question to answer, a picture to name), *prompting* the child to make the appropriate response, *rewarding* successive approximations, and *fading* the prompts.

In speech training, the teacher or parent at first reciprocated exchanges with a powerful reinforcer, namely the child's meal. Mothers were asked to bring the child's meal to the Laboratory with him, to bring food the child liked, and to make sure that the child had eaten nothing since his last meal. Because learning to speak is difficult, in the early stages the sessions lasted only 20 minutes. If the child was doing especially well during a session, it was extended. Once the child progressed to where speaking was not as difficult, the sessions might be expanded to 45 minutes or longer.

There were several stages in speech training. If the child were originally mute or nearly so, he would be led from the stages of spontaneous vocalization, to imitative speech, to labeling or naming, to conversational speech.

Stage 1: Spontaneous vocalizations. This stage was designed to increase the child's rate of spontaneous sounds as a first approximation to speaking and to facilitate the next stage, imitative speech. The procedures were essentially the same as in the eye contact stage. That is, the parent waited until the child vocalized, then praised the child and gave him a small bite of food. Initially, the parent might prompt the child to vocalize by talking to him or bouncing him on his knee, reinforcing the child for each vocalization. As the child's rate of vocalizations increased, the parent faded the prompt and reinforced the child on thinner schedules, e.g., after about three or four vocalizations.

If a child began to make the same one or two sounds over and over, the parent gave the child praise (e.g., smiled and nodded), but waited until the child made a slightly different sound, and then reinforced the new sound with praise, an imitation of the new sound, and then a bite of food. For example, the child says, "Eee, eee, eee, eee [the parent is nodding], eee-yah!" The parent responds "Eee-yah!" and gives the child a bite of food (Kozloff, 1974). With vocalization shaped in this way, the child gradually learns to say a large number of sounds, and to string them together ("Ah-yee, buh-buh, mmm-eee").

Stage 2: Imitative speech. The next stage of speech training involved teaching, by imitation, first the phonemes and basic syllables in the English language, and then words. The training was in a small room with minimal distracting stimuli. If the child was uncooperative, or if progress was slow, the child would have two or more sessions (meals) per day in the Laboratory-school. The basic procedures used by the parents were as follows.

First, the sound to be taught was specified. In the beginning the easiest sounds were worked on: vowels and bilabial consonants that the child already said fluently and frequently. The child and the parent sat across from one another at a table, with the child's food within easy reach of the parent but out of the child's reach. The parent next waited until the child was sitting calmly and attending to him. The parent then held up a small bite of food to his lips so as to draw the child's attention to the parent's mouth. When the child was looking at the parent's mouth, the parent said, slowly and clearly, the sound that the child was to imitate.

If the child made no vocal response in about five seconds, the parent lowered the food and waited about five seconds before holding up the food again and repeating the signal (model). Two procedures were used to evoke imitative responses. First, the parent prompted vocalizations by gently pushing the child's abdomen, bouncing her on his knee, by stroking her throat, singing to her, etc. If the child seemed unable to imitate the sound, the parent, when possible, might physically prompt the child by molding the child's lips, tongue, cheeks, or chin so that the correct response or an acceptable approximation was produced.

Finally, when the child said the correct imitative response or approximation—prompted or not—within the five-second interval, the parent immediately reciprocated with praise, a hug, and a small bite of food. This sequence was designed to build up praise, physical contact, and the parent's voice as conditioned reinforcers. The cycle of (1) the parent presenting the child with a vocal stimulus to imitate; (2) the child making a correct (prompted or unprompted) response; and (3) the parent reciprocating with positive reinforcement, was repeated over and over, giving the child practice imitating the sound. Note that the sequence constituted a structured exchange. Each person presented a stimulus to the other according to an underlying rule or contingency, and each stimulus presented by one person was a reinforcer for the other (food from the parent and sounds from the child).

Gradually, as the child gained expertise imitating a sound, the parent *faded out* the prompt. *Differential reinforcement* was used throughout. That is, closer approximations to the parent's model and less-prompted imitations were given higher-quality and more frequent reinforcement. At first, gross approximations were reinforced strongly; that is, the child was not expected to give an exact imitation in the beginning. Otherwise, the child would almost never be rewarded; would suffer unnecessary deprivation and frustration; and would soon refuse to cooperate since imitative responses, vocalizing, sitting at the table, and looking at the parent would all be extinguished.

Besides gradual change in the definition of a rewardable response, there was a gradual change in the *schedule of reciprocation*. While the child was in the acquisition phase (i.e., learning to make the appropriate imitation), continuous reinforcement was used. As the child became more fluent, the parent began to reciprocate on an intermittent schedule of about one reinforcement for three good imitations—not three in a row, but an average of three.

Speech training is hard work for parent and child alike. Disruptive behavior—getting up from the table, gaze avoidance, tantrums, repeated errors—was handled in several ways. First, the parent ignored the disruptive behavior. Instead of telling the child to come back to the table, or punishing the child for incorrect imitations, the parent waited until the child returned to the table or, in the case of repeated errors, waited several seconds before presenting the next model for the child to imitate.

Second, the parent increased the *attractiveness* of the speech exchanges by: (1) going back to easier sounds or words for a few days; (2) giving the child more prompts; (3) reinforcing with more enthusiasm and for grosser approximations to the vocal model; or (4) switching to other reinforcers or to other tasks for a few days. These procedures usually reestablished a more enjoyable teaching situation and steadier progress in the child. Behaviors such as tantrums, which made it impossible to continue a teaching session, were handled by immediately timing out the child for a few minutes contingent upon each tantrum. The emphasis at all times, though, was to encourage cooperation by making the exchanges attractive, rather than to force cooperation by making noncompliance aversive for the child.

Once an imitative response had been learned, the parent chose another sound to work on. The criteria for defining a response as "learned" vary from teacher to teacher and school to school. We taught parents to define a sound as learned by imitation when the child could emit ten consecutive unprompted correct responses, or could imitate the sound correctly and unprompted 80 percent of the time. Naturally, sounds had to be worked on periodically to increase the child's fluency. Typically, it took fewer and fewer trials for the criteria to be reached with new and harder sound models, perhaps indicating "insight" into the structure of the exchange or the development of a "learning set" (Harlow, 1949).

When a child's imitative repertoire contained approximately five sounds, the parent began to work on words (one-syllable words at first) and new sounds. At first, progress imitating words was uneven.

It was characterized by periods of incorrect responding, bursts of correct responding, then more incorrect responding, until eventually the child was emitting longer and longer series of correct responses. Also, the definition of a rewardable response moved up and down; that is, the parent lowered the required level of approximation when the child made too many incorrect responses at a higher level.

Words were *built* by adding component sounds to form the unit word. First, the parent made sure the child could reliably imitate each component. Next, he or she tested to see if the child could imitate the word without further work. If the child could not say the word, the parent chose one of the component sounds as a foundation and had the child repeat it over and over. The writer taught parents to choose between the beginning and final sounds in the word and select the one that was *weaker*. The rationale was that it would be easier to add the second sound to the foundation sound if the second sound were easier for the child to say. Thus, some words were built forward ("B-B-B-Blue") and some backward ("D-D-D-fooD").

After the child repeated the foundation sound fluently many times, the parent had the child similarly imitate the second sound. Then the parent began to combine the two sounds. First, she had the child say the sound which occurred first in the word, and rewarded the child. *Immediately* thereafter, she had the child say the following sound in the word, and rewarded the child. This was done many times to give the child some idea of the order of the sounds in the word.

Next, the parent had the child imitate the first sound, and, if the child said it correctly, the parent *immediately* had the child say the following sound. If the child also said the second sound correctly, he was rewarded. For instance, the child might have imitated "m" then "e" to form "me." Then he was rewarded. If, however, the child failed to imitate the first sound, the parent waited five seconds and then repeated the sound.

It was a bit more complex if the child imitated the first sound but not the second. If the parent gave no reward, the child's first response would have gone unrewarded. To solve this, the parent used prompting and shaping; that is, she helped the child make the second sound and was willing, in the beginning, to accept a rough approximation. Thus, at first the child might be rewarded for saying "m" and "uh" or "muh" instead of *me*.

Once the child was reliably repeating the two sounds in succession, the parent presented the whole word to imitate. Again, prompting and shaping were used to generate good pronunciation. The criteria for learning a word by imitation were the same as for a single sound.

The following table summarizes the three steps in building a word.

	Parent Says	**Child Says**	**Parent**
Step 1	"m"	"m"	Rewards
	"e"	"e"	Rewards
Step 2	"m"	"m"	
	"e"	"e"	Rewards
Step 3	"me"	"me"	Rewards

The next words selected by parents usually sounded very different from earlier words. This was to help the child learn to hear the difference. Later, old words or parts of words served as parts of new words. Hence "eat" added to "m" is "meat" and, with a slight vowel change, "ball" added to "loo" is "blue." Again, the parent worked on old words and sounds from time to time to increase fluency and retention.

Stage 3: Labeling. Imitative speech seems to be a precondition of functional speech. If a child's training stopped with imitative speech, however, he would merely have acquired another symptom of autism: echolalia. Functional speech requires that the words said by a person have *meaning* for him and others in his speech community; i.e., the words signify or symbolize classes of things, events, and relationships.

The acquisition of a labeling vocabulary may well be, in the Meadian sense, the beginning of the acquisition of mind. At any rate, learning names of things is a first step in the development of functional speech, i.e., speech that enables a child to communicate. The use of sentences in conversational speech depends, of course, on the prior acquisition of meaningful words.

In making the transition from imitation to naming and in helping the child to build a labeling repertoire, the writer again borrowed from the prior research of Lovaas and Risley and Wolf cited above. The problem was to teach the child to associate a particular word (and later, its synonyms) with a particular set of stimuli. Generally, the following steps were used: (1) waiting for the child to attend to the teacher or parent; (2) holding up an object or picture; (3) waiting for the child to attend to the object; (4) asking the child what the object was and immediately prompting by supplying the correct answer; (5) rewarding him when he imitated the prompt correctly; (6) fading the prompt until the child was able to give the correct answer when asked "What is this?"; (7) holding up other objects in the same class so the child would learn to generalize the word to include a wide range of members of the class. Typically, it took a child many trials to learn the first functional word. Gradually, the child learned words faster and faster until his rate stabilized. Acquisition was facilitated by teaching him words that were of immediate relevance, such as the names for foods, parts of the body, objects in the home, and so forth. Besides nouns, the child was also taught several common verbs, such as "eat," "go," "want," and "help," which he could *use* to acquire objects or activities he had learned to name.

Words that were more abstract—such as prepositions or adverbs—were not usually taught in this stage. It was felt that the child should be able to use words in order to communicate as soon as possible. Then, once "communicating" became more frequent, more difficult concepts could be taught.

Stage 4: Conversational speech. In this stage the child was taught to use sentences in typical ways—to answer questions, ask questions, ask for things, and so forth. At first, the child was taught simple sentences of immediate relevance: for instance, to answer "What is this?" with "That's bread." The same techniques used in Stage 3 were used here. The child was asked a question, prompted with the correct answer, and rewarded for answering appropriately. This was repeated until he could answer without a prompt.

Similarly, the parent taught the child how to ask for things by saying to him, "What do you want?... I want food." When the child imitated with "I want food," he was given food. By slowly fading out the answer (e.g., saying it more softly or delaying it longer), the child learned to say "I want food" when he was asked what he wanted. More important was teaching the child to *initiate* with the sentence. This was done by fading out the question "What do you want?" in the presence of a desired object (food), until the child spontaneously said, "I want food." Once the child initiated with a sentence he had made a breakthrough, because he usually began to initiate more and more and generalize the grammatical frame "I want _____" to other things and to other situations. He might be heard to say, "I want eat," "I want cookie," "I want more."

Basically, teaching a child to use sentences involved teaching him grammatical frames which could be filled with thousands of different words. At the same time, the child was encouraged to use sentences. The parent prompted and required the child to use sentences before rewarding him with objects and activities he had formerly been getting "for nothing" or for undesirable behavior.

Parents were taught the above techniques in several stages. They were given articles to read and lists of steps to use; they observed the teacher working with the child; and they were coached to work on speech with the child. Progress at home was observed periodically, and additional coaching and instruction may have been given. Specific procedures used by parents in teaching imitative speech, labeling, and conversational speech are found in Chapters 5, 6, and 7.

Inappropriate Behavior

Much of an autistic child's behavior (tantrums, breaking things, self-stimulation) is not only incompatible with but hinders learning adaptive, prosocial behavior. With the exception of negative practice, the parents were trained first in the Laboratory and then at home to use ignoring, time out, differential reinforcement of alternative behavior, and other techniques described in Chapter Two for reducing and replacing problem behavior. Usually, the major problem was not teaching parents *how* to apply the techniques, but *when*—i.e., for which inappropriate responses should extinction be used? When should punishment be used? When should satiation be tried? Parents' handling of inappropriate behavior is discussed further in Chapters 4, 5, 6, and 7.

Termination of the Training Program

The termination of research and training with each family was contingent on the progress of parents and children—the parents' skill at applied behavior analysis and exchange management, and the child's developing a repertoire of appropriate behavior. We planned to work with a family until the child (1) had progressed at least to the third stage in speech training; (2) had begun to spend substantial time in constructive activities; and (3) had substituted constructive behavior for much of his bizarre-disruptive behavior.

Methodology

Various considerations of methodology entered into the design and progress of the research.

Experimental Design

In general the research was experimental, in the form of an ABCAC design for each family. I adopted this design because I felt that it would best enable me to effectively evaluate my research hypotheses. In the A_1 period, observations were made of exchanges between parents and child prior to the Parent Training Program. In the B and C_1 periods, exchanges were again observed—this time after parents had passed several phases of the Training Program. As discussed, the A_2 and C_2 periods involved an experimental reversal of exchanges in the home. The reversal constituted an intra-subject replication enabling the researcher to (1) determine the reliability of any changes observed in the B and C_1 periods; (2) possibly produce an intensification effect; and (3) give parents confidence in their ability to apply the educational techniques. The experimental periods were followed by a follow-up period to assess the stability of changes in the home.

Sampling

Four families participated in the program. No attempt was made to obtain a representative sample, for several reasons. First, the amount of time and effort involved in training the large number of families required for representativeness would have far exceeded the capacity of a single investigator. Second, the universe of families with autistic children had not adequately specified. Third, and most important, the internal and external validity of findings was dealt with by means of *experimental control,* not by a statistical analysis of differences between an experimental and a control group whose members presumably differed only by chance. Experimental control was exerted in two ways. First, extraneous variables were controlled by constancy; that is, the same conditions were to obtain in all the experimental sessions. Second, a basis for inferring the validity of findings was obtained by showing that behavioral processes in each family could be *reliably (repeatedly) changed* or controlled by the investigator and the parents. This latter refers to intrasubject replication by reversal. In addition, of course, each family served as an intersubject replication (Sidman, 1960) for the others.

Recording Data

Observations were recorded in both the Laboratory and the homes. In the Laboratory, data were taken on an Esterline-Angus twenty-channel event recorder connected to a panel with twenty permanent switches. The Esterline allowed recording of both the frequency and the duration of variables. At the same time, audiotape and dictaphone recordings of most sessions were made. From these, the researcher could determine the tasks at hand and the communication of caregivers and children.

At first, home observations were recorded onto a portable tape recorder in sportscaster fashion. This yielded a running description of the events, from which the researcher could later determine the frequencies and durations of selected variables.

This method had several drawbacks. First, each session required at least six hours of transcription. Since a hundred or so home observations were envisioned, this made recording all home observations onto tape prohibitive. Moreover, although the inter-observer reliability of scoring from recordings was high, over time fatigue was bound to reduce reliability.

A more efficient method of recording home observations evolved shortly after the research began. Since the variables for each session were specified and defined beforehand, it seemed reasonable that events and their durations could be recorded *directly* onto a standardized recording sheet using abbreviations for the different variables. In this way, the observer would merely have to make abbreviations and a few comments along a recording sheet as the interaction progressed.

The standard recording sheet is presented in Table 1 on the next page. The steps in each exchange were recorded horizontally across the three columns. In exchanges beginning with an exchange signal by a parent, recordings were made in all three columns: (1) how the parent initiated the exchange; (2) what the child's response was; and (3) how the parent reciprocated the child's response. In exchanges initiated by the child, information was put only in the center and right-hand columns (the child's response and the parent's reciprocation). The temporal progress of exchanges through the session was recorded vertically. By scanning the sheet, one could note the pattern or sequence of events during the session. This enabled the investigator to determine, for instance, what sequence of exchanges led to a child's tantrum, or how the child escalated disruptive behavior until it finally produced a reward (Bijou, Peterson, & Ault, 1968).

There were standard categories and abbreviations for each column. Parents' initiations with Directives (D), Questions (Q), and Contracts (C) were recorded in the left-hand column. Who initiated was also recorded, e.g., mother (M) or father (F). The exchange responses by the child were recorded in the middle column. Examples are as follows. The child could cooperate (Coop) with a parental exchange initiation, or he could be noncooperative (Noncoop). He could use Speech (Words, Phrases, Sentences). He could engage in Constructive Activities (Play, Chores). He could engage in atavistic behavior (Bizarre, Aggressive, Self-destructive). And finally, he could engage in behavior that was generally disruptive (Tantrums, Playing in water, Screaming, etc.).

Two response classes could be scored for one exchange response of the child. For instance, if the child cooperated with a parental directive by performing a chore, both Cooperation and Chore would

---

Table 1: Standard Recording Sheet

Family _____ Purpose of Observation _____

Date _____ Session No. _____ Time Begun–Time Ended _____

Parental Exchange Signals	Responses of Child	Parental Reciprocations

be recorded. Or if the child screamed following a parental directive, both Noncooperation and Disruption would be recorded. All responses of the child could be further categorized and scored as appropriate, correct, or constructive (A) or inappropriate (I).

Finally, parental reciprocations were recorded in the right-hand column. The child's behavior could be followed by a Reward (R) or a Nonreward (Nonrew). As to Nonrewards, the parents could Ignore (I) the child; they could Punish (P) him; they could Time Out (TO) the child; or they could Remove (Rem) him or a particular object from the situation.

To summarize, the typical variables for each segment of parent-child exchanges are presented (on a representation of a recording sheet) in Table 2 on the next page.

On the recording sheet the observer also indicated the duration of certain responses, e.g., the length of time the child engaged in play. In addition, the observer wrote down, in an abbreviated fashion, what the parent said to the child in signaling exchanges, what toys the child was playing with, what chore he was performing, and whether the parent prompted the child to make correct responses. This way, one could describe both the *structural* aspects of the interaction (the relative frequencies of the different exchange variables) and the *content* of the interaction.

To give the reader an idea of how data were taken, a sample recording sheet selected from a portion of the observation of one session is presented in Table 3 (p. 92).

Tabulation of Data

Originally, the researcher and several reliability checkers summarized the data by meticulously reading each recording sheet and tabulating frequency and, when applicable, duration for each variable. Then, either by computing percentages (e.g., the percent of inappropriate responses which were rewarded), or by comparing the frequency of a particular response of the child with the frequency of the different parental reciprocations, the structures of the exchanges could be seen. After several months a data sheet was devised to simplify tabulation and the subsequent description of exchange structures. A sample data sheet is presented in Table 4 (p. 93).

From the data sheet one can readily see the overall structure of exchanges in this family. The child was rewarded for inappropriate behavior quite frequently, but was also ignored for engaging in appropriate behavior. At the same time, it is evident that the child seldom engaged in appropriate behavior. He seldom cooperated with parental exchange signals, and he engaged in inappropriate behavior a great deal.

Table 2: Typical Variables in Parent-Child Exchanges as Recorded on the Standard Recording Sheet

---

Family _____ Purpose of Observation _____

Date _____ Session No. _____ Time Begun–Time Ended _____

Parental Exchange Signals	Responses of Child	Parental Reciprocations
Directive (D)	Appropriate Behavior (A)	Reward (R)
Question (Q)	Cooperation (Coop)	Attention
Contract (C)	Speech	Food
	Words	Music
Mother (M)	Phrases	
Father (F)	Sentences	Nonreward
Sibling (Name)	Constructive Activity	(Nonrew)
	(Constr)	Ignore (I)
	Play	
	Chore	
	Inappropriate Behavior (I)	
	Atavisms	
	Bizarre	
	Self-destructive	
	Aggressive	
	Disruptions (D)	
	Tantrum	
	Destructive	
	Screaming	
	Water play	
	Noncooperation	
	(Non-coop)	

One drawback of this data sheet, however, is that it does not indicate whether cooperation or noncooperation with the various *types* of exchange signals is reciprocated differentially. The researcher would have to return to the recording sheet to determine this. In addition, one cannot tell if the behavior of the two parents is differ-

---

Table 3: Data from Observation During Part of One Session as Actually Recorded on Recording Sheet

Hare Family   Progress during C_1 (uncoached)
Saturday, November 9, 1968   Session 7   12:00-2:00 p.m.

Parental Exchange Signals	Responses of Child	Parental Reciprocations
MD "Carry this in."	Coop. A	MR Attention, "Thank you."
MD "Put these away."	Coop. A	MR Attention, praise
	Spins lid (1 minute). I	I
	Puts piece of pottery in its proper place on counter. A	MR Attention, praise
	Gets into cabinets. I	TO (3 minutes)
MC "As soon as you're done, I'll see what you want." (Brings him to work table and hands him a pegboard to work on.)	Coop. Plays (2 minutes). A	MR Attention, praise MR Attention, praise MR Attention, praise MR Attention, praise MR Attention, praise MR Attention, praise, music
MD "Close the door, please."	Coop. A	MR Attention, praise
	Self-initiated play with puzzle (2 minutes). A	MR Attention, praise MR Attention, praise MR Attention, praise, music
	Dumps box of crayons on floor and scatters them. I	I
MC "As soon as you pick them up, you can play with water."	Noncoop. I	I

ent. This is remedied, of course, by having a separate data sheet for each parent.

Reliability

Naturally, procedures to ensure experimental control are undermined if the accuracy of observations is open to question. Reliability checks were made, therefore, during each training stage and experimental period with each family. Inter-observer reliability checks were made by comparing the data recorded by two observers. To avoid the possibility that observations made early in the training lacked reliability, the observers (uninformed of the hypothesis) were trained to take the type of data under study *prior* to the reliability checks. Intra-observer

---

Table 4: Sample Data Sheet

Family _____ Purpose of Observation _____

Date _____ Session No. _____ Time Begun–Time Ended _____

BEHAVIOR		Parents' Behaviors							
		Exchange Signals			Exchange Reciprocations				
Child's Behaviors		D	Q	C	Rew	I	P	TO	Rem
Inappropriate	Non-cooperative	5	10	3	10	5	3		
	Shrieking				8	2			
	Playing in water				10				
	Getting into things				10	2			
	Destructive				4				
	Bizarre sounds/ actions				3	3			
	Jumping on bed								
Appropriate	Cooperate	5				5			
	Play				1	5			

reliability was periodically assessed via audio and videotapes of the sessions.

Presentation of Data

Aside from anecdotal data used to illustrate interesting and/or important points, most data are presented in the form of tables and graphs. Moreover, in many cases the data are presented so that the reader can ascertain changes in various classes of the children's behavior, and note how the children's behavior changes as a function of the exchanges managed by the parents (see especially Figures 1, 2, 3, 8, 13, 14, and 16). In other words, most of the graphs and tables enable one to observe changes in the behavior of *each* member of the exchange as well as covariation in the behavior of both members. Most graphs concerning verbal behavior, for example, present the frequency of the child's verbal responses and the frequency of parental reinforcement.

Observer Effects

Whether or not the observations were accurate, it is possible that the behavior observed was influenced by the presence of the observer. Several precautions were taken to weaken observer effects. First, as noted earlier, observations were made for several days prior to the baseline observations in order to accustom family members to the presence of the observer. Second, the observer (unless he was coaching) refrained from interaction with family members. And third, the observer located himself at a place away from family interaction, e.g., in another room.

Jules Henry (1967), moreover, has argued that (1) family interaction patterns are relatively stable and are not likely to be easily disturbed by the presence of an observer; (2) family members do not necessarily know what the observer is looking for and so they do not know what to conceal; and (3) many parental behaviors are habitual and will be performed especially when a parent is under the strain of the child's disruptive behavior. In other words, not only were precautions taken to lessen observer effects, but a good case can be made that the presence of the observer did not readily change habitual patterns of behavior.

Ethical Considerations

The researcher is confronted with the fact that he intruded on the lives of a number of people and did so with the express intent of changing their lives. How is such intervention justified? First, observations of the private lives of the families were conducted in the spirit of helping the family members overcome important problems. Second, the parents came to the researcher for help, and were fully informed of the nature and purpose of the research and the procedures. And third, available evidence indicated that unless the behavior of the children changed in a positive direction, they would spend most of their lives in some form of residential facility.

In the second place, the ethics of experimental reversals might be questioned. The issue is whether the canons of scientific method overshadowed the welfare of the families. It should be remembered that complete reversals of the productive systems of exchanges were not conducted, precisely because of the possibility of destructive effects. Instead, reversals were conducted on isolated aspects of a child's repertoire, and the reversals were of short duration. In addition, past research has shown that experimental reversals often have beneficial effects, further accelerating appropriate behavior and decelerating inappropriate behavior.

4 Michael Hare

Michael Hare was unique among the four autistic children in the program. In contrast to the other three children, Michael had almost no constructive behavior at the time the writer began working with his family. Therefore, the program for teaching his parents and educating Michael was the most comprehensive of the four, focusing on bizarre and disruptive behavior, and establishing functional speech, cooperation, and play behavior. In a sense, the program with the Hares was prototypical. In fact, several techniques that were successful with the Hare family were used with other families with similar needs.

Description of the Child

Michael, a Caucasian male, the last of three children (two sisters, ages sixteen and eleven), was born on January 21, 1962. Michael's mother listed her occupation as "housewife." She had received some college education prior to her marriage. Mr. Hare had been a secondary school teacher until his switch to guidance counseling, having received a graduate degree in that field in early 1968. Concerning the family's medical history, the Hares indicated that none of Michael's parents, siblings, grandparents, uncles, or aunts had been seriously mentally ill or retarded. Michael's development is summarized in Appendices 1 and 2.

Equally as important as Michael's development were his parents' reactions to his development, for these reactions played a large part in Michael's reinforcement history. Mr. Hare reports that he felt something was wrong with Michael from the day of Michael's birth, as he was so quiet and did not even cry. The first major incident noted by the Hares was that when Michael was three weeks old, his father was seriously burned in a shop accident; as a result, Michael was cared for by a series of aunts, grandparents and friends for the next two weeks. His mother related, however, that "Nothing unusual occurred—I remained calm and feel Michael wasn't upset in any way... He cried and did all normal things—but was quiet and reserved. His father is this way, and I told myself Michael's personality was showing itself at an early age."

The next thing the Hares noticed was the slowness of Michael's development in the areas noted in Appendices 1 and 2: his lateness sitting up, seeming lack of motivation, not walking. They suspected that Michael was simply stubborn. "It was never that he *couldn't*; it was that he *wouldn't*. (He) refused to walk." Yet the Hares' response to Michael's "refusal" to walk had been to carry him about the house. It was not until Michael was 22 months old that Mrs. Hare, revealing a fine practical knowledge of behavior shaping, "forced" him to walk by standing him a few steps from the bed and, after he had walked that distance, gradually increasing the distance until he could walk by himself. Nevertheless, assuming that children, on the average, begin to walk between 12 and 15 months (Ilg & Ames, 1955; Frankenberg & Dodd, 1967), for at least 6 months during this early stage of his development, Michael and his parents interacted in a way that reinforced whatever behavior signified Michael's "refusal" to walk.

Appendices 1 and 2 also reveal that Michael was quite unresponsive to his environments. Not only was he rather aloof toward others, but he had little interest in manipulating objects constructively or following instructions. Instead, Michael's repertoire seems to have been oriented to the passive consumption of available reinforcers such as music, food, and objects to chew upon. And for their part, the Hares supplied Michael with those reinforcers, often following his demands for them.

The Hares' interactions with Michael may have been affected by their early experiences with professionals whose help they sought. The Hares' early definition of Michael and their reactions to him had been ambiguous. On the one hand, familiar with the fact that there is a higher rate of children with disabilities born to middle-aged parents, and remembering Mr. Hare's feeling that Michael seemed strange even as early as birth, the Hares seriously entertained the notion that Michael was retarded in some biological way. At the same time, they sensed that Michael's behavioral deficits reflected stubbornness and not inability. Consequently, they were very supportive of him but also felt that he was responsible for much of his behavior. His mother (and the rest of the family) may have acceded to his demands, but his mother also forced him to learn to walk.

However, once they began making the rounds of professionals, and once Michael was labeled "aphasic," their definition of him as biologically impaired was validated. At this point they became less likely to require that he learn to behave appropriately, and began to reinforce his behavioral retardation. This is a clear example of what can happen when parents receive a diagnosis for their child's developmental deviance but no training and support for productively interacting with and teaching their child.

At the time he entered into the educational program at the Social Exchange Laboratory, the outstanding features of Michael's behavioral repertoire were as follows:

1. Michael was and had always been mute, neither imitating nor using words.
2. He engaged in almost no appropriate play with the wide range of conventional play objects available to him, and instead occupied himself frequently and for long periods of time by mouthing and chewing plastic and leather objects, spinning lids, plates, ash trays and compacts, fingering and mouthing silky material and hair.
3. He very frequently engaged in stereotyped hand-wrist flapping and squealing in response to increased visual stimulation—for instance, shiny objects and spinning lids. He oriented to and gazed fixedly at moving lines (for example, slowly turning fan blades) and often produced such patterns by waving his fingers in front

of his eyes or by rocking his head from side to side in front of a screen door.

4. He listened to music frequently and for long periods, rocking sideways from one foot to the other, often with his thumb in his mouth, when the tempo, pitch, or volume changed sharply.

5. Michael had a strong pattern of teasing which consisted of smiling and looking out of the corners of his eyes at persons observing him while he engaged in undesirable behaviors such as climbing on kitchen counters or getting into pantries, behaviors which had in the past produced negative attention.

6. Although he ran slowly and awkwardly, he was careful and graceful when climbing to precarious places.

7. He seemed to enjoy being held, frequently cuddling with and clinging to his mother, father, and sisters.

Michael changed considerably between the age of two and his entrance into the Laboratory-school, as shown in Appendix 1.

Following is an outline of the research and training with the Hares.

Jan. 24-29, 1968:	Baseline observations at the Laboratory on interaction between Michael and his mother.
Jan. 31, 1968:	Michael begins educational program with staff teacher in Laboratory. Parents informally observe sessions.
Feb. 10–11, 1968:	General observations at the Hare home. Mrs. Hare begins recording observations during sessions.
Mar. 28–Apr. 1, 1968:	Baseline taken at the Hare home (A_1).
April 1, 1968:	Mrs. Hare begins training in the Laboratory.
June 4–7, 1968:	Observations at the Hare home to assess progress in applying basic techniques learned in Laboratory and to identify remaining problems in parent-child exchanges (B).
June 10–16, 1968:	Coaching at the Hare home to restructure exchanges (beginning of C_1)
July 16, 1968:	Michael begins language training with staff teacher in the Laboratory. Parents observe sessions.

July 30, 1968:   Mrs. Hare is taught language training techniques.

Sep. 16–Feb. 9, 1969:   Weekly observations and occasional coaching at Hare
                          home (continuation of C_1).

Feb. 9–16, 1969:   Experimental reversal at home to test parents' influ-
                          ence on bizarre-disruptive behavior and constructive
                          behavior (A_2).

Feb. 17–Apr. 12, 1969: Return to orthogenic system of exchanges (C_2).

May 4–June 22, 1969:   Follow-up.

As can be seen, Mrs. Hare observed and recorded some teaching sessions prior to the beginning of the Parent Training Program on April 1. It is likely that she acquired some knowledge of the teaching procedures by observing these sessions. Greater control was not exerted over Mrs. Hare's entry knowledge because Michael was admitted to the Lab school a month before the writer began the research. It is fair to say, however, that what the Hares learned through their informal observations was minimal. They were not told what they were watching or why and how the techniques were supposed to work. Neither were they given instructions for applying techniques at home. Indeed, the general home observations and home baseline observations revealed that the Hares did not utilize the most basic of teaching techniques which, to a trained eye, were being used constantly in the Laboratory. At any rate, the baseline observations allow for the evaluation of change due to training, regardless of anything already learned.

Pre-Training Description of the Home (A_1)

As noted in Chapter 3, a picture of the home situation prior to the training was obtained through parents' logs, general home observations, and home baseline observations.

Parents' Logs

Mrs. Hare began writing logs on February 13, 1968. The following analysis of her logs covers the period between February 13 and March 28 (the day of the first structured home observation). Mrs. Hare's logs give us a picture, from her point of view, of the more glaring counterproductive exchanges in the home. There were many exchanges, for instance, in which inappropriate behavior was *immediately* reinforced by one of the Hares. Michael continually attempted to, and usually succeeded in, playing with water either in the kitchen, bathroom, basement, or outside. Typically, his mother gave him attention for this by chasing after him and yelling at him to stop. Sometimes she reinforced him with a much stronger, material reinforcer. One day she wrote that Michael was playing in the sink again:

> ... by now I'm very upset. It's been a long morning and Michael hasn't stopped once. I asked Lena to put a record on for him to slow him down.

In other words, Michael's water play produced music as a reward.

Besides water play, Michael was rewarded for climbing onto the refrigerator, the mantel, the piano, the kitchen counter, and the roof of the family car. Usually, Mrs. Hare yelled at Michael for climbing, or carried him down—i.e., she gave him negative attention. That negative attention was rewarding to Michael is clear from his smiling whenever Mrs. Hare yelled or went after him, and from his invariably climbing back up after she carried him down. Mrs. Hare also rewarded Michael for not cooperating. Once, for instance, she gave him food to stop his fighting with her.

> [Michael had been spinning a lid.] I take it away but he fights me and gets another. Michael has become physically defiant lately, very aggressive over things he really wants. I ask him if he wants Grape Nuts Flakes, to calm him down. He refuses; gets Graham Cracker box instead. I give him one.

In order to control Michael's defiance, Mrs. Hare was using a strategy of *placation,* a strategy which would decrease Michael's disturbing behavior temporarily but increase it in the long run.

A final example of the immediate reinforcement of inappropriate behavior concerns Michael's eating patterns. Michael was given many opportunities to eat during the day. All he had to do was to pester, whine, cry, or pull on his parents, and they would feed him. At the same time, the Hares allowed Michael to be choosy about what he would and would not eat. If he did not care for what was on the supper menu, he would wait until it was over and then pester his parents for something else. Mrs. Hare wrote that Michael sat still during one meal and refused to eat anything but lettuce, cornbread, and tea. When everyone else left the table, he returned and got tuna salad from the refrigerator and ate it. Then Mrs. Hare fixed him a bowl of ice cream. Later still, she gave him three pieces of bread and jelly. As she notes, she had always been concerned about nutrition, even to the point of physically forcing her two older daughters (when they were younger) to eat.

At least as important as the immediate reinforcement of maladaptive behavior, is the *escalation* of maladaptive behavior by either delaying the reciprocation and/or inadvertently requiring a higher frequency or intensity of the behavior. Over time, in other words, Mrs. Hare taught Michael to escalate his behavior by "giving in" only after the behavior was more intense or prolonged than before. For instance, Mrs. Hare writes:

> Neighbor brings us a bowl of jello and Michael wants some immediately. Keeps getting it out of the refrigerator and begging until I *give in* and give him a bowl.

Or, with respect to climbing:

> Watches "Captain Kangaroo" for intervals and gets up and tries to climb on top of piano. *Repeats* this routine one-half dozen times. I *finally* spank on leg and make him get

off piano. [...] Climbs on top of refrigerator. I leave him there for a few minutes hoping he will get down by himself. He doesn't. He jabbers and makes different sounds while there. I take him down.

From her logs we can also get a rough idea of the rate of Michael's behaviors. Three weekdays and three weekend days were chosen at random to average out the fact that Michael went to the Laboratory-school on weekdays. Keeping in mind that Michael was not always in his mother's presence and that she may not have recorded everything, we can (under-) estimate that Michael, on the average, engaged in five climbing episodes, three spinning episodes, seven water play episodes, and seven eating episodes per day. He never played with toys (which were available) like "other" children. His "play" consisted of letting his younger sister or his father tickle and play horse with him. Spinning, chewing on things, water, food, and music were his main forms of entertainment.

As to cooperation, Mrs. Hare noted that Michael cooperated with requests a few times during the day. But his cooperation was always directly relevant to his own interests. For example, he was willing to bring the jello or the electric mixer when asked, but only when these items were to be used to make food for him at *his* request.

Using his mother's logs, we can synthesize a typical day in Michael's life.

5:30-9:30 a.m.	awakens
	goes to bathroom
	mother dresses him
	eats
	watches "Captain Kangaroo" for short periods of time
	climbs on various objects
	chews objects
	lounges in bed or on couch
	attempts to obtain more food
1:30 p.m.	watches and often disrupts preparation of lunch

	eats lunch and often disrupts it
	plays in water
	eats snacks
	looks at grocery ads
	"plays" with sister
	cuddles with mother
	aimlessly wanders around basement or outside (for water)
	spins objects
	climbs on objects
	"arranges" music and plunks on piano
5:00 p.m.	watches and often disrupts preparation of dinner
	eats dinner
	plays in kitchen water during clean-up
	eats snacks
	bath
	climbs on objects
	spins objects
9:30 p.m.	bedtime

We see from Mrs. Hare's logs that Michael has many learning deficiencies. He does not know how to play; he does not know how to talk; he does not know how, or is unwilling, to cooperate. *But he does know how to consume.* He can eat eight or ten meals a day, listen to music all day long, watch rapidly changing reflections of light on spinning objects or spilling water. At the same time, one cannot miss the harried futility of Mrs. Hare's life with Michael— always trying to keep up with him as he rushes about the house, ready to give in to his nagging demands for food, paradoxically rewarding him with attention for the very behavior she dislikes.

General Home Observations

I spent two days (February 11–12) making general observations. I observed three hours the morning of the first day and two hours the early afternoon of the second day, when the Hares agreed that Michael was at his worst. In general, it was found that all of the Hares treated Michael the same way. They either acceded to demands for food and music or gave him attention for disruptive behavior. In addition, they were very supportive of him, helping him do the simplest of things. For instance, during lunch, either his mother or father would ask if there was anything he wanted, and when he indicated that there was, they would get it for him. They would get the salt for him and sprinkle it on his French fries, or get the mustard and put it on his hamburger—things most six-year-old children are expected to learn for themselves.

The following incident is presented as it was recorded during the first general home observation. The incident points out the extent to which Mrs. Hare complied with Michael's demands, was overly supportive of him, and rewarded maladaptive behavior. Analysis of exchanges is included in parentheses.

> Michael walks into the kitchen with his mother following him. Michael opens up a pantry door and gets out a can of soup. His mother tells him, "You don't need any of that. You just ate lunch." *(Rewards getting into pantry with attention.)* But he goes to the drawer and gets out a can opener, and she is allowing him to do it. She says to him, "Do you really want me to open that up?" She asks him if he'd really eat some if she were to fix it. He gets the chair from the table and moves it over to the counter where the chicken soup can is. He is up on the chair, watching her while she's opening up the can of soup. *(She's doing exactly what he wanted her to do.)* She says to him, "You know, I spend half my day cooking for you; I spend half my day keeping up with your eating habits." *(Rewards him with attention for climbing on a chair.)* Michael goes back over to the pantry and starts fooling around with objects inside it. His mother says she thinks he's fooling and he's not really

hungry. *(Rewards him with attention for getting into pantry.)* She says to him, "Your chicken soup is ready. Come on." He is still standing there in the pantry by one of the shelves. His mother starts pouring the soup out into a bowl, and she says, "Listen to this, Michael. Do you hear the soup splashing? Come over here." *(Rewards him with attention for standing in pantry.)* She tells him if he wants it, he'll have to come over to the table. She says, "Now we'll find out if you're really hungry." He is still standing in the pantry. His mother says, "The soup is on the table." *(Rewards him again with attention.)* He is opening and closing the door of the pantry. His mother finally opens the door and tells him, "We've played enough." *(Rewards him with attention for playing in pantry.)* She takes him out and tells him the soup is over there. She leads him to the table, but he walks away. She says, "I thought so. I knew you were playing a game with me."

Home Baseline

The home baseline observations were more structured. Observations were made for five consecutive days (March 28–April 1) at the same two-hour period each day (1:30–3:30 P.M.). As during the previous general home observations, I asked the Hares to go about their normal activities. I recorded a flat description of the ongoing interactions onto a portable tape recorder. These narratives were later examined in terms of the variables under study. Four exchange patterns were scored:

1. the overall structure of the system of exchanges in the home;
2. cooperation exchanges;
3. exchanges involving bizarre and/or disruptive behavior; and
4. exchanges involving constructive activity.

High inter-observer reliability was obtained during general home observations and was checked again during the baseline. Two observers listening to the tape-recorded descriptions of the ongoing exchanges scored each exchange in terms of the set of variables. Reliability was computed by comparing each consecutive scoring. The average percent of agreement was 92.

Table 5 (p. 108) presents a number of exchanges which repeatedly occurred during the home baseline. Briefly, with respect to Michael's behavior, the home baseline revealed that: (1) the rate of inappropriate behavior was much higher than the rate of appropriate behavior; (2) he spent a large amount of time engaging in bizarre and/or disruptive behavior, some of which seemed aimed at teasing or tormenting his mother (climbing, getting into food), and some of which seemed merely to help him fill time (playing in water, spinning); (3) he seldom played or performed chores; and (4) he rarely cooperated with exchange initiations. At the same time, Mrs. Hare (1) rewarded inappropriate behavior a high percentage of the time; (2) did not systematically reward Michael's appropriate behavior; (3) seldom gave Michael explicit opportunities to engage in appropriate activity (e.g., chores) in return for some reward; and (4) gave Michael much noncontingent attention as well as other types of rewards. These, then, were major problems to work on during the Parent Training Program.

Training in Basic Techniques of Exchange Management

Training in the Laboratory

At her request, Mrs. Hare had observed teaching sessions with Michael from the time he entered the Lab school. However, her formal training did not begin until April 1, 1968, after baseline observations at home. In the interim, a teacher had been working with Michael on eye contact and simple manipulative tasks, e.g., puzzles and blocks.

The training of the Hares followed the stages described in Chap-

Table 5: Description of Typical Exchanges in the Hare Home
Prior to Parent Training

Child's Behavior	Parents' Reaction
Plays in bathroom or kitchen water.	Chases after him, yells at him to stop: "Michael Hare, you get out of that water this very instant!" (Usually, he simply begins again.)
Pulls and pushes for records.	Gives him record--about 50% of the time.
Whines and cries if he is not given what he wants.	Cuddles him and asks what is wrong.
Gets into food as it is prepared.	Chases after him, yells at him to stop. (Usually, he simply begins again.)
Gets into pantry/lower cabinets.	Yells at him to stop. (He usually continues.)
Climbs on top of refrigerator, chairs, mantel, or hood of car.	Yells at him to come down, asks him to come down over and over again, or eventually carries him down.
Spins objects (plates, compacts, vases).	Goes after him and takes object away, about 50% of time. Ignores about 50% of time.
Climbs onto kitchen counter, or pulls chair up to counter so as to climb up more easily.	Usually tells him over and over to get down. Usually he does not. Eventually, she takes him down bodily.
Plays with his food during a meal (slaps it with spoon, pours it back and forth with spoon, spills drink)	Repeatedly tells him to stop.
Gets into records, pulls them out, creating mess by record player	Goes after him and tells him to stop. Eventually she ends up yelling at him as he continues to get into the records.
Stands up and rocks back and forth, often with thumb in mouth.	Ignores.
Sits idly fingering silky material.	Ignores, unless it is something she is wearing.
Stands outside and urinates (usually onto sidewalk).	Gives him attention: "Why, Michael Hare...I just don't understand you...!"
Pours, spills, and dumps things onto floor right in front of her (looks at her to see if she is getting upset).	Usually gets upset after he makes a mess. She says: "Michael Hare, you're just doing that to tantalize me." Often hollers at him to clean it up.
Usually runs away or otherwise ignores parents when they encourage him to play with his toys or to perform a simple task.	Give up in exasperation.

ter 3. First, Mr. and Mrs. Hare (and their daughters) read introductory theoretical materials and discussed them with the researcher, observed sessions between the teacher and Michael, and recorded observations of sessions onto tape. Next, Mrs. Hare received extensive training in applying exchange management techniques by working with Michael on the same simple manipulative tasks as the teacher, with coaching from the researcher who observed from behind a one-way mirror.

It will be remembered that baseline observations had been made of Michael's and his mother's exchanges at the start of Michael's schooling in January 1968. These observations revealed that Mrs. Hare frequently initiated exchanges with questions and seldom rewarded Michael for correct task responses. Thus, the coach first focused on teaching her to initiate exchanges with directives or contract statements and to reciprocate immediately with food and praise for every correct response. It was felt that all further training depended upon such changes.

At first, Mrs. Hare was uneasy working with Michael. She repeatedly asked the coach what to do and if she were doing all right. She was especially concerned that Michael get up from the table or behave in a bizarre fashion. She was coached to ignore him if he did. She rapidly became skilled at managing exchanges. In six days the number of exchanges initiated with questions fell from 18 to zero; directives increased from zero to between 36 and 61; and contract statements rose from three to about seven per session.

Figure 1 (p. 110) clearly shows Mrs. Hare's acquisition of exchange management techniques, especially reciprocation, and the concomitant effect of her behavior on Michael's task behavior. Note in Figure 1 that Mrs. Hare's earlier observations of sessions and her reading were not alone sufficient to provide the skills necessary for managing productive exchanges. For in only one day of the C period, Michael's previous rate of fifty correct responses with the teacher fell to the same low level as during the pre-training baseline with his mother. Note also, however, that Michael's performance rate rose steadily and eventually exceeded that with the teacher. In the D pe-

Figure 1: Training the Mother of an Autistic Boy in the Basic Techniques of Exchange Management

In condition A, observations were made of the untrained mother having her child work at simple tasks. In the B condition, the mother observed a teacher working with her child on the same tasks. In the C condition, the mother was coached while working with her child, In the D condition, she was coached to use intermittent reinforcement. In the B condition, reinforcement was continuous.

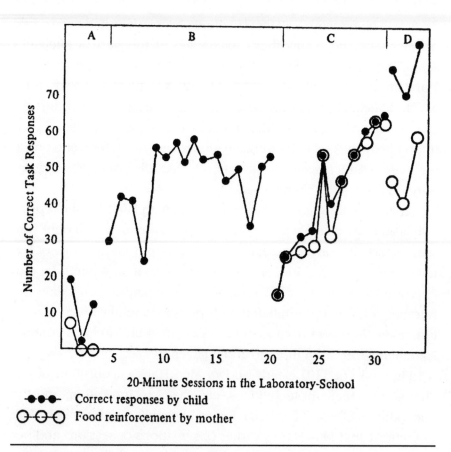

riod, Mrs. Hare was coached to reciprocate intermittently, in order to avoid satiating her child and to increase his rate of performance.

Mrs. Hare's daughters also worked with Michael for several days. Their coach was Mrs. Hare. At the same time she was coaching her daughters to manage exchanges, Mrs. Hare was coached in *how to coach* by the researcher standing in another room. Both Mrs. Hare and the researcher could hear exchanges in the classroom and could communicate with each other electronically. Thus, Michael's siblings were given practice at managing exchanges, and Mrs. Hare was given the additional practice of teaching others to apply the techniques. In fact, Mrs. Hare later coached two other mothers for several weeks. It was hoped that this practice teaching others in the Lab would help Mrs. Hare teach her husband at home.

Description of the Home After Training in Basic Techniques (B)

Progress and the Generalization of Training

Four home observations, involving the same recording techniques, variables, and time as the home baseline, were made for three reasons: (1) to assess the extent to which the Hares' training in the Laboratory had generalized to the home, (2) to identify changes in Michael's behavior, and (3) to locate additional problems requiring coaching at home.

It was found that ignoring inappropriate behavior and rewarding appropriate behavior had generalized to a large extent. The Hares' rewarding of disruptive behavior had decreased by about 70%. At the same time, Michael's disruptive behavior had decreased by a factor of about three. Moreover, several disruptive behaviors had been completely extinguished, e.g., playing with the stove. Finally, Michael's rate of cooperation with parental exchange signals had doubled.

On the basis of these data, one would think the training program was successful. So why continue? In fact, many parent training programs in applied behavior analysis *do* stop at this point. The reason for continuing was that I was not convinced that the thirty or so days of training would be sufficient to maintain the behavioral gains already made and enable the parents to teach their child more complex imitation and language skills.

Remaining Problems

The Hares still made many mistakes. For instance, they occasionally initiated exchanges with questions, and they rewarded disruptive behavior an average of 29% of the time. It was expected that these mistakes could be corrected easily with a little coaching at home. However, other problems remained which would take more time to solve and had greater significance for Michael's socialization. These are summarized in Table 6 below.

In general, then, exchanges in the Hare home did not yet constitute an environment that would systematically foster Michael's competence (e.g., play, activities of daily living, communication) and participation in social activities (e.g., attention, interest, cooperation). It is true that the overall structure of the exchanges had been altered so that new bizarre-disruptive behaviors were not likely to be strength-

---

**Table 6: Basic Problems in the Hare Home Following
Training in the Laboratory**

- Much of Michael's behavior was not under stimulus control. He had not been taught to regard the kitchen, for instance, as a room where one eats or helps but does not get into the food, climb, or disrupt meals, or the bathroom as a place to wash or perform bodily functions but not to play with water.

- Michael had an almost complete absence of complex appropriate skills. He did not play, dress himself or perform chores.

- Several classes of disruptive behavior were strong despite the substantial reduction in reinforcement, e.g., playing in water and getting into the food.

- The Hares still did not know how to initiate work or play exchanges of long duration (at least five minutes) outside of the Laboratory.

- The Hares still did not know how to spot reinforcers, or how to manage back-up reinforcers.

- Michael still had no speech and the Hares used no systematic techniques for teaching him to speak.

- The Hares gave Michael a lot of non-contingent attention.

ened by reinforcement. Yet it had not changed to the extent that Michael would acquire appropriate behaviors to replace existing bizarre-disruptive and uncooperative behavior.

The Hares and I planned a broad and long-term program for further changing exchanges in the Hare home. This program was the second stage in the parents' training. The goals were to teach the Hares to:

1. decrease Michael's remaining disruptive behaviors and any new ones that should develop;
2. teach Michael complex constructive activities (play, chores) to replace disruptive ones; and
3. teach Michael to talk.

Training to Restructure the System of Exchanges (C_1, A_2, and C_2)

This period lasted ten months, from June 10, 1968 to April 12, 1969. Except for the last few months, when an experimental reversal was in progress, all time and effort were devoted to the goals identified above. Structured observations were made approximately once a week, and when Mrs. Hare reported special problems, several days of coaching were provided.

The first seven consecutive days of this period involved directly *coaching* the Hares to handle disruptive behavior and, more importantly, to structure counter exchanges to promote constructive behavior. To prepare the Hares for the changes to be made, on June 10 they were given a "prescription" which *specified* (tentatively) techniques to use to further restructure exchanges between themselves and Michael. The prescription, which was discussed with them, is reproduced in Table 7 (pp. 114-115).

The training methods used and the progress in each problem area will be discussed in detail. Data will be summarized periodically in the form of graphs.

Table 7: Tentative Prescription Given to the Hares to Restructure the Exchange Patterns in the Home

Instructions:

To Ignore: Do not look at or talk to Michael while he is engaged in inappropriate behavior. Do not tell him to stop, or try to verbally divert his attention, or scold him, or threaten him with punishment.

To Reward: For the present, give Michael approval (verbal, strokes, etc.). For certain things, food may be given (an afternoon snack for working puzzles for a while, a drink of juice for a household task, etc.). Make sure, of course, that the reward follows the behavior immediately—within a few seconds.

To Time Out: Without speaking, but with some vigor, take Michael to time out room. Leave him in 2 minutes for first offense, 4 minutes for second offense, etc. Do not let him out if he is whining or tantruming.

Child's Behavior	Your Response
Pulling and/or pushing for records	Set aside several periods of the day during which Michael can work for a record (e.g., by picking up toys, clothes, working puzzles). Tell him, "As soon as you ____, you can have a record." At any other time, ignore him until he asks at an opportune time of the day. (Eventually, working for records was established 10 minutes after lunch. It was initiated with Mrs. Hare saying, "It's time to work for a record." She would lead Michael to the table and prompt him to work puzzles.)
Pulling and/or pushing for bath	Ignore. Then, when it is proper time, tell him he may take bath or whatever you usually say.
Crying and/or whining	Ignore. This will probably occur after he is ignored for pulling.
Playing with stove, getting into food in refrigerator or pantry, climbing on cupboard, getting into food being prepared (assuming any of these are disturbing to you)	Time out from the kitchen by removing Michael from kitchen and locking door from inside. Open in approximately 3 or 4 minutes and repeat each time he repeats inappropriate behavior. Don't let it escalate; don't wait and let him do it for awhile. Remove him immediately. This will work if he likes being in the kitchen. If he does any of these when you are not in the kitchen with him, remove him and lock the door.
Climbing on refrigerator	Ignore.

Child's Behavior	Your Response
Playing with own food (spilling it, slapping it, etc.) or getting up from the table to mess around	Take food away. No food until next meal. Ignore all appeals for food in between.
Spinning objects	Do not chase him or have a tug of war. Take object away quickly and without speaking. Then say, "As soon as you _____, you can spin this." (Have him perform a simple task.)
Water play	Temporarily, remove him from room and lock door. If he does this during a meal, remove him from the kitchen, lock him out, and take his plate away. Use this until we attack problem outright.
All bizarre behavior	Ignore.
Self-initiated working at puzzles, looking in magazines, picking up clothing, helping in kitchen, speech (any approximation)	Reward verbally and with strokes; if convenient, with a bite of food. If he is engaged in such activity for more than a few minutes, reward him several times. Don't just wait until he stops. Reward him during activity if it is longer than 10 seconds or so. Be on the lookout for appropriate behavior and reward it consistently.

Handling Bizarre-Disruptive Behavior

During the seven days of home coaching, the Hares were helped to use the prescription. In general, they were coached to ignore most of Michael's bizarre-disruptive behavior. In addition, they were asked to set up a time out room, for behavior that was too disruptive to tolerate or proved to be resistant to extinction. They chose the landing of a stairway between the kitchen and basement, enclosed by two doors which could be locked from the outside. During the ten months of this period, only a few behaviors required handling with the time out room (getting into food, playing in water).

Using the prescription, Michael's parents and sisters helped him to reduce his rate of bizarre-disruptive behavior by a factor of four during the seven days of home coaching (a greater decrease than between the baseline and the check for generalization). For instance, Michael's climbing onto the refrigerator and car rapidly extinguished.

The first time he was ignored when he climbed onto the refrigerator, he remained there quite a while, watching out of the corner of his eye to see if his mother was watching him. His mother went about her business. Eventually, Michael came down and walked out of the kitchen. He climbed for only a few days thereafter and for shorter and shorter durations. The same thing was observed with respect to climbing on the car. His mother left him standing on the burning hot roof waiting for her to get him.

Michael's disrupting of meals was also eliminated rapidly. Whenever he left the table or played with his food, his mother or father removed his plate, ending Michael's meal. Mrs. Hare had to be reassured that this technique (Type 2 punishment) was likely to work quickly, because she was so concerned that her children eat well-balanced meals.

To handle water play, we deviated from the prescription somewhat. The Hares were still asked not to give Michael any negative attention for it. In addition, Michael was given the opportunity to work for water play by learning new behavior. It was hoped that this would yield partial satiation on water play and teach Michael alternative play behavior. At the very least, water play would be under stimulus control. Mrs. Hare was coached to teach Michael to ride his tricycle on the driveway. Shaping combined with most-to-least manual prompting was used. That is, the first day she pushed him; the second day he had to do more of the pedaling; and future days would require him to ride farther and farther by himself. Each time he completed a successful approximation, he was allowed to play with the hose or with a bucket of water for a few minutes. Not only did he learn to ride the tricycle (as well as to play on the swings), and not only did he begin to initiate this exchange, but his desire for water play decreased. He began to walk away from the hose or bucket after just a few seconds, and he attempted to get into water indoors less often. This exchange—working for water—remained in effect throughout the program.

In November, with the approach of winter, Michael had less opportunity to play outside. Consequently, his rate of getting into water indoors increased. Although, as will be discussed later, the Hares were teaching Michael constructive activities indoors, it was now decided that Michael should be timed out each time he attempted to get into water. Gradually, playing in water decreased to near zero, as determined from logs and home observations.

Getting into food also required several techniques before it was brought under control. At first, as prescribed, Michael was timed out (removed) from the kitchen for a few minutes contingent upon each infraction. With this technique, getting into food being prepared (e.g., sticking his hands into food) quickly weakened. No doubt this was in part a result of Mrs. Hare's teaching Michael the alternative behavior of helping her in the kitchen by stirring food, putting things away, getting things for her, etc. Getting into cabinets, however, remained strong. He would be removed from the kitchen only to return and go right back to the cabinets to play with the food inside, pour out the contents, and tear open packages. Timing him out in the time out room was tried. As with water play, getting into the cabinets gradually decreased in frequency, although occasionally when Michael was generally uncooperative, getting into cabinets increased for several days.

It should be pointed out that Mrs. Hare was not the only one following the prescription. Under her coaching, all of the family learned to handle Michael's bizarre-disruptive behavior. In fact, Mrs. Hare and her daughters instructed neighborhood children who came to the house how to interact with Michael, especially to ignore it whenever he behaved in a bizarre fashion. Similarly, the Hares coached Michael's grandparents whenever they came to visit.

Additional effects of training are revealed in ways the Hares *generalized* techniques to new behaviors. At one point, Michael started refusing to leave the car when he and his mother returned home from the Laboratory. Mrs. Hare simply walked into the house, leaving Michael alone in the car. This behavior was extinguished in a few days. Later, Michael developed a bedtime problem. One night he got out of bed, came into his parents' room, turned on the lights, and tried to wake them up. Without a word, Mrs. Hare led Michael out of the room and into the hall, told him to go to his room, went back into her room, and locked the door. The next morning they found Michael asleep in the hallway with his blanket. From then on, he remained in his own room at night.

Developing Constructive Behavior

Although bizarre and disruptive behavior may be the more visible signs of an autistic child's disorder, learning deficiencies, which include a lack of constructive activity, are a more important and more difficult problem.

Building a play repertoire. Developing a repertoire of constructive behavior began with teaching Mrs. Hare to teach Michael to play. At first, this involved having Mrs. Hare structure exchanges in which Michael interacted with her at play activities in return for rewards from her (much as had been done in the Laboratory). During the seven days of home coaching, Mrs. Hare was asked to set aside a specific time of day when the play exchange was to be in effect. She chose a period approximately fifteen minutes after Michael's lunch. She was asked to place a number of play objects on the same table each day just before the time arrived for the exchange. She was coached to initiate the exchange by leading Michael to the table and to use either a directive ("It's time to work some puzzles") or a contract statement ("As soon as you've worked some puzzles, you can have some music").

To increase Michael's participation in the activity, his mother was coached to praise him often as he played and make the interval of play required for back-up reinforcement small (e.g., a few minutes at first). Gradually, the interval was increased to as much as twenty minutes before Mrs. Hare reciprocated with back-up reinforcers. In addition, she was coached to rotate the back-up reinforcers. For example, one day Michael would hear music, the next he would play in water, and the next he would eat dessert. If he refused to enter the exchange or left the table before the requisite interval, his mother was instructed to ignore him. It was expected that the back-up reinforcement and Michael's gradually learning to enjoy playing would motivate him to participate.

The above techniques were quite successful. During the seven days of home coaching, the length of time per day that Michael played in this situation ranged from twenty to forty minutes (an increase of a factor of five over the baseline). In addition, Michael's pulling and pushing for things was weakened by his parents ignoring the pulling and pushing and, instead, initiating a counter exchange (the play exchange) so that Michael would have to engage in desirable behavior to earn what he wanted. Furthermore, and perhaps as a result of this latter, Michael began to initiate the exchange himself. He would sit down and work a puzzle or stack blocks and then go to his parents for his reward (which they were instructed to give him). In other words, self-initiated play was developing. In fact, Mrs. Hare's logs indicated that within a few months of the week of home coaching, most play was initiated by Michael. Michael had apparently developed an "exchange set"; he expected his parents to reward him for playing. And finally, play itself seemed to have become an enjoyable activity. The logs and several home observations indicated that Michael would sometimes play appropriately with his toys alone in his room, without attempting to obtain a reward from his parents.

This play exchange was in effect every day. If Michael played either by himself or with others, he was rewarded. Moreover, he could initiate the exchange at any time, not only at the originally specified time. As the months went by, the amount of time Michael spent playing increased. Mrs. Hare's logs indicated that while there was some fluctuation in the total time from day to day, Michael sometimes played indoors for as long as several hours a day. In addition, the number of play activities Michael learned increased; his play repertoire grew larger and began to include more difficult activities. Not only was this important for Michael's development and education, but the periodic change in play activities also helped to prevent boredom and an eventual weakening of play behavior. Table 8 (pp. 120-121) presents, in temporal order, the toys and play activities that Mrs. Hare worked on with Michael.

Table 8: Toys and Play Activities Worked On by Michael Hare at Home

Date	Toy	Description
Sept. 16	Pegboard	Flat blocks with holes in them. Hand-eye coordination and color discrimination.
Sept. 20	Tinker toys	Hand-eye coordination and creativity.
Sept. 22	Play-doh	Tactile stimulation, fine motor coordination. Learned to use rolling pin, knife, and cookie cutters.
Sept. 24	Coloring with crayons	Visual stimulation, fine motor coordination, and creativity.
Oct. 5	Sewing cards	Hand-eye coordination.
Oct. 18	Shape box	A variety of small wooden shapes that drop through corresponding holes in box lid. Hand-eye coordination and color-form discrimination.
Oct. 28	Pegboard landscape	Pegboard on which a landscape can be built using pegs and a variety of small shapes, e.g., houses, trees, boats, cars. Hand-eye coordination and creativity.
Oct. 29	Complex puzzles	Many pieces to make a picture (switched every few weeks). Hand-eye coordination.
Nov. 11	Plastic eggs	Eggs of different sizes fit inside one another.
Nov. 16	Musical viewer	Hand-operated viewer that plays music and shows slides. Visual and auditory stimulation.
Dec. 12	Punch-out puzzle	Pieces are punched out of cardboard puzzle and replaced to complete figures. Form discrimination.
Dec. 29	Talking lion	Pull string and lion talks. Auditory stimulation.
Jan. 2	Toy accordion	Auditory stimulation. Did not learn tune, but at least how to make different sounds to amuse himself.
Jan. 7	Sorting box	Box with compartments for sorting shapes of different colors. Color/form discrimination.
Jan. 11	Lite-Brite set	Pegboard, illuminated from behind, into which colored plastic pegs can be inserted to create designs. Visual stimulation, creativity.
Jan. 22	Motor imitation	Mrs. Hare teaches Michael to imitate a wide variety of gestures, in an attempt to have him develop generalized imitation.
Jan. 25	Pointing to objects in picture book	Mother names one of many objects on page and asks Michael to point to it. Object discrimination and development of labeling vocabulary.

Date	Toy	Description
Feb. 20	Picking up object named and placing it in box	Mother names one of a number of household objects and has Michael pick it out from among a number of such objects, and replace it in a box. Object discrimination and development of labeling vocabulary.
Mar. 12	Coloring book	Learns to color within the lines.
Mar. 13	Imitation of object manipulations	Learns to imitate simple arrangements of blocks by mother (stack, line them up), and to imitate by using blocks of the same color.

It should be pointed out again that the growth of Michael's play repertoire was due in large part to his mother's creativity and perseverance. She had been trained in the Laboratory and coached at home for seven days, but after that she was largely on her own in teaching Michael new play activities.

Imitation training. Mrs. Hare's work with Michael on imitation deserves special attention. Several writers whose works are classics in the field of child development have discussed the importance of imitation in the socialization process (Bandura & Walters, 1959, 1963; Sears, Maccoby, & Levin, 1957). This is especially clear with autistic children. Through imitation, a child can learn single behaviors and complex sequences much faster than he could through prompting and/or shaping alone. In fact, without the ability to imitate appropriate models, the socialization of autistic children is inconceivable. By the time a typical child is six or seven years old, he or she has a repertoire of hundreds of behaviors arranged into larger and larger classes and sequences, and that repertoire expands continually. If one were to try to socialize an autistic child by teaching new behaviors one by one, it would take an extraordinarily long time, if not forever.

Cognizant of this, many individuals involved in the education of autistic children have utilized techniques to teach children to imitate appropriate models (Baer, 1968; Baer & Sherman, 1964; Hingtgen et al., 1967; Kennedy & Shulka, 1995; Laski, Charlop, & Schreibman, 1988; Lovaas, 1968; Metz, 1965; Risley, 1968; Sigafoos & Meikle, 1996).

In December 1968, I was working with Michael on speech, and Michael's progress in learning to imitate sounds was slow. It was felt that he might benefit from training on motor imitation in general. On December 13, a pre-test was made of Michael's imitative behavior. A number of models such as clapping hands, patting the table, and touching the nose were repeatedly presented to him. He made no attempt to imitate the models. Thus, Michael's imitative baseline was essentially zero. I decided to give Mrs. Hare the job of teaching Michael to imitate. It was hoped that Michael would eventually develop "generalized imitation," i.e., imitating even when he was not reinforced. This generalized imitation would help Michael learn to imitate speech.

On December 14, Mrs. Hare was given the following prescription for teaching Michael to imitate a model. The instructions followed the technique used by Hingtgen et al. (1967).

1. Wait until he is attending to you.
2. Then present the stimulus (model) for him to imitate. Make it an easy one at first.
3. Wait a few seconds for him to imitate the stimulus. If he does not, verbally and physically prompt him. Reward him after he has made the response.
4. Gradually fade the prompts.
5. When he can reliably imitate the stimulus correctly and without a prompt, begin working on another.

I coached Mrs. Hare for ten minutes that same day in applying the steps. Later that day, she coached her husband.

Five weeks later, on January 22, 1969, Michael's progress was observed at home. Mrs. Hare was asked to run an imitation session with Michael, presenting different models at random, and rewarding Michael with praise and food for correct responses. A model was considered learned by imitation when Michael imitated it correctly and unprompted ten times. Of the ten models Mrs. Hare and Michael had been working on, Michael had learned seven.

Later still, on February 9, 1969, another test was made to determine the size of Michael's imitative repertoire and whether he had acquired generalized imitation. The same instructions were given to Mrs. Hare as during the first test, only this time she was to select two models and never reward Michael for correctly imitating them. The test revealed that Michael had learned at least seven new imitative responses, bringing the total to fourteen, and that he had developed generalized imitation because he consistently imitated the two models which were not rewarded. Michael's list of imitative responses was as follows:

By January 22:	clapping hands
	patting head
	patting object
	stamping one foot
	waving goodbye
	swinging one arm
	swinging leg
By February 9:	patting table
	touching nose
	patting chest
	warwhoop
	placing hand on head
	jumping up and down
	bending down and touching toes

It is likely that Michael's acquisition of a play and chore repertoire was facilitated by imitation training. Partial support for this statement lies in the observation that after Mrs. Hare learned to teach Michael to imitate, she integrated those techniques into her teaching of other constructive activities. When teaching him to color within the lines, for instance, she first performed the correct response with Michael watching, and prompted him to do the same.

Although Mrs. Hare taught Michael most of his new play skills, she was not the only one to play with him. Quite often when they were home from school, Michael's sisters—especially his younger

sister, Lena—played with him, rewarding him with praise and sometimes with food and other reinforcers for appropriate play. In fact,
Lena taught him to play hide and seek, a game he was not able to
play prior to the Training Program. Michael would stay in his room
and wait for her to hide. After several seconds he would slowly emerge
from his room, peering around corners and behind doors and furni-
ture until he found her. Then he would run laughing back to his room to
play again. Although he was not yet able to take the role of the "hider,"
his participation as the "seeker" marked a significant decrease in
autistic aloneness: he was not oblivious to the presence of others.

Mr. Hare also played with Michael—working puzzles, the pegboard, etc., in exchange for music, food, praise and roughhousing.
Michael enjoyed roughhousing so much that Mr. Hare could sustain
Michael's playing with toys for hours by rewarding him occasionally
with a bout of wrestling or a horseback ride.

Michael's father and sisters were usually able to manage play
exchanges without coaching from Mrs. Hare. When she did coach
them, her instructions involved telling them to reciprocate more frequently or not to prompt so much (for she believed that Michael
often feigned inability).

Building a chore repertoire. In addition to play activities, Mrs.
Hare taught Michael a number of chores. The importance of chores
in the education of an autistic child cannot be emphasized too
strongly. Chore behavior is in sharp contrast to the behavior characteristic of many autistic children. Instead of the aimlessness, repeti-
tiveness, and simplicity of the autistic child's self-stimulatory behavior and "play" (Tilton & Ottinger, 1964), chores often involve complex sequences or chains of responses to be performed at a specific
time and having a definite end. Uncoached (except in a very few
cases), Mrs. Hare taught Michael the following chores, which he eventually performed on request or even at his own initiation:

- dressing himself;
- putting laundry (towels, washcloths, sheets) away;

- scouring the toilet bowl with cleanser and brush;
- setting the table with plates, utensils, and food;
- clearing the table and returning plates, utensils, and food to the kitchen;
- loading the washer with clothes and detergent and starting it;
- loading and starting the dryer;
- carrying trash baskets to the trash can outside;
- packing his lunch box with food and utensils;
- stacking dishes in the drain;
- washing the dishes.

Setting the table was learned by back-chaining the steps into a composite chore (Napalkov, 1959). Specifically, Mrs. Hare had Michael perform only the last response (setting out the food) until this was learned. Then she had Michael learn the second to last step, and perform it and the last step in sequence. This process was continued until Michael could begin with the first step by laying out the tablecloth, then the plates and the utensils, etc., until the chore was completed. Though he occasionally needed an instruction, Michael could perform this chore fluently and was observed to do so by himself. In fact, several times when his mother signaled that they would be eating soon, Michael started the chore by himself.

Mrs. Hare used a different method to teach Michael to dress himself. Michael was simply not allowed to leave his room until he was dressed, when he had been told to put on a particular garment or to get dressed. His clothes were laid out and Mrs. Hare prevented him from leaving the room. When Michael finally began to handle the clothes, signaling his participation in the exchange, his mother physically prompted him to put the different items on, using the strategy of graduated guidance. Over a period of weeks, Michael learned to put on the various garments by himself, although in April 1969 he was still having trouble with his socks. Usually Michael's dressing was initiated by his mother's directive. Several times, however, when he got his shirt or pants wet while playing with water, he got another garment, or had his mother get him one, and put it on by himself.

In building Michael's repertoire of constructive activity, Mrs. Hare demonstrated a fine understanding of exchange principles. Teaching Michael to wash the dishes was one example of Mrs. Hare's ability to spot reinforcers with which to structure new exchanges. Michael enjoyed playing in water. It was also his chore to clear off the table after a meal, a chore for which he was rewarded. One day Mrs. Hare decided to *allow* Michael to wash the dishes as a reward for clearing the table. Because he enjoyed water play so much, he quickly learned the new dishwashing chore and became more willing to clear the table. Another example was her use of the television as a reward. Prior to training, Michael usually watched his favorite program, "Captain Kangaroo," in the morning. After training, however, she made "Captain Kangaroo" contingent upon constructive activity.

Mrs. Hare also understood how to vary the amount or value of rewards to increase the rate of the behavior that produced the rewards. Throughout the afternoon, she wrote, she rewarded Michael with food and records for playing. To increase his rate of *self-initiated* play, she began to hold the duration of the music reward at a minimum, except for self-initiated play.

The reader may recall that Michael engaged in little constructive activity before his parents were trained. Following is a list of Michael's constructive activities from Mrs. Hare's log of a day chosen at random from late in the training phase of the research (January 10, 1969):

8:15 a.m.	Performs about eight small tasks for me, carrying things upstairs and down to basement. I love & compliment him.
9:15 a.m.	Works Jack Horner puzzle—record reward.
9:25 a.m.	Sorts silverware for me—record reward.
	Wants another record. Gets a simple puzzle. I make him do landscape set instead. He works well at it—record reward.
10:05 a.m.	Works pegboard and puzzle—record reward.
10:15 a.m.	Works chicken puzzle—record reward.
10:16 a.m.	Works chicken puzzle just for fun.
	Helps dress himself for school.

Works pegboard (he initiates it) and wants to hear "Sabre Dance" again.

| 1:30 p.m. | Helps change his clothes. |

2:15 p.m.   I tell him to work landscape set for music. He gets a simple puzzle from his room and works it. I refuse him the record. He gets another simple puzzle. I take it away and point to the landscape set. He works it easily and I reward him with record.

3:00 p.m.   Works chicken puzzle—record reward.

Helps set table.

5:45 p.m.   Clears table from dinner—record reward.

Goes upstairs with Lena and plays with Lite-Brite set.

Picks up toys from bedroom floor—marshmallow reward.

7:40 p.m.   Initiated play at landscape set. Wants a record reward; turntable won't work so I give him water (to play in).

Lena begins to work with him on imitations—gives him marshmallows and pie as a reward. He always enjoys working with her.

They play with the (cardboard) box. Every time he wants to be tipped, he does an imitation.

They turn somersaults and Michael has a ball doing this. First time he has ever done it by himself. He received marshmallow rewards for them.

9:15 p.m.   Initiates a couple of puzzles for records, but receives marshmallows instead.

It is clear from the above that Michael was occupying his time with a good deal of constructive activity, and was systematically rewarded for it (though, perhaps, he was given music too often). Toward the end of January, however, Michael became rebellious—running from his parents when asked to do something, whether a chore or a simple task. He would not come when called, and would try as hard as he could to run away when he was walking with them. He taunted them by staying away from the table during meals or by getting up and leaving in the middle. The same was happening at the Laboratory. Michael would leave the table and walk around, trying to get the teacher's attention. He would not take off or put on his coat. And he began to refuse to cooperate with requests or do the opposite of what was asked. To make matters worse, the usual procedures for reinforcing steady progress—switching tasks and reinforcers, more prompting, more immediate reinforcement—had no effect.

Major Experimental Reversal in the Home (A_2 and C_2)

The negative change in Michael's behavior prompted us to try an experimental reversal. There were two reasons for this. First, Michael's rebelliousness seemed to be a consequence not of task difficulty or lean reinforcement schedules, but of a long history of continuous reinforcement at home. Ever since the training began, he had been on a schedule of continuous reinforcement for new tasks. He seemed to be satiated. In addition, much of Michael's constructive behavior was *contractual*. That is, his behavior was no longer merely being "conditioned," for he knew the terms (the structures) of the exchanges. This was evidenced by his initiating exchanges (e.g., working a puzzle and then going to his parents for a reward) and by his now only occasionally participating in an exchange when told what the reinforcer would be.

Knowing he was engaging in exchanges or contracts with his parents, and expecting a reward *every* time he participated in one, gave Michael the luxury of choosing to participate or not, to cooperate or not. If, at a given moment, he did not care to hear music, eat marshmallows, receive praise, and so forth, he would simply refuse to engage in the exchange at no cost to himself. Michael was one step ahead of his parents. The structure of the exchanges had to be changed so that participation would be more reinforcing. The proposed solution was to move to a *variable ratio* or *variable interval* schedule of reciprocation, for then Michael would no longer be able to predict when he would be rewarded.

The second reason for the reversal was to test the major hypothesis that Michael's behavior was in fact strongly affected by the structure of exchanges in the home. Were the changes in his behavior (the increase in constructive activity and decrease in bizarre-disruptive behavior) due to extraneous variables, or to the exchanges managed by the Hares?

In general, the A_2 period involved giving Michael little attention except for the two 20-minute food exchanges Mrs. Hare had with Michael for his breakfast and supper. In particular, the Hares were asked, and for several days coached, to (1) make no attempt to encourage Michael to engage in constructive activity; (2) give him no reinforcement for engaging in either constructive activity or bizarre-disruptive behavior; and (3) give him no noncontingent attention, e.g., talking or playing with him. These conditions went into effect February 9 and remained in effect until February 16, 1969. Data for this period consisted of Mrs. Hare's logs and four home observations by the researcher.

A negative change in Michael's behavior occurred on the first day. He began to play in water, whine, cry, and spin objects, and his constructive behavior decreased. Typically, he would work at some constructive activity as before and come over to his parents for a reward; receiving none, he would begin to pull and push them and whine. Finding that this too was ignored, Michael returned to his old patterns of self-stimulating and attention-getting behavior. As the days went by, bizarre-disruptive behavior rapidly increased, while constructive behavior fell to zero.

On February 17, 1969, the exchanges were reversed back to the productive exchanges existing in period C_1. This final period, then, was known as C_2, and data were taken until April 12, 1969. During the C_2 period, the Hares were taught to manage variable reward schedules, to strengthen Michael's constructive activity and make it less likely that satiation or rebelliousness would recur.

Figure 2 (p. 130) shows the results of the Parent Training Program with respect to bizarre-disruptive versus constructive behavior. To summarize: In the A_1 period, before any training, Michael had a very high rate of disruptive behavior. His parents reinforced this at

Figure 2: Changing the Structure of Exchanges Involving Constructive and Disruptive Behavior in the Home

The A_1 observations of the exchanges between the mother and child were made before the mother was trained in the Laboratory-school; the B observations, immediately after training. For the first 7 days of C_1, the mother was coached at home in changing the pattern of behavior observed in A_1. In A_2, the mother was asked to ignore both disruptive and constructive behavior. In B_2, she was instructed to again reciprocate constructive behavior and to ignore disruptive behavior.

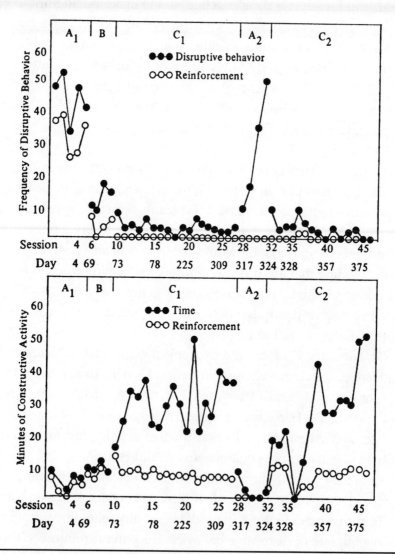

a similarly high rate with attention and sometimes food. At the same time, Michael seldom engaged in constructive activity. In the B period—after Mrs. Hare was trained in the Laboratory to ignore him or to time him out for disruptive behavior—Michael's disruptive behavior decreased from approximately 50 to 15 episodes per 2-hour period. Note, however, that with only this training, Michael's time at constructive activity did not increase significantly in the B period. So for the first seven days of the C_1 period, I coached the Hares at home to structure and maintain exchanges involving constructive activity, e.g., chores and play. During the C_1 period, the time Michael spent at constructive activity increased from about ten minutes to almost 40 minutes per 2-hour home visit. Notice, also, that the number of disruptive behaviors decreased further as the time at constructive activity increased. During the A_2 period, the Hares ignored both disruptive and constructive behavior. As Figure 2 shows, time spent on constructive activity fell to zero, while disruptive behavior rose to its pre-training level. In the C_2 period the Hares again reciprocated exchanges for constructive activity. Constructive activity then increased and disruptive activity decreased. It should be noted that by the end of the C_2 period, the duration of Michael's constructive activity was about 50 minutes, whereas constructive activity had stabilized at around 40 minutes per session during C_1.

The sudden drop in both constructive activity and reinforcement, and the increase in bizarre-disruptive behavior during Session 36, requires some explanation. For several weeks the Hares had, one by one, come down with the flu. As a result, they were too ill to structure and manage exchanges involving constructive activity with Michael. From Michael's point of view, this was another reversal: no one was paying any attention to him. Thus, the observation on Session 36 shows the result of the several weeks of illness in the family. Once the Hares recuperated, Michael's constructive activity rapidly increased and disruptive behavior decreased.

Building Cooperation

During the home baseline Michael seldom cooperated with parental exchange initiations (only 49% of the time on the average). In particular, he cooperated with directives and contract statements almost three times as often as with questions; he was not always rewarded for cooperating (rewarded for cooperating 60% of the time); and he was often rewarded for not cooperating (47% of the time on the average). To correct this situation, during the seven days of home coaching (C_1 period), the Hares were asked to use differential reinforcement to strengthen cooperation and weaken noncooperation. They were coached to ignore all instances of noncooperation, to initiate exchanges only with directives and contract statements, and to reward Michael each time he cooperated.

The data on cooperation indicate the following: (1) the Hares' questions rapidly fell to zero, while directives (predominantly) and contract statements increased; (2) the percent of reinforcement for cooperation rapidly increased; and (3) concomitantly, the percent of initiations with which Michael cooperated gradually rose. Figure 3 shows the results of the training on Michael's cooperation. Observation days were the same as in Figure 2.

Figure 3 indicates that when exchanges were changed to reward cooperation, ignore noncooperation, and initiate exchanges with directives and contract statements, Michael's cooperation increased; by the end of the C_1 period, it had stabilized at 100%. There was no *complete* reversal of the new exchange structure as such; that is, there was no period when the Hares were instructed, for instance, to reward noncooperation. Nevertheless, the conditions during A_2 affected Michael's cooperation later, when the C_2 period was begun. In A_2, it will be remembered, the Hares were instructed not to initiate exchanges with Michael. Consequently, he experienced no reward for cooperation during that period. During C_2, cooperation with initiations took several weeks to be re-strengthened, and stabilized at around 98%.

Figure 3: Changing Cooperation Exchanges in the Home

The A$_1$ observations of the exchanges were made before the Hares were trained. The B observations began immediately after the Hares were trained in the Laboratory-school. For the first 7 days of the C$_1$ period, the Hares were coached in the home to ignore non-cooperation, to initiate exchanges with directives and contract statements, but to avoid using questions, and to reward Michael each time he cooperated. No data are reported for A$_2$, as the Hares were instructed not to initiate any exchanges at all. During the C$_2$ period, they were again instructed to ignore noncooperation, to use directives and contract statements, and to reward cooperation.

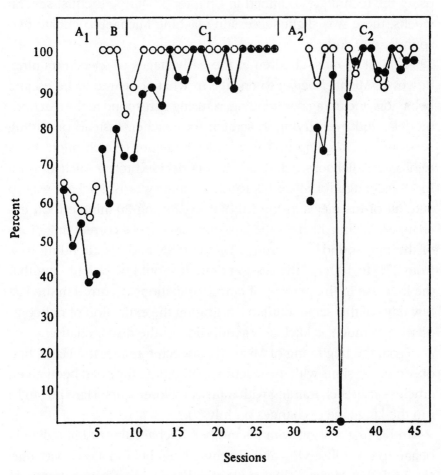

-●●●- **% cooperation with parents' initiations**
-○○○- **% reinforcement of cooperation by child**

Speech Training

For the first six months of Michael's education at the Lab school, teachers worked on encouraging eye contact and spontaneous vocalizations, extinguishing bizarre-disruptive behavior, and learning simple manipulative tasks. As the reader may recall from the Rimland checklist, Michael had never learned to speak, and was mute at the time he was admitted to the Laboratory. Speech training was begun in early July, 1968. The teacher began working on imitative speech, using the techniques outlined in Chapter 3. During the first several weeks, there was slight success in teaching Michael to imitate two sounds, *mm* and *uh*.

Typical of most children in the early stages of speech training, however, Michael began to engage in what appeared to be escape behaviors, including disattending, refusing to respond to the teacher's models, and even trying to scratch the teacher. Instead of ending sessions or switching to a new task altogether (which might have reinforced Michael's behavior), it was decided to try Michael on a food exchange for all of his food. In other words, Michael was to take all of his meals in the Laboratory, during 20-minute food exchanges. Within 12 days (31 sessions), Michael's correct imitations of the two sounds rose from 13% to 100%, and his attending rose from 27% to 100% of the session time. It should be pointed out that the increase in the percent of correct imitations occurred in the last few days of this stage, perhaps indicating the extinction of noncompliance as much as Michael's acquisition of the discrimination.

From the beginning of Michael's speech training, the Hares had observed sessions with the teacher. In addition, they had been given articles on speech training with autistic children. Mrs. Hare began to run the language exchanges on July 30.

In his first session with his mother, Michael almost immediately began to cry. Observing and coaching from behind a one-way mirror, I felt that Michael's behavior may have been a consequence of his mother's never having worked with him on speech before. A simple desensitization procedure was immediately tried. I entered the classroom and instructed Mrs. Hare only to reward Michael with food and praise for each correct response. I took over the task of presenting the vocal models for Michael to imitate. Michael's crying stopped, and he began to imitate correctly. Next, Mrs. Hare took over the exchange again, but instead of requesting speech, she requested that Michael look at her in order to receive food. In other words, the difficulty of the task was reduced. I stayed in the classroom and coached Mrs. Hare gradually to introduce more and more sounds for Michael to imitate as long as he remained calm. By the end of the session, Mrs. Hare was running the exchange by herself and was working on speech, and Michael was at ease.

In the second and third sessions, Mrs. Hare was coached from behind the one-way mirror. Specifically, she was coached to reward approximations to accurate imitations, to reward Michael only if he responded with a good approximation within five seconds, to use small bites, and to make sure that he was attending before she presented the model for him to imitate. Since Mrs. Hare seemed to have mastered the basics of speech training, and since Michael's correct responses were rather high during the last two of the three sessions (75 and 80 percent), it was decided that Mrs. Hare should begin running language exchanges at home for two of Michael's meals and occasionally for snacks.

Observations of Michael's progress at home on imitative speech began in mid-September. Standing in another room, I recorded three variables: the frequency of requests or models for each sound or word, the frequency of correct responses, and the frequency of incorrect responses. Though Mrs. Hare was not coached during sessions, she was asked to limit sessions to 20 minutes unless Michael was doing very well, and to end sessions if he left the table. Typically, she would present the same vocal model to Michael only a few times in a row, and then move to another one.

A word was defined as learned when the number of unprompted correct responses was at least 80% of the requests. Figure 4 (p. 136) summarizes the data taken over a period of seven months on Michael's acquisition of imitative speech.

It is obvious from Figure 4 that Michael's acquisition of imitative speech was extremely slow, especially when contrasted with that of Luke Nash, another mute child who will be discussed in Chapter 6. Difficulty in teaching mute children to talk was noted by Lovaas (1966a, 1966b). Moreover, studies by Kanner and Eisenberg (1955) indicated that a child's age has important implications for prognosis. Autistic children who had not developed speech by the age of five almost without exception failed to improve their level of socialization in later years. And Brown (1960) had found that even with psychotherapy, autistic children who had not developed speech by the

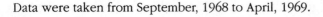

Figure 4: Cumulative Frequency of Words Taught to Michael Hare by Imitation by His Mother at Home, Uncoached

Data were taken from September, 1968 to April, 1969.

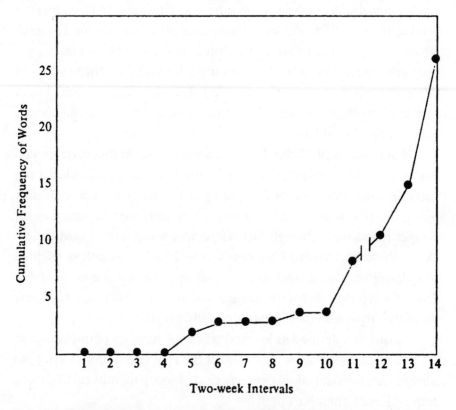

age of three remained generally unimproved. Michael, it will be remembered, was six years old when he entered the Laboratory, and speech training did not begin until he was six and a half.

Michael's main problem was acquiring the basic sounds or phonemes of the English language. Once he was fluent at saying and imitating the phonemic components of a word, he had little difficulty imitating the whole word (cf. Binder, 1996; Johnson & Layng, 1992). But his pre-training repertoire of sounds had been so limited that months were spent teaching him to imitate sounds that were not in his repertoire, e.g., *t, d, f,* and *s.* Note, however, that during the last two months of observations, Michael's acquisition was positively accelerating. It was becoming easier for him to speak. The reader should also bear in mind that Figure 4 underestimates Michael's repertoire. His mother was never asked to run through *all* the words she had been working on with Michael, and the number of words that could be observed was limited to the duration of the mealtime sessions at home.

On January 18, 1969, an experiment was conducted to test whether Michael's imitative speech was, indeed, under the control of the exchanges managed by his mother. The experiment was conducted at the usual time for Michael's lunch. It had an ABAB design. In the A periods Michael was given his plate of food and allowed to eat. Mrs. Hare was asked to present vocal models to Michael whenever his mouth was not full. In the B periods, Mrs. Hare moved the food in front of her and made each bite contingent upon a correct imitative response. All words and sounds Michael was to imitate were already in his repertoire.

Data consisted of the frequency of correct imitative responses for consecutive 30-second intervals. The clock was not running when Michael was eating. Inter-observer reliability was computed by comparing the percent of agreement of two independent observers on the number of correct responses recorded for each 30-second interval. The average percent agreement was 96. Data for the experiment are presented in Figure 5 on the next page.

As can be seen from Figure 5, the structure of the food exchange exerted powerful control over Michael's imitative speech. When food was not contingent on correct imitations, he made none—but when the structure of the exchange required that he produce correct imitations to receive food, his rate of correct imitations immediately increased. Although Mrs. Hare was not asked to present the same number of models to Michael each 30-second interval, the differences

---

**Figure 5: Cumulative Frequency of Correct Verbal Responses
in the Home During an Experimental Reversal**

In the A periods the child's food was given to him and his mother attempted to evoke imitative speech. In the B periods she moved his food in front of her and made each bite contingent upon a correct imitative speech response.

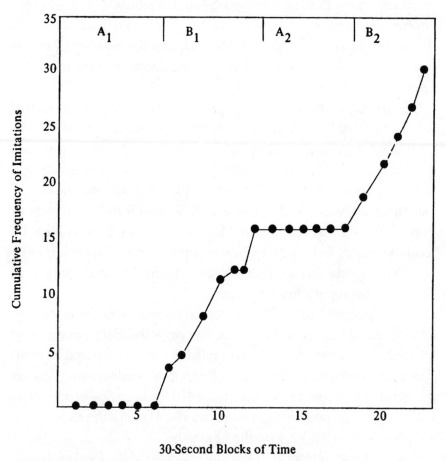

between periods cannot be attributed to her presenting more models in one period than in another. She presented 21, 19, 19, and 19 models to Michael in the A_1, B_1, A_2, and B_2 periods respectively. It should be added that there were only five 30-second intervals in the B_2 period because Michael, evidently full, left the table, ending the exchange.

By the time the Program with the Hares ended, Mrs. Hare was beginning stage two in Michael's speech and language instruction: teaching him names for things. No acquisition data had yet become available. Mention should be made, however, of several activities, all of Mrs. Hare's creation, that she engaged in with Michael to teach him names for things. Both are noted in Table 8 (pp. 120-121). One consisted of her naming objects in a book of pictures of everyday household items, and then asking Michael to point to the objects named. In this way, Michael learned to discriminate objects on the basis of the name.

The second activity, begun in February 1969, was an extension of the first. Mrs. Hare filled a large box with some of the objects that appeared in the book. The box was kept in Michael's room. Almost every day, she would empty the box in front of Michael, have him point to and name an object in the book, and then have him pick up that object from the pile and replace it in the box. This was continued until all of the objects had been replaced. Periodically, she would rotate the objects in the box. By mid-April, Michael's correct responding—i.e., picking up objects named on the first trial without a prompt—was 89%, indicating that he was learning to make object discriminations on the basis of the name.

Follow-up Description of the Home

Observations during the C_2 period ended on April 12, 1969. Follow-up observations were begun almost a month later on May 4 and lasted until June 22, 1969. Five follow-up observations were made, approximately a week apart, at the same time of day and for the same duration as previous observations. Except for one problem, the findings were quite encouraging.

In the first place, the rate of Michael's disruptive behavior remained at a very low level—an average of only one disruption per session. At the same time, he was never rewarded for his disruptions. He was either consistently timed out or ignored, and counterexchanges were made available to him. Second, his constructive activity had increased above the duration at the end of the C_2 period. At the end of the C_2 period, Michael engaged in constructive activity about 50 minutes per two-hour session; by the end of the follow-up period, constructive activity was up to about 62 minutes per session. Simultaneously, the Hares continued to reward Michael with praise while he worked or played and to reward him with a back-up reinforcer such as food, music, or water play when he had finished. They were learning, moreover, to use intermittent reinforcement on a variable-interval schedule. Michael usually had to work for longer periods of time before he received the back-up reinforcer. The Hares, in other words, were following my advice on how to prevent Michael from becoming satiated and uncooperative. They were preventing Michael from working contracts with them at his leisure, for he could no longer predict when his constructive behavior would be rewarded.

As to cooperation with exchange signals, it remained at the same percent as during the C_2 period. The average rate of cooperative responses during the last five days of C_2 was 95%, and it also averaged 95% during the five days of the follow-up period. The average rate of reinforcement for cooperative responses was also the same for the last five days of the C_2 and follow-up periods—96%.

Finally, Michael was continuing to make progress in speech training. Only four language exchanges were run for Michael's lunch during the five follow-up sessions (he was not hungry one of the days and did not come to the table for lunch). According to the criteria for learning words by imitation, the four language exchanges revealed that Michael had learned 11 new words. Michael's speech had also changed *qualitatively*. Michael was observed to initiate exchanges with the word "chip" many times to obtain potato chips. In addition, he used the word "mama" several times when, during imitation sessions, Mrs. Hare pointed to herself. In other words, as a result of Mrs. Hare's play periods with Michael, those in which objects were pointed to and named, Michael was beginning to use speech to communicate.

In sum, the follow-up period indicated that the Hares were still effectively applying techniques they had learned through the Parent Training Program, and were using their imagination and creativity to teach Michael new skills.

With all of the success of the Training Program, one major problem remained in the Hare home. From the beginning, the Hares had given Michael a great deal of attention, often for bizarre-disruptive behavior. In addition, they gave him much noncontingent attention. They *constantly* talked to him, cuddled him, and so forth. Although the Training Program taught the Hares not to give Michael attention for bizarre-disruptive behavior, the Hares persisted in giving Michael noncontingent attention.

Usually there would be nothing wrong with giving a child noncontingent attention. Obviously, parents should not always require their child to engage in some form of appropriate behavior before they reciprocate with attention. But with an autistic child, the situation is different. Attention is sometimes a powerful reinforcer. If the child receives it noncontingently, the parents are, in effect, *wasting* a reinforcer they could use to strengthen appropriate behavior. In fact, if the parents give their child enough noncontingent attention, the child may become satiated on attention, in which case when they give attention for appropriate behavior it will have little strengthening effect.

The Hares' noncontingent attention was discussed with them in the early stages of training. They were also reminded of it before and after home observations, and were directly coached to reserve most of their attention for Michael's appropriate behavior. None of these methods was effective enough. Suggestions to improve the Training Program will be considered in the summary chapter.

Conclusions

From both theoretical and practical standpoints, the Training Program with the Hares was successful. Theoretically, the hypotheses that (1) by training the parents, changes in the system of structured exchanges in the home would be produced, and (2) these changes would produce beneficial changes in the behavior of the child, were affirmed. The Hares changed patterns of interaction with Michael that had been in effect for years. They learned not only how to structure or initiate exchanges with Michael to produce cooperation, but also how to reciprocate exchanges to strengthen appropriate behavior and weaken inappropriate, autistic behavior. In addition, they learned a variety of methods for *teaching* Michael new skills—imitation, chores, play, speech.

From an emotional standpoint, the quality of life in the Hare family had improved. For Mr. and Mrs. Hare, there was a decrease in the confusion, disruptiveness, and chaos in their family, for they had learned how to control Michael's behavior. There may also have been a decrease in their feelings of frustration, guilt, and hopelessness as evidenced by their logs. There were also important changes in Michael's life. Most of his energy was now spent in constructive activity. His bizarre-disruptive behavior had markedly decreased; he had acquired many self-care skills, could work and play with others, and was learning to communicate.

5 Peter Gordon

By the time I began to work with the Gordons, Peter had been attending the Social Exchange Laboratory for almost two years, and his mother had received some training in exchange management in the Laboratory. She had read introductory materials, observed and recorded sessions, taken data for a number of sessions, and been given instructions on how to handle a few of Peter's disruptive behaviors at home. Yet I felt that including the Gordons was important for several reasons. First, Peter was extremely difficult for Mrs. Gordon to handle at home. Second, no data had been taken in the home on Mrs. Gordon's application of techniques she had learned in the Laboratory, nor had data been taken on Peter's progress at home. And third, Peter had a problem that is typical of many severely impaired children: namely, the generalization of behavior acquired in the school environment to other settings in the larger community, such as the home.

Description of the Child

Peter Gordon, a Caucasian male, was six years and eleven months old when he entered the program at the Social Exchange Laboratory. He was the younger of two children, with a brother three years older. Both of Peter's parents had a college education. Mrs. Gordon was a librarian prior to her marriage. Mr. Gordon was a judge. The Gordons indicated that there was no history of serious mental illness in the family.

A description of Peter's development is contained in Appendices

1 and 2. Briefly, Peter seemed to be developing normally during his first two years. In fact, Mrs. Gordon noted that he learned to stand and walk at an earlier age than his brother. The Gordons suspected that something was wrong with Peter when, by the age of two, "His speech just didn't come." As he grew older, Peter's repertoire of behavior became more and more autistic. He was no longer a happy, inquisitive child. He became withdrawn, demanded sameness in his environment, and developed ritualistic behaviors. The Gordons could not explain the changes in Peter's behavioral repertoire and development. They were certain, however, that there had not been any sudden, unusual, or traumatic experiences or illnesses.

The Gordons then made the rounds of professionals. After several years they concluded that their efforts to obtain help had been unsuccessful. Mrs. Gordon remarked that no one gave them concrete instructions in how to deal with Peter. The result was increasing frustration for the Gordons, as Peter became progressively more autistic.

During the four years that Peter was developing an autistic repertoire, the Gordons tried to educate him. They attempted to teach him to speak. They encouraged him to play by supplying toys and showing him how to use them. Mrs. Gordon reported that Peter merely stared into space when they were trying to instruct him. When left to his own devices, Peter spent his time stripping the beds, throwing things down the laundry chute and under the couch.

In handling Peter's disruptive behavior, the Gordons were remarkably permissive, yet they inadvertently *escalated* much of his disruptive behavior. They rarely punished Peter, but when they could no longer tolerate his disruptive behavior, they would spank him. Mrs. Gordon felt that the occasional spankings, which were not severe, kept Peter's disruptiveness under some control. She also reported, however, that over the years these same behaviors had gotten more frequent and violent. In other words, the occasional spankings probably taught Peter that he could engage in disruptive behavior for longer and longer periods of time (and be reinforced many times) before he would receive a punishing consequence. The longer the Gordons waited before they finally spanked Peter, the more violent, habitual, and resistant to extinction Peter's disruptive behavior became.

By the time he began his education at the Laboratory, Peter was extremely withdrawn, avoiding eye contact and physical contact. He often held his arms in a stereotyped position encircling his eyes and ears, a position which had often produced attention when people tried to pull his arms down. Although he could hum the tunes and say a few lines from several television commercials, Peter was essentially mute. He seldom made any sounds at all, except when grunting and slapping his hip. He spent much of his time moving and disarranging objects around the house in a ritualistic way. As soon as his mother cleaned up after him, he would begin again. He frequently engaged in self-destructive behaviors such as biting his index finger, palms, and the backs of his hands, striking himself on the sides of his head and on the cheekbones with his foreknuckles, and slapping his face, never breaking the skin but raising huge callouses and welts. When thwarted, Peter frequently slapped people near him, bit his finger, and threw himself onto the floor kicking and yelling.

Peter had been working with other teachers in the Laboratory for almost two years before the Gordon family became part of the Training Program. In those two years, eye contact had been established; several of Peter's stereotyped behaviors (including encircling his head) had been all but eliminated; he had been taught simple manipulative tasks and had progressed through several stages of speech training. Peter's imitative speech was quite strong, and he had learned a number of functional words and phrases.

Nevertheless, Peter had several severe problems, which was why the Gordons asked to join the Program. Peter had recurrent periods of even worse bizarre-disruptive behavior, and his speech had not generalized to the home. From the beginning, the rates of Peter's appropriate behaviors in the Laboratory had been cyclical. He typically worked and learned steadily for two weeks to a month, and then began to engage in bizarre-disruptive behavior, threw tantrums, became uncooperative (leaving the table, avoiding eye contact), and emitted only enough appropriate responses to earn food to kill his appetite. Though practitioners had referred to this sort of pattern (Rice & McDaniel, 1966), there were few good explanations. Since Peter's behavior so closely resembled that of a child worked with by Hewett (1965), Hewett's explanation and procedure were used. That is, Peter was defined as negative, rebellious, in a struggle to maintain the control he had had over everyone in his environment for years. The procedure in the Lab school had been to terminate interaction immediately contingent upon noncooperation. In this way it had been expected that Peter's self-deprivation would bring him around. And usually within a week or so Peter would indeed begin to participate and learn again.

At home, Peter went through similar cycles. For several weeks he was relatively calm and cooperative, looking through books and magazines, performing small tasks at his mother's request, or at least accompanying her as she did housework. Then, abruptly, he began throwing tantrums at the slightest inconvenience; stripping beds, removing slipcovers and pillows from the chairs and couch; throwing almost everything he could get his hands on under the couch, into the closet, or down the laundry chute; taking his father's law books out of the bookcases and piling the books on the floor, on tables, or tossing them behind the couch; and refusing to participate in constructive exchanges. After a few weeks of this, Peter would again calm down.

Peter's teacher had been advising Mrs. Gordon to ignore as much of this disruptive behavior as possible, but to systematically time Peter out whenever he started to disarrange the house. No coaching or observing at home had been done, however, to determine how well Mrs. Gordon was following the instructions or whether they were effective. More important, Mrs. Gordon had received no systematic instruction or coaching in how to teach Peter constructive behavior.

Finally, although Peter was learning to speak in the Laboratory, he rarely used speech at home. His mother reported that she was rarely able to prompt vocal imitations or functional speech.

As determined from her logs and from discussions with Mrs. Gordon, the situation in the Gordon home by September 1968, was as follows:

1. The Gordons knew how to ignore Peter and time him out for disruptive behavior, but his disruptive behavior still occurred at a high rate.
2. The Gordons did *not* know how to structure and manage counter exchanges with Peter to strengthen appropriate behavior.
3. As a result, Peter seldom used speech and rarely engaged in constructive activities at home.

Although no structured baseline observations were made prior to the research and training with the Gordons, the problems were rather clear.

Training to Restructure the System of Exchanges

The Training Program with the Gordons was conducted in their home. The goals were to teach Mrs. Gordon to structure and manage counter exchanges with Peter, increase Peter's functional speech at home, teach Peter to play, and decrease the more disruptive classes of inappropriate behavior.

Building a Play Repertoire and Decreasing Disruptive Behavior

The procedures used to teach Peter to play and to decrease disruptive behavior were exploratory. In the first place, with the exception of Lovaas et al. (1967) and Hudson and DeMyer (1968), little research had been done on teaching autistic children to play. Second, as said earlier, there was the problem of determining which variables control different classes of disruptive behavior.

Essentially, Peter performed three kinds of disruptive behavior: tantrums, removing his clothing, and ritualistically disordering the house. During his periodic uncooperative phases, all three were present. Tantrums and disordering the house were the most frequent of the three. The latter was most problematic because it occupied so much of Peter's time, thereby preventing his learning much appropriate behavior, and because it forced Mrs. Gordon to continually straighten the house. The main research hypothesis was that there would be an inverse relationship between the amount of time Peter spent playing and the frequency of his disruptive behavior. Three stages were involved in teaching Peter to play and in testing the hypothesis.

Stage 1: Self-initiated play. Instead of motivating and teaching Peter to play by structuring a contract with him, as we did with Michael Hare ("As soon as you play, you can have a record"), the procedure was to shape self-initiated play. Basically, Peter was rewarded not for completing a task or for playing a certain length of time, but for initiating play by touching or approaching a play object.

The procedure for shaping self-initiated play and teaching Mrs. Gordon how to maintain it involved two researchers (myself and an associate, Dr. Daniel Ferritor) running play sessions with Peter at home several times a week for three weeks. The steps were as follows:

1. Three play objects were put on the kitchen table within Peter's reach.
2. Mrs. Gordon was asked to watch the researchers work with Peter, using them as models.
3. The researchers stood near the table, holding food to be used to reward Peter.
4. Peter was rewarded with praise and food for approaching or touching any of the play objects.
5. Using praise and prompts, the researchers sustained Peter's contact with the objects, and tried to teach him how to play with them.
6. Every few minutes that Peter played with the objects, he received another bite of food.

7. After ten minutes of play, or if Peter left the table before ten minutes elapsed, the researchers removed the first play object and left the table, giving Peter the chance to initiate play with the remaining objects.

8. During the day Mrs. Gordon was to leave the toys on the table and continue as the researchers had done if Peter initiated play.

The self-initiated play stage lasted 35 days, from September 11 to October 15, 1968. Mrs. Gordon recorded Peter's time at self-initiated play each day and the frequency of his initiations. Data for weekends were excluded from the analysis because of the change in household routine. In addition, a reversal was performed from September 23–27 because Peter's play had begun to decrease. The reversal consisted merely of removing all toys—giving him no chance to play at all. It was hoped that the contrast would increase his playing when toys were reinstated. Data for the self-initiated play stage are presented in Figure 6 on the next page.

As can be seen from Figure 6, the procedure for strengthening self-initiated play was not successful. Gradually, Peter initiated play less and less. For several days after the reversal, self-initiated play increased, but it then decreased as before, stabilizing at 15 to 30 minutes a day. The average frequency of self-initiated play episodes was only four per day.

The data lent themselves to several additional generalizations. First, if played with on consecutive days, a toy lost its appeal. Some toys required more time before Peter became bored with them. Peter satiated on a pegboard landscape in 2 days, and on a lockboard (a board containing different types of locks that could be opened) in 3 days—but it took 23 days for him to satiate on pasting, and he never satiated on Play-doh. Second, once Peter satiated on a particular toy, its absence for a few days did *not* increase its appeal (though this may have depended on the length of time the toy was removed). And third, toys which were simple to operate (the cost of playing with them was low) and which offered much novelty or "natural" reinforcement, kept their appeal longer (cf. Hutt, 1967). The total

Figure 6: Strengthening Self-Initiated Play in an Autistic Boy

Mrs. Gordon was instructed to make toys available to Peter and to reward him for touching and/or approaching them. She was then to sustain his play. with the toy, rewarding him intermittently with food and praise. For three days a reversal was instituted in which no toys were made available.

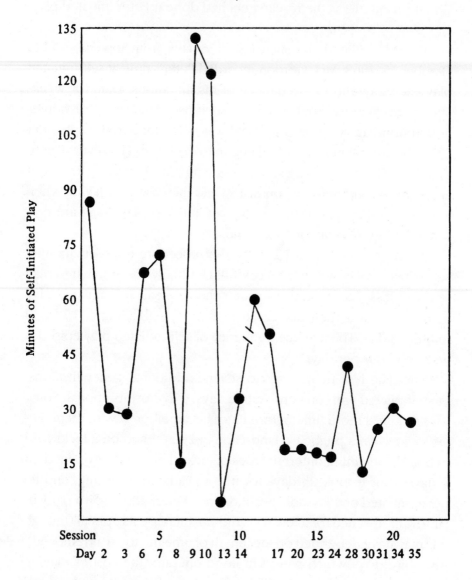

duration of play with Play-doh and paste (including weekends) was 1,045 and 244 minutes respectively. These objects provided stimulation in a variety of ways—tactile, olfactory, visual, and novelty. The total duration of play with sewing cards and a buttoning board, however, was two and one minutes, respectively. With these generalizations in mind, a second stage was instituted.

Stage 2: Toy rotation. Mrs. Gordon did not take data on the frequency of Peter's disruptions during the self-initiated play stage. However, in logs and discussions with her, she noted that Peter had become much easier to live with. She wrote that all classes of disruptive behavior had decreased and that Peter and his father were spending more time together in constructive activities. During this second stage, Mrs. Gordon took data on Peter's disruptions.

This stage was guided by two ideas. First, if Peter satiated quickly on each toy, then toys must be rotated *before* he was bored. Second, it seemed that any toy or activity involves costs and rewards. Some effort is expended in operating the toy, and at the same time, a toy provides feedback which may be naturally reinforcing. Therefore, the ratio of cost and reward in playing with particular toys was an important consideration. Furthermore, it was felt that play behavior might be strengthened if Peter were first allowed to play with toys having low cost and high reward values. Then, gradually as he mastered the skills for playing with simple toys, more complicated toys could be introduced.

Stage 2 was in effect from November 6 to December 2, 1968. The conditions were as follows:

1. Toys were rotated at least every two days.
2. At first, simple battery-operated and wind-up toys were introduced. The determination of how much natural reinforcement each toy supplied can be questioned, as it was based on my judgment, not Peter's. Toys that were easier to operate and generated more stimuli (noise, motion) were tentatively considered more reinforcing.

3. Peter received food and praise for initiating with a toy, and inter-
    mittently while he played, with Mr. Gordon taking over the play
    exchanges in the evening.
4. Peter was timed out immediately for any instance of the three
    forms of disruptive behavior mentioned earlier.
5. To test the effects of the time out contingency when Peter had no
    available alternative exchange, a reversal was performed from
    November 11-13, in which all toys were removed.

Data from the toy rotation stage are presented in Table 9 on the next
page (a graph is not presented because many data points overlap).
As in Stage 1, data from weekends are not included.

As Table 9 shows, the toy rotation stage did not increase the
duration of Peter's playing. The duration of play generally remained
within the range of the last nine sessions of Stage 1. The average
duration of play for the last five days of the period was 15 minutes
per day. There were more play initiations in the toy rotation stage,
however. The average frequency of play initiations was six per day,
in contrast to four during Stage 1. Thus, although the relative simplicity and systematic rotation of the toys did not increase the length
of time Peter played, he seemed to be playing a little more frequently.

Second, the combination of time out for disruptions and reinforcement for playing weakened only Peter's removing of clothing.
As time went by, tantrums and disarranging the house very gradually
increased in frequency. This may have been because play was still
not strong enough. Nevertheless, the availability of the play exchange
did control Peter's disruptive behavior somewhat. For, during the
reversal, when only the time out procedure was in effect, all disruptions increased. Thus, as was the case before the Training Program,
time out by itself was not sufficient to weaken Peter's disruptive behavior.

In sum, there was little success teaching Peter to play and weakening his disruptive behavior. When toys were not rotated, strengthening the *initiation* of play (i.e., the first response in a chain) was
not enough to build a durable play repertoire; introducing and sys-

tematically rotating toys graded according to their natural reinforcement qualities was not sufficient to increase the duration of Peter's
playing. What he seemed to need was special education in playing—something he had not gotten in the first two stages. In addition,
Mrs. Gordon needed special training in teaching him to play. A third
stage, therefore, was planned.

Table 9: Play and Disruptions During the Toy Rotation Stage

Day	Session	Play Behavior		Disruptive Behaviors			
		Mins. at Play	Play Initiations	Tan-trums	Remove Clothes	Disarrange House	Total Disruptions
1	1	11	11	0	4	0	4
2	2	7	5	1	0	0	1
3	3	21	10	0	3	0	3
7	4	22	8	0	0	1	1
8	5	23	8	0	0	0	0
9	6	74	9	1	0	2	3
10	7	21	7	2	0	1	3
13	8	30	10	0	2	0	2
Reversal: All Toys Removed But Time Out Still In Effect							
15				0	0	3	3
16				3	1	4	8
17				2	0	6	8
Toys Again Made Available for Playing							
20	9	26	9	2	0	1	3
21	10	7	3	0	0	0	0
22	11	35	5	7	1	3	11
23	12	17	2	1	0	0	1
24	13	2	1	0	0	1	1
26	14	13	2	1	0	5	6

Stage 3: Structured play. In this stage, Peter was rewarded for initiating play during the day; toys were introduced and rotated according to their natural reinforcement qualities; and Peter was given special education in learning to play.

From December 4, 1968 to January 13, 1969, Mrs. Gordon ran food exchanges at home with Peter involving play. A total of 17 sessions were held. No data were taken on weekends, and a Christmas break occurred from December 21 to January 6. This break constituted a reversal, as Mrs. Gordon was asked not to run sessions with Peter. Toys were available for him to play with, however.

Each session was 20 minutes long. For the first several sessions, the researcher coached Mrs. Gordon in managing the exchange— i.e., how to initiate the exchange, how to prompt Peter to make correct responses, how to reward him for correct responses, and how to rotate the toys that were worked on. After the first few days, Mrs. Gordon ran the exchanges without coaching.

The toys used in the early sessions were simple ones: Play-doh, pop-beads (large plastic beads to be strung together), simple puzzles, plastic building blocks, and Tinker toys. Later, more complicated toys were introduced: jigsaw puzzles, a pegboard landscape, peg- and-pull blocks (a larger version of Tinker toys), and a machine to cut out various shapes of paper. Besides changing the complexity of the tasks, Mrs. Gordon was asked to gradually change the schedule of reciprocation from almost continuous reinforcement in the beginning to a fairly thin variable ratio schedule toward the end.

A number of variables were recorded during each session: the frequency of Mrs. Gordon's verbal prompts (e.g., "That piece goes in there"); the frequency of Peter's correct responses (for instance, each puzzle piece put in the right place, each bead snapped together, and each piece of paper cut out were scored as correct responses); and the frequency of reciprocations with food for correct responses. The data on Peter's rate of correct responding and Mrs. Gordon's rate of reciprocating are presented in Figure 7 on the next page.

As shown, Mrs. Gordon was quite successful in motivating and teaching Peter to play during the structured play sessions. In only 12 sessions, she increased his rate of correct responding from 20 responses to 90 responses per 20-minute session. This is even more significant in light of the fact that Peter was introduced to new and

---

Figure 7: Teaching an Autistic Child How to Play

Observations of sessions designed to teach Peter Gordon how to play with various toys. Sessions were run at home by Mrs. Gordon who was coached only for the first few days. Mrs. Gordon was instructed to gradually put Peter on a variable ratio schedule. The Christmas break occurred between Days 17 and 35. Essentially, the break constituted a reversal.

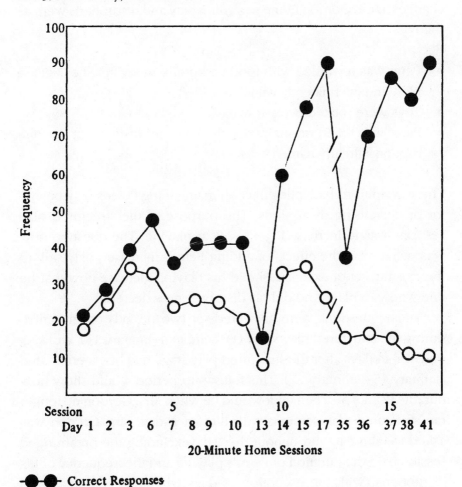

-●●- **Correct Responses**
-○-○- **Reinforcement**

more difficult toys every few days—toys requiring more time to complete a correct response. Peter's increasing skill is revealed by both his rate of correct responses and the amount of verbal prompting from his mother. Within the 17 sessions, the percent of correct responses that were verbally prompted fell from 71% to 13%. At the same time, the percent of correct responses that were rewarded was reduced from 95% to 12%. In other words, by Session 17 Peter was responding correctly at a high rate, was receiving few prompts and little food reinforcement, and had mastered ten different toys.

The reader will recall that as a result of Stages 1 and 2, the exchanges in the Gordon home regarding play and disruptions were as follows:

- Peter was rewarded with food and praise every time he initiated play, and intermittently while he played.
- Toys were rotated every few days.
- Peter was timed out immediately for every instance of the disruptions already named.

These conditions had little effect on maintaining Peter's play behavior or decreasing disruptions. The purpose of the structured play sessions was to increase Peter's *skill* at playing. The question now was, what were the effects of adding Peter's increased play skill to the existing set of exchanges? Did his playing increase now that he knew how to play? And did his disruptiveness decrease?

These questions were answered for two periods of time: first, during the structured play stage (December 4–January 13), and second, for 44 days after the structured play stage had been terminated (January 15–February 27). This follow-up period would show how durable Peter's play behavior would be when Mrs. Gordon no longer ran structured play sessions with him each day. Mrs. Gordon was asked to take data throughout the day (excluding the prearranged sessions) on the duration of Peter's playing and the frequency of his disruptions. With the exception of days when she was unable to take data, Table 10 (pp. 157-158) presents the duration of Peter's

Table 10: Play and Disruptions During and Following the Structured Play Stage

Day	Session	Play Behavior		Disruptive Behaviors			
		Mins. at Play	Play Initiations	Tan- trums	Remove Clothes	Disarrange House	Total Disruptions
Structured Play Stage							
1	1	68	5	0	0	2	2
2	2	210	13	0	0	0	0
3	3	56	3	1	0	1	2
6	4	99	10	0	0	1	1
7	5	71	8	0	0	0	0
8	6	53	7	0	0	2	2
9	7	87	4	0	0	2	2
10	8	29	3	0	0	2	2
13	9	68	4	0	0	0	0
14	10	75	2	0	0	0	0
15	11						
17	12						
Christmas Vacation: Essentially an 18-Day Reversal							
35	13						
36	14						
37	15	80	2	0	0	0	0
38	16	85	2	0	0	0	0
41	17	80	2	0	0	0	0
Follow-Up Period							
43	18	120	8	0	0	0	0
44	19	45	2	0	0	1	1
49	20	5	1	0	0	5	5
50	21	40	7	0	0	2	2

Table 10 (Continued)

Day	Session	Play Behavior		Disruptive Behaviors			
		Mins. at Play	Play Initiations	Tan-trums	Remove Clothes	Disarrange House	Total Disruptions
Follow-Up Period							
51	22	30	3	0	0	0	0
52	23	30	1	0	0	0	0
55	24	30	1	0	0	1	1
56	25	10	1	0	0	3	3
57	26	10	2	0	0	8	8
65	27	135	3	0	0	10	10
66	28	120	2	0	0	0	0
67	29	90	3	0	0	0	0
68	30	120	2	0	0	0	0
69	31	120	2	0	0	0	0
72	32	180		0	0	0	0
73	33	80	2	0	0	1	1
74	34	40	3	0	0	1	1
76	35	61		1	0	0	1
77	36	33		1	0	0	1
78	37	27		0	0	0	0
80	38	66	8	0	0	0	0
83	39	73	9	0	0	0	0
84	40	70	4	0	0	1	1
85	41	110	5	0	0	0	0
86	42	60	2	0	0	0	0

self-initiated play and the frequency of his disruptive behaviors during and following Stage 3.

With respect to play, Table 10 indicates that teaching Peter how to play during the structured play stage *did* increase the duration of self-initiated play relative to both previous stages. The average duration of play per day during Stage 3 (as determined by averaging the last five days of that period) was 60 minutes, in contrast to 15 minutes during Stage 2. Although Peter's playing during the follow-up period was less stable than in Stage 3, there was a further increase in the average duration of play. The average of the last five days during the follow-up was 75 minutes per day.

Thus, the program to build Peter's play repertoire was at least moderately successful. Beginning with a baseline of essentially zero, by the end of the program Peter played for over an hour a day on the average, by himself, with his brother, and with both parents. This change was accomplished after three systems had been introduced and finally combined into one program. On the other hand, it is clear that the program was quite successful in controlling two of the three classes of Peter's disruptive behavior: removing clothes and throwing tantrums. These were nearly reduced to zero. Even though Peter's stereotyped disarranging of the house occurred periodically, toward the end of the follow-up it too was weakening. Thus, the system of exchanges that combined time out for disruptions and reinforcement for appropriate alternative behavior—namely playing—was generally effective in reducing Peter's disruptiveness.

Speech Training

Peter was well into the third stage of speech training in the Laboratory (labeling). However, his mother reported that she and Mr. Gordon were unable to evoke speech from him at home. This is an example of the problem of generalizing skills acquired in the classroom to other everyday social situations. Therefore, the goal was to teach Mrs. Gordon to structure and manage language exchanges with Peter so that she could teach him to talk both during speech training sessions and throughout the day, and teach her husband to use the same procedures.

The research and training with Mrs. Gordon on speech was based on an ABAB design. All sessions were 20 minutes long, held from approximately 10:20 to 10:40 A.M. Inter-observer reliability was checked periodically and was computed as a percentage of agreement between the two observers on the frequencies recorded for each variable. The average agreement was 91%.

Baseline (A$_1$). Seven baseline observations were made between October 25 and November 7, 1968. During the baseline Mrs. Gordon used picture cards and picture books, and was instructed to ask Peter questions about the pictures. (Today I would strongly recommend using actual objects.) Some questions concerned the names of the objects in the pictures (e.g., "What is this?"); others concerned action (e.g., "What do you do with a comb?"). She was also asked to prompt him to give the answer and to reward him if he did so. She received no coaching, however, on how to gain and hold Peter's attention or how to ask questions.

The observations revealed several things. First, Peter's rate of appropriate responses to questions was quite low, averaging only four per session, although he was receiving food for each appropriate response. Moreover, his attending was low. He often got up from the table and walked around, and he threw a total of 11 tantrums over the seven sessions. Typically, Mrs. Gordon tried to maintain Peter's attention by going after him or telling or asking him to come back. He rarely returned.

Second, Mrs. Gordon asked many "multiple" questions. When Peter refused to answer or imitate a prompt, Mrs. Gordon asked the same question over and over in a series. The average length of each series of multiple questions was four, but one time Mrs. Gordon repeated the same question 17 times in a row. The number of series of multiple questions per session was one variable measured. The number of "single" questions asked each session was also measured. A single question consisted of Mrs. Gordon's asking a question once and then going on to another if Peter did not emit an appropriate response.

Single questions (B_1). The B_1 period consisted of 12 sessions between February 24 and March 14, 1969. The reason for the delay between A_1 and B_1 was that the writer was working with Mrs. Gordon and Peter on playing, and it was felt that working on play and speech at the same time would put too much strain on Peter. The reader may wonder whether Mrs. Gordon's language exchange behavior changed in the interim. The answer is that it did not. For during the structured play sessions Mrs. Gordon also asked Peter questions, and she asked multiple questions at a high frequency. In fact, the average number of series of multiple questions per play session was the same as during the A_1 period on speech: seven.

Mrs. Gordon was coached for the first few days of the B_1 period. In particular, she was coached not to hold up a picture or ask a question until Peter was attending to her. She was also instructed to ignore it when he left the table. Second, she was coached to ask *only* single questions. If Peter did not give an appropriate verbal response within five seconds of the question (or the prompt), she was to wait five seconds and then ask a question about a different picture. She was still to reward each appropriate response with praise and a bite of food.

Experimental reversal (A_2 and B_2). During A_2 (March 17–28), Mrs. Gordon was asked to return to asking multiple questions should Peter not give an appropriate response. And finally, during the B_2 condition (March 31–April 15) she was instructed to ask only single questions. Data on the relationship between Peter's rate of appropriate verbal responses and Mrs. Gordon's single vs. multiple questions are presented in Figure 8 on the next page.

Figure 8 shows that the technique Mrs. Gordon used to initiate verbal exchanges was an important determinant of Peter's rate of correct responses. During the A_1 period, when multiple questions were predominant, Peter correctly answered an average of only four

Figure 8: Appropriate Verbal Responses of an Autistic Boy Under Various Exchanges Managed by His Mother

In the A_1 condition Mrs. Gordon gave Peter bites of food for each correct verbal response to questions about pictures. She was uncoached. In B_1 she was coached for two days to ask each question only once. In A_2 Mrs. Gordon was instructed to ask multiple questions as in A_1. In B_2 she was instructed to return to asking each question only once.

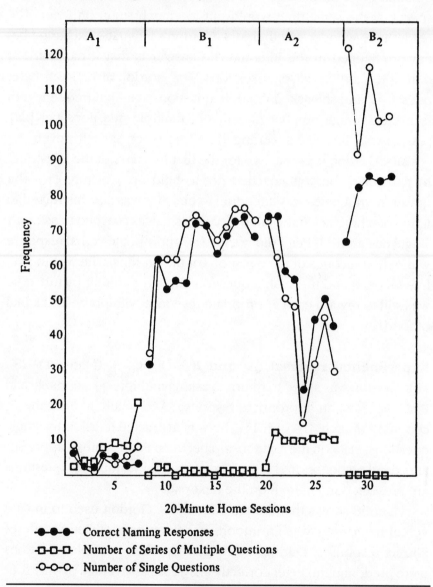

20-Minute Home Sessions

—●—●—●— Correct Naming Responses
-◻-◻-◻- Number of Series of Multiple Questions
-○-○-○- Number of Single Questions

questions per session; during the B_1 period, when single questions were predominant, the number of correct responses rose to approximately 70 per session. When Mrs. Gordon used multiple questions again (A_2), Peter's rate of correct responses fell to about 40 per session. And finally, when he was asked only single questions again, Peter's rate of correct responses rose to slightly over 80 per session. Thus, the reversal not only demonstrated the effect of the independent variable (the type of question asked), but produced a slight intensification of Peter's speech as well.

A possible explanation of the efficacy of single questions over multiple questions is that multiple questions reinforce errors and non-responding. Once a child begins not responding, a vicious cycle may develop in which not responding is reinforced more than correct responding. But if every time the child answers incorrectly or does not answer and the picture is turned down, he is timed out for five seconds and is asked another question, then inappropriate or nonresponses may be extinguished.

Having been trained to promote imitative speech, Mrs. Gordon was next asked to apply the techniques throughout the day—to ask Peter about a variety of objects and events, prompt him, and reward him. Thereafter, her logs and discussions with her indicated that Peter was answering a number of questions without prompting, that his imitative speech was becoming quite strong (he would attempt to imitate any vocal model directed to him), that he was beginning to use words to ask for things, and that Mr. Gordon was also managing the language exchanges effectively.

Conclusions

At the beginning of the research with the Gordon family, exchanges between Peter and his parents were such that Peter was neither acquiring new, appropriate behavior nor generalizing behavior learned in the Laboratory to the home. In fact, Peter's disruptiveness at home was driving his parents to distraction. The Training Program with the Gordons was aimed at (1) strengthening both Peter's imitative and functional speech at home—i.e., bringing his speech under the stimulus control of his parents; (2) decreasing his disruptive behavior; and (3) teaching Peter to occupy his time constructively with play activities.

The Training Program was partially successful in all three areas. Mrs. Gordon learned how to teach Peter to play and how to maintain his play behavior. It should be pointed out, however, that Peter, having essentially no play repertoire at the beginning of the research, required several weeks of intensive play training sessions before playing became a stronger part of his repertoire. Moreover, Mrs. Gordon learned how to promote and strengthen imitative speech. Peter's imitative speech was facilitated by teaching Mrs. Gordon to initiate speech exchanges only with "single" in contrast to "multiple" questions. And finally, Peter's disruptive behavior was reduced to near zero. This was accomplished only after Peter's playing had been strengthened. His playing, then, seemed to be a substitute for disruptive behavior.

In sum, by the end of the training and research with the Gordons, Peter had made important steps in his socialization, his mother and father had learned how to manage exchanges involving speech, play, and disruptive behavior, and the frustration and futility in their efforts to teach Peter had been lessened.

6 Luke Nash

Luke Nash, an African-American male, was seven when I began to work with his family. He had already attended the Social Exchange Laboratory for one year. Luke was the third of four children, with a sister, 11, and two brothers, 10 and 6. Both parents had three years of college education. Mr. Nash was an aircraft mechanic for a large corporation. The parents indicated that there was no history of serious mental illness in the family. However, his older brother had been diagnosed with mental retardation and was attending special education classes, but was soon to enter a regular fifth-grade class. Indications of retardation in this boy's development appeared after the birth of Luke. Similarly, Luke's behavioral retardation began, or was noticed, just after the birth of his younger brother.

Description of the Child

A detailed description of Luke's development can be found in Appendices 1 and 2. To summarize, Luke seemed to be developing normally in all areas—speech, motor skills, relatedness to others—until he was approximately 1½ years old. A dramatic change in his development was noticed at 14 months, shortly after the next sibling was born. Luke became inactive and withdrawn, slept a great deal, stopped smiling and talking, and seemed to be "in a trance most of the time."

Mrs. Nash, believing that Luke needed extra attention to soften the blow of being displaced from his position as youngest child, began to give him a great deal of attention *while he was withdrawn*.

She related that she spent much time with him, cuddling him and trying to coax him out of his room. Luke was taken to a physician, who advised the Nashes to wait before seeking special services. The Nashes waited for another year.

Meanwhile, Luke developed a repertoire of bizarre-disruptive behavior. For instance, he began having what his parents called "fits." He shrieked in increasing intensity, overturning household objects until, with a vacant stare, he contorted himself into rigid postures. His parents' response to the fits (or tantrums) was to give Luke attention. They talked to him, trying to calm him, and sometimes physically restrained him. In addition, Luke began sitting in fixed positions, sometimes rocking for long periods of time. He also became aggressive towards his older brother when the brother was receiving attention from Mrs. Nash. As noted in Appendices 1 and 2, when not withdrawn Luke was generally hyperactive: running and shrieking through the house, jumping on beds, getting into drawers and spilling the contents, and sometimes destroying objects.

When Luke was three, the Nashes returned to the physician, who put Luke on medication for a year. The fits did not disappear. Nor did Luke begin to develop normally again. Several years later, the Nashes were referred to a child guidance clinic, where Luke was diagnosed with autism. The clinic directed the Nashes to the Social Exchange Laboratory, with the clinic speech pathologist predicting that speech was not likely to become Luke's main means of communication.

By the time he began attending the Social Exchange Laboratory in September 1967, at the age of seven, Luke's skill repertoire was as follows. Luke could eat properly, dress and undress himself, and use the toilet. He could work puzzles, stack blocks, and—interestingly enough—draw human figures on a level normal for his age. His speech was limited to a very few words such as "mama" and "daddy," although, in the main, his vocalizations were in the nature of lalling. Even the words "mama" and "daddy" were not functional, for Luke did not use them to name or call his parents; they were merely words that he occasionally said.

For the first nine months of his education in the Social Exchange Laboratory, Luke worked with a teacher other than myself. Luke's education centered on three areas: imitation, manipulative tasks, and speech. For imitation, Luke was taught to imitate a large number of body movements by the teacher (touching the face, patting the tummy) and manipulations with objects (putting them on the floor, arranging them in certain ways). Within a few months, Luke acquired what Metz (1965) and Baer (1968) called "generalized imitation." He would attempt to imitate anything the teacher did, even those gestures of the teacher which were consistently not reinforced. Second, Luke was taught to work attentively at manipulative tasks, such as puzzles, boxes and blocks to stack, and so forth. Little success, however, was attained in speech training. After approximately six months, Luke learned to imitate only a few simple sounds (ē, a, ī, ō), and a few two-syllable utterances (*baba, mama, dada, wawa, cookie*).

I began working with Luke in June 1968. Several days were spent on speech. Luke was quite disruptive and inattentive, frequently leaving his seat, shrieking, and closing his eyes tightly. Thus, it was thought best to strengthen the sorts of behavior necessary for speech training, which we began again later, in September 1968.

During the summer of 1968, Luke's preparation for speech training went through several stages. First, Luke's gaze aversion was dealt with. The procedure was as follows. Luke and the teacher sat across from each other at a table in front of the Laboratory's "token machine." The token machine was a piece of masonite, a little larger than a door, which stood across the corner of two walls, leaving enough room behind it for an observer to sit. Across the center of it were several small vertical slits and a cup dispenser. The child was taught to drop tokens through the slits, and when he had deposited a specified number, the observer would drop a cup of food down the dispenser for the child. The setup was quite effective in teaching children to work token exchanges. Bites of Luke's lunch were contingent upon attending to the teacher, i.e., looking at the teacher's eyes either spontaneously or on request.

The teacher, holding a token up to his own eyes, would say to

Luke, "Look at me." If Luke looked at the teacher within five seconds, he was rewarded with praise and a token. He also was rewarded for looking spontaneously. Gradually, he was required to look for longer periods before he received a token, and gradually the exchange ratio with the token machine was increased from one token per cup of food to four tokens (on a variable ratio schedule). At the same time, Luke was timed out in a time out room immediately upon getting up from the table, closing his eyes tightly, or shrieking. After a week, Luke's attending behavior was quite strong and his disruptive behavior was reduced to zero.

In the second stage, Luke's generalized imitation was used to teach him more complex tasks such as putting together multi-piece picture puzzles, pasting, and coloring. Results in this stage were also good. His attention to the teacher remained high (each additional piece of the puzzle or shape to paste was presented contingent upon Luke's looking at the teacher); his disruptions remained low; and his skill at these tasks became quite high. He could work most puzzles and paste shapes onto pages without prompting, and he could add the missing parts of a simple human figure drawn by the teacher.

During August, I introduced into the sessions sounds for Luke to imitate. At first, sounds were presented intermittently, and they were sounds already in Luke's repertoire. Luke was rewarded, of course, for correct imitations. Since Luke's attention remained high and disruptions remained low, a larger proportion of the sessions were devoted to verbal imitation training. By September, I felt that speech training and training Luke's parents could begin in earnest.

The following is an outline of the stages of research and training with Luke and his parents.

Sept. 19, 1968:	Speech training begun in the Laboratory with Luke.
Oct. 2–3, 1968:	General observations at the Nash home.
Oct. 5–9, 1968:	Baseline taken at the Nash home (A_1).
Oct. 11, 1968:	Mrs. Nash begins training in the Laboratory.
Nov. 19, 1968:	Observation of Mrs. Nash at home on imitative speech training (uncoached).

Dec. 6, 9, & 10, 1968:   Mrs. Nash trained in Laboratory to teach Luke functional words.

Dec. 10, 1968:   Observation of Mrs. Nash at home on functional speech training.

May 5–8, 1969:   Observations to check for progress and the generalization of training, and to locate remaining problems in the system of exchanges (B).

May 13–29, 1969:   Coaching and observing at Nash home to restructure system of exchanges (C_1).

June 3–5, 1969:   Experimental reversal at home to test control by parents over bizarre-disruptive behavior, constructive behavior, and speech (A_2).

June 6–25, 1969:   Return to orthogenic system of exchanges (C_2).

Pre-Training Description of the Home (A_1)

The Nashes' participation in the Training Program is an interesting example of how principles of exchange theory apply to both training parents and educating their children. When parents enter a program, they incur costs and (hopefully) gain rewards. In essence, they enter into an exchange with their consultant. The consultant helps them remove some of the disturbances from their home life and gives them the satisfaction of seeing their child begin to develop. At the same time, however, the consultant may require them to: (1) open their homes to his or her eyes; (2) allow him to increase their workload with educational tasks to perform at home and in the Laboratory; and (3) change established behavior patterns or ways of interacting with their child.

Now it seems that once parents are told what the consultant may require of them, they will enter the exchange only when they expect that the benefits or rewards—namely, help, a reduction in discomfort, and so forth—will outweigh the costs. The Nashes were hesitant to enter such an exchange. When I began working with Luke, I told the Nashes that I would like to work with them in the home. Though the subject was broached several times, the Nashes were not interested. They could never find time for me and an assistant to make home observations.

The reason, perhaps, was that during the preceding nine months Luke had progressed so little in learning to speak, an important sign of progress. Thus, the Nashes had little expectation of success. However, after I had worked with Luke for about a month and taught him to imitate 11 words, the Nashes were quite willing to be part of the Parent Training Program. They suddenly found time. In fact, Mrs. Nash began to accompany her husband every day when he brought Luke to the Laboratory, and she seemed very enthusiastic as she arrived for each day's session, especially when she began working with Luke herself.

General Home Observations

General home observations were made at the Nash home from 11:00 A.M. to 1:00 P.M. and from 1:00 P.M. to 3:00 P.M. on October 2–3, 1968. The observer, standing in a corner of the living room, recorded observations on a portable tape recorder. Although a less conspicuous place of observation would have been preferred, Luke's tendency to run from room to room would continually have brought him into contact with the observer.

Analysis of the observations reveals the following generalizations. First, Luke did *not* perform very many different kinds of bizarre-disruptive behavior, but the frequency of this behavior was high. His bizarre-disruptive behavior consisted of shrieking; playing in water in the bathroom sink and toilet; getting into the refrigerator and pantries in the kitchen; jumping on the beds, putting the sheets and covers in disarray; rolling on the floor, grabbing for his mother's legs; and giggling inappropriately. Though inappropriate and somewhat of a nuisance to his parents, Luke's giggling and rolling on the floor were not considered worthy of immediate attention. And although his parents later noted that Luke often threw tantrums, had some bizarre behaviors and was sometimes destructive, none of these were observed at this time.

As to constructive behavior, Luke was observed to engage in what must be called play behavior. It was not a ritualistic manipulation of objects. Rather, he put blocks of wood together into a rectangular construction and then moved a plastic car in and out of his construction. This play was of short duration, and though a sister and brother were playing nearby, Luke made no attempt at cooperative play. Rather, his play was of a parallel type.

It should be pointed out that the short duration of Luke's play might have indicated a limited play repertoire and not a short attention span. In fact, for Luke to have continued building his construction over and over and moving his car in and out of it ritualistically for a long period of time would have been more problematic.

Finally, as to his parents' reactions to Luke's behavior, both parents consistently gave negative attention for inappropriate behavior, either by going after him or telling or yelling at him to stop. He was *never* rewarded for playing. His parents merely watched television or talked to the other children while Luke played. In effect, constructive playing was ignored.

Home Baseline

Based on the general home observations and discussions with the Nashes concerning their assessment of Luke's major problems, several variables were selected for measurement during baseline observations taken at the Nash home. The Nashes' baseline, like the Hares', was to describe exchanges in the home between Luke and his parents—exchanges which presumably were important conditions that fostered or hindered Luke's development. Observations were made from 2:00 to 3:30 P.M. on October 4–8, 1968.

Unfortunately, no other observers were available for direct measures of inter-observer reliability. Therefore, the researcher, during Day 1, recorded a flat description of events onto a portable tape recorder. He then transferred data from the tape onto a recording sheet. Later, an observer who had had instruction concerning definitions of the variables was asked to take data off the same tape and transfer it to the recording sheet. To obtain a measure of reliability, the frequencies of occurrence scored by each observer for each variable were compared. The average percent of agreement for the 13 categories in which any events were recorded was 93. For the remaining four baseline sessions, observations were recorded directly onto recording sheets—a more efficient method since no data were lost in the transfer from tape to sheet.

Variables on the parents' side of the exchanges were (1) attempts to structure or initiate exchanges with directives, questions, and contract statements and (2) types of reciprocations—rewarding, ignoring, punishing, removing, and timing out. Variables concerning Luke's involvement in exchanges were: cooperation with parental exchange initiations, shrieking, playing in water, getting into things, destructive behavior, bizarre sounds and/or gestures, playing, and speaking.

Table 11 lists exchanges that repeatedly occurred in the home

Table 11: Description of Typical Exchanges in the Nash Home Prior to Parent Training

Child's Behavior	Parents' Reaction
Plays with water in bathroom: splashes water out of sink, flushes toilet, fills shoes with water.	Chases after him or yells at him to get out of bathroom or to stop what he is doing, almost 70% of the time. (He usually begins again.)
Gets into things: attempts to get into refrigerator, pantries, and dressers in order to remove, consume, or disarrange contents. Watches to see if parents are looking.	Chases after him or yells at him to stop, almost 100% of the time. (He usually begins again.)
Shrieks: often runs through house shrieking at the top of his lungs.	Tells him to "shut up" or "cut that out" about 45% of the time.
Destructive: sometimes throws or overturns objects, e.g., records, chairs.	Yells at him to stop 100% of the time.
Bizarre sounds and/or gestures: ritualized hand-flapping and moaning.	Ignores 100% of the time.
Plays with cars, blocks. (Very infrequent and of short duration.)	Ignores 100% of the time.
Cooperates with parental exchange signals.	Ignores 100% of the time.

during the baseline observations. The following conclusions were drawn concerning the exchanges in the Nash home prior to training:

1. The frequency of Luke's social interaction during observation periods was low (14 on the average), as he spent much time listening to records or watching television.

2. Bizarre-disruptive behavior consistently (i.e., day by day) greatly outweighed appropriate behavior. Homans' second proposition in *Social Behavior: Its Elementary Forms* (1961) states that the frequency with which a person directs a response toward another is proportional to the frequency with which the other reciprocates with a reward. Luke's case bears this principle out. With the exception of destructive behavior, the frequency of each class of inappropriate behavior was directly related to the proportion of times that responses in each class had been rewarded. For instance, getting into things occurred 23 times and was rewarded 95% of the time; playing in water occurred 19 times and was rewarded 69% of the time; shrieking occurred 10 times and was rewarded 43% of the time; and bizarre sounds and/or gestures occurred 3 times and were never rewarded. In other words, the relative frequencies of Luke's behaviors are nicely predicted by the "matching law" (Hernnstein, 1961), which has been shown to apply to human behavior in many settings (Dishion, Spracklen, Andrews, & Patterson, 1996; McDowell, 1988).

3. Bizarre-disruptive behavior was rewarded an average of 72% of the time, while appropriate behavior was never rewarded. Only bizarre sounds and gestures were ignored, perhaps because they did not interfere with family activities or arrangements.

4. Some of Luke's inappropriate behavior—e.g., getting into things and playing in water—seemed to be attention-getting behavior, as he (like Michael Hare) would watch to see if anyone were looking at him before he engaged in the behavior, and would smile when his actions produced negative attention.

5. Luke emitted no appropriate verbal responses, nor did his parents attempt to prompt speech.

6. The Nashes made no attempts to encourage Luke to engage in constructive activities.
7. The Nashes never rewarded Luke when he cooperated with a parental exchange signal.

In sum, it was clear that Luke's parents played little more than a custodial role—never encouraging or rewarding Luke, only attending to and attempting to stop disruptive behavior. It was as if the Nashes sought only to preserve the peace and quiet which Luke so often disturbed.

Yet it would be both unfair and inaccurate to blame the Nashes for the nature of their interaction with Luke. The home baseline revealed only a few hours of exchanges that were governed by many factors operating over many years. Having two children with learning deficiencies, one of whom (Luke) had "fits" at all hours of the day and night for years, and having taken Luke to several specialists to no avail, the desire for a little peace and quiet was not unreasonable, however ineffective the methods they used to obtain it.

Training in Basic Techniques of Exchange Management

The problem was to change the role played by Luke's parents from custodians to educators. Luke's behavior in the Laboratory-school indicated that he had the capacity to learn to play, and his inappropriate behavior at home (getting into and disarranging things) was of the type that had been shown, in the cases of Michael Hare and Peter Gordon, to be relatively easy to replace by ignoring and/or timing out coupled with structuring alternative exchanges. Therefore, it was decided that the first major objective should be to work on Luke's most serious behavioral deficit, namely speech.

Having read and discussed introductory training materials, the Nashes were given basic instructions for handling Luke's disruptiveness at home. So, instead of spending several weeks coaching the Nashes at home, I decided to see how much they could do on their own, on the basis of their reading and observing of sessions, and with prescriptions from me. If observations at a later date (during the B period) showed that neither Luke's nor his parents' behavior had changed sufficiently, then more active training at home would be undertaken.

Speech Training

Luke's speech training capitalized on his special abilities and addressed his special problems. Hewett (1965) has commented on a "power struggle" which took place in the education of one of his students. Luke's earlier nine months of speech training had been one long power struggle. He had been able to endure the small meals that were a consequence of his disruptive behavior; thus, he had progressed little in speech training.

As stated earlier, Luke's speech training with me began in early September 1968, after the behavior incompatible with speech training had been all but eliminated. To avoid the development of another fruitless power struggle, Luke's training was begun in a relaxed fashion, to prevent the speech training situation from becoming aversive to him. Thus, I was especially careful to be very warm with Luke—laughing with him, cuddling him, shaking his hand, and roughhousing.

Phase 1: Imitation training. The first phase of Luke's speech training consisted of teaching him, by imitation, the phonemes and basic syllables in the English language and then words. Training in spontaneous vocalization, which usually precedes verbal imitation training (see Chapter 3) was not necessary since Luke already vocalized at a high rate and had a large phonemic repertoire. During September, simple vowels and consonants such as *oo, ee, ah, buh, o, i,* and *duh* were worked on. Perhaps because of his strong generalized imitation, Luke learned quickly to imitate these sounds reliably. Luke took both breakfast and lunch in the Laboratory. Each session lasted approximately 20 minutes.

Luke's parents had already read the materials given them. At this point, they observed sessions with Luke from behind a one-way mirror. The techniques used and Luke's progress were discussed with them after the sessions. They were, in addition, asked to note such things as the way the teacher physically prompted Luke to emit appropriate imitative responses, rewarded him with small bites of food, rewarded him for successive approximations and not just for perfect responses, and ignored him or timed him out for disruptive behavior. Toward the end of September, Mrs. Nash was asked to record observations of ongoing sessions onto a dictaphone, and was praised for using proper terms to describe the events.

In late September, we decided to begin teaching Luke words by imitation. The words "eat" and "food" were worked on first, as they were most relevant to the situation and could easily be transformed into mands (that is, used to ask for food). At this point, Luke's fast progress in imitation training all but stopped. He could imitate component sounds separately and in close succession (Step 2), but he could not or would not say them together to form a single word. Instead, he consistently reversed the order, repeating "tea" instead of "eat" and "do" instead of "food."

Another power struggle was avoided when I inadvertently hit upon a new word that Luke readily imitated. As Luke sat down for his breakfast, I waved and said, "Hi." Luke immediately waved back and said, "Hi," smiling and laughing. Work continued on the words "hi" and "bye" and others, leaving "eat" and "food" for future sessions. No further response reversals were observed. By October 18, he had acquired an imitative repertoire of 13 one-syllable words. Luke was never "forced" to learn or perform; the exchanges were made as attractive as possible to maintain cooperation and promote learning.

Beginning October 21, 1968, Mrs. Nash began working with Luke on imitative speech. Data were taken each session to track Luke's progress with his mother. In addition, measures of intra-observer and inter-observer reliability were taken periodically. For 17 days, I coached Mrs. Nash at the Laboratory-school to run the food exchange and to teach Luke new words by imitation. These sessions were held at approximately 1:30 P.M. and lasted 20 minutes. I sat in the room with her and Luke and coached her directly.

Based on the experience of Mrs. Hare in her first session with Michael on speech, care was taken to make the situation familiar to Luke. Thus, Mrs. Nash was introduced gradually as the teacher. For almost ten minutes I, as usual, presented Luke with models to imitate (words already in his repertoire). Each time Luke responded correctly, I prompted Mrs. Nash to reward Luke with a bite of food. It took only a few minutes for Luke to accept his mother as a reciprocator in the food exchange. In addition, Mrs. Nash quickly learned to discriminate between correct and incorrect responses. Hence, I was able to fade out my prompts for her to reward Luke.

For the remainder of the session, Mrs. Nash gave Luke words to imitate and rewarded him for each correct response. She was coached to wait for Luke to look at her before she presented the model, to hold the bite of food up to her mouth while she presented the stimulus, to enunciate slowly and clearly, to reciprocate quickly and with a small bite, to praise Luke for each correct response just prior to giving him the bite of food, and to ignore any irrelevant behavior Luke might engage in. I praised her as she performed successively closer approximations to correct teaching procedures.

In the second session, Mrs. Nash learned to teach Luke a new word by breaking it down into its components, teaching Luke each component, and then synthesizing the components into a whole word. For example, she introduced the word "door" and worked with Luke on "do" and "r." By the end of the session, however, Luke had not learned to say the two components together as a word.

From the third through fifth sessions Mrs. Nash was coached on shaping; i.e., she was coached to notice and reinforce successively closer approximations to the desired response. For instance, she was coached to reward Luke, at first, for rudimentary attempts to put "do" and "r" together into a word, and gradually to increase the level of proficiency required before she would reciprocate. By the end of the fifth session, Luke had learned his first word from his mother in the Laboratory.

For the remaining sessions, Mrs. Nash practiced the skills she had acquired. She continued to introduce new words and teach them to Luke. As always, I praised her progress in applying the various techniques. After 17 days of training in the Laboratory, Mrs. Nash was running sessions by herself, with few prompts from me. It was thus decided to end Mrs. Nash's training in the Laboratory. She was asked to run a food exchange with Luke at home for his lunch each day at approximately 1:30 P.M.

Beginning November 19, an assistant and I observed Mrs. Nash and the food exchanges she ran at home. As in the Laboratory, data were taken on the frequency of correct and incorrect responses so as to trace Luke's progress, and inter-observer reliability was measured periodically. During these sessions, I did *not* coach Mrs. Nash. Prior to some sessions, I did suggest possible words to teach Luke. And I often praised Mrs. Nash after the sessions were over for correctly applying techniques learned in the Laboratory.

Observations were made for seven days (to December 5), at which point Luke entered the third stage of speech training: training in functional speech. In early March 1969, however, sessions on imitation training were resumed for several days. Furthermore, reversal experiments were conducted on March 11 and 12 to assess the extent to which Luke's imitative speech was affected by the exchanges managed by his mother. Figure 9 on the next page presents data on Luke's acquisition of words by imitation under three conditions:

(A) in the Laboratory with myself as teacher;
(B) in the Laboratory with Mrs. Nash as teacher, coached by me;
(C) at home with Mrs. Nash as teacher, uncoached.

Several processes are shown in Figure 9. In Condition A, Luke's imitative speech seems to have been in the acquisition phase. At first it took him several days to learn a word; as the days went by, it took progressively less and less time and fewer trials. It became easier for him to speak. Luke's speech in condition B also appears to represent acquisition, but there is an interaction effect; Luke was learning to

Figure 9: Acquisition of Imitative Speech by a Seven-Year-Old Autistic Boy

In the A period a teacher worked with the boy in the Laboratory-school while his mother observed. In the B period his mother, coached by the teacher, worked with him in the Laboratory-school. In the C period his mother, uncoached, worked with him at home. Sessions were 20 minutes long.

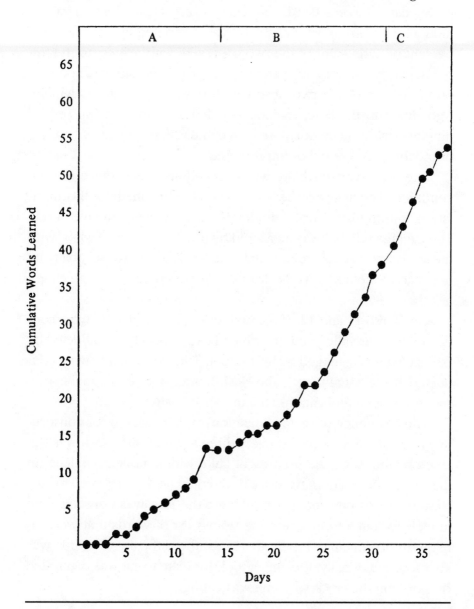

speak with his mother as teacher, and his mother was learning to teach him to speak. By Condition C, the rate of Luke's learning new words seems to have stabilized; i.e., he learned new words at a constant or nearly constant rate.

As stated earlier, inter-observer reliability was measured periodically across the three conditions. Reliability was determined by comparing data on correct and incorrect responses taken by two trained independent observers. Reliability was computed in two ways: (1) percent of agreement of the two observers with respect to the frequency recorded for each variable, and, when possible, (2) percent of agreement of the two observers for each *successive* judgment. Agreement in the latter method entailed agreement along several dimensions simultaneously—e.g., whether the response was correct or incorrect, prompted or unprompted.

Inter-observer reliability was checked six times, twice in each condition. The first two checks involved the first method of computation, and the last four (with Mrs. Nash as teacher) involved both. The average reliability as measured by the first method was 91, with the lowest percent of agreement being 86. The average reliability by the second method was 89, with the lowest percent of agreement also being 86.

On March 11 and 12, 1969, two reversal experiments were conducted to assess the extent to which Luke's speech was affected by the exchanges managed by his mother. The experiments were conducted at the usual time at the Nash home. Both experiments (the second being a replication) had an ABAB design.

The frequency of correct imitations was measured for consecutive intervals of 30 seconds. Every three seconds Mrs. Nash was signaled by the researcher to present Luke with a model to imitate. In this way, differences between periods could not be attributed to Mrs. Nash's rate of presenting models, for the rate was constant. The models for Luke to imitate came from a list of words that were already in his imitative repertoire. Thus, the difficulty of words was also constant. Finally, the time it took for Luke to eat was controlled by stopping the clock when he was eating.

In the A periods, food was handed to Luke on a plate and he could eat at will. In other words, he could obtain food without speaking. The clock was running only when he was not eating. In the B periods, Mrs. Nash moved the plate in front of her and made each bite contingent upon a correct imitative response.

Inter-observer reliability was measured during the second experiment. It was computed by comparing the percent of agreement between two observers on the frequency of correct and incorrect responses recorded for each 30-second interval. The average agreement was 98% for correct responses and 96% for incorrect responses, or 97% overall. Data for the two experiments are presented in Figures 10 (p. 182) and 11 (p. 183), respectively.

As can be seen from the two graphs, Luke's imitative speech was strongly affected by the structure of the exchange. He made correct imitative responses when food was contingent upon it. And when he no longer had to speak in order to eat, he gradually stopped speaking. Furthermore, the first experiment shows an intensification effect in both the A and B periods. In A_2, Luke's imitative speech was reduced to zero after fewer responses than in A_1. On the other hand, in B_2 his rate of correct imitations began at a higher rate than in B_1. In the second experiment, Luke's speech did not reduce to zero in A_1, but in A_2, it reduced to zero after far fewer responses than A_2 of Experiment 1. In addition, there was no intensification of B_2 over B_1.

Phase 2: Labeling. By early December, Luke was rapidly acquiring an imitative speech repertoire. It was thus decided to move to the next stage of language training, the development of a labeling vocabulary (see Chapter 3). In this phase, Mrs. Nash was trained and took over a large part of helping Luke acquire a labeling vocabulary from the beginning. On December 6, 1968, she sat at a table with me while I worked on labeling with Luke in the Laboratory. On December 9 and 10, Mrs. Nash, coached by me, worked with Luke by herself. Also on December 10, she was given a prescription of written instructions for teaching Luke the names for things. Those instructions were as follows.

1. Hold up the object and wait until he is looking at it. Make him look at it for two seconds before you say "What is this?" followed quickly by the name (prompt).
2. If he does not imitate the word (prompt) correctly, look down at the table and lower the food for two or three seconds. Then re-

---

Figure 10: Frequency of Correct Imitative Speech Responses in the Home During An Experimental Reversal

---

In the A periods the child's food was given to him and his mother attempted to elicit imitative speech. In the B periods she moved his food in front of her and made each bite contingent upon a correct imitative speech response.

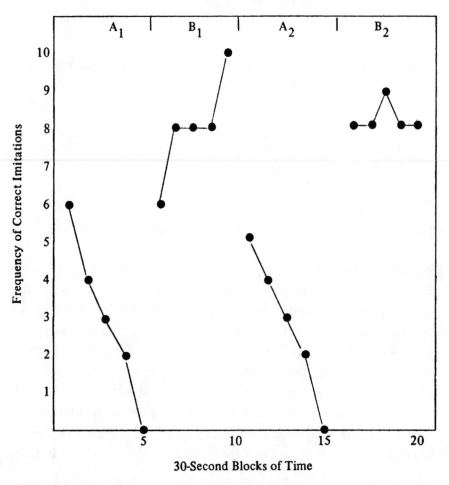

peat "What is this?" followed quickly by the name (prompt).

3. Once he is correctly imitating the prompt, start to fade the prompt. Gradually say less and less of the word, and gradually lower your voice, until all you have to say is "What is this?"

4. Once he can name the object correctly without a prompt 10 times

---

Figure 11: Replication of Experimental Reversal in the Home on Imitative Speech

---

In the A periods the child's food was given to him and his mother attempted to elicit imitative speech. In the B periods she moved his food in front of her and made each bite contingent upon a correct imitative speech response.

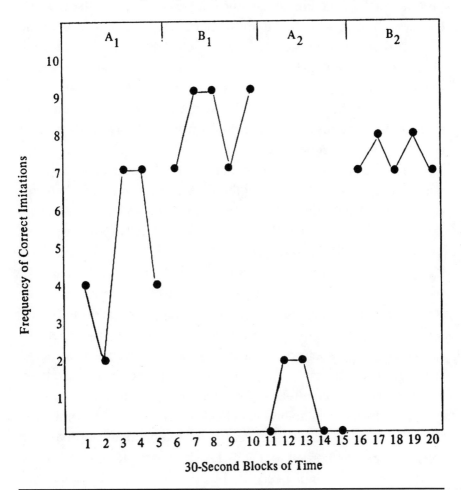

consecutively, add a new word.

5. Test his use of the word by switching back and forth between the current word and an old word.

It should be pointed out that the criteria for deciding that a word has become a name, label, or concept for the child are rather arbitrary. There is always the question of time (i.e., over how many days must a child remember the association) and the number of similar objects to which the child must generalize the word before it is considered learned.

The criteria chosen by the researcher placed much responsibility on Mrs. Nash for giving Luke sufficient practice so that the association would become habitual and generalize to other objects in the class. A name was considered learned when two criteria were met: (1) Luke used the word correctly, and unprompted, ten consecutive times—e.g., he answered the question "What is this?" correctly ten times in a row; and (2) Luke used the word correctly, and unprompted, five consecutive times when the object was *alternated* with another one already in his repertoire.

Again, these criteria required that Mrs. Nash give Luke daily practice so that he would remember the names and generalize them appropriately. Mrs. Nash's skill and effort at this are revealed in an assessment of Luke's labeling vocabulary conducted in February 1969. Those results will be presented later.

Observations of Mrs. Nash's sessions with Luke in this phase began December 10, 1968. Sessions 20 minutes long were held at the Nash home at the same time as in Phase 1 (approximately 1:30 P.M.). Mrs. Nash was not coached during the sessions. She was sometimes given suggestions before a session as to possible words to work on, or suggestions after a session concerning techniques to try next time. She was also praised after each session for her and Luke's progress.

Inter-observer reliability was checked three times by computing the percent of agreement between two independent observers on the frequencies recorded for each of several variables for each word worked on. The variables recorded were whether the response was correct or incorrect, prompted or unprompted. The average percent of agreement was 85.

Data on Luke's acquisition of a labeling vocabulary are presented in Figure 12 (p. 186). As can be seen, Luke's rate of acquisition was slow at first, but gradually increased and stabilized at about two words per session. Actually, this equilibrium rate is rather high considering that sessions were only 20 minutes long and that part of most sessions was first spent teaching Luke new words by imitation. At any rate, assuming Luke could learn new words at the rate of two per day, his vocabulary would, in a year, equal that of a child between two-and-one-half and three years of age (Thompson, 1962). Prior to training, with no words, his vocabulary was smaller than that of a child of eight months.

As mentioned earlier, the maintenance of Luke's vocabulary was left largely to Mrs. Nash. Her job was to give Luke practice on words every day. On February 24, 1969, we assessed the strength of Luke's labeling vocabulary. I chose 15 words at random from the list of words Luke had learned, and gave the list to Mrs. Nash at the beginning of the language exchange for that day. She was asked to present at random the stimuli for Luke to name (pictures, objects) and, as usual, to reward correct responses. For each stimulus, I recorded the frequency of unprompted correct responses. Overall, the percent of unprompted correct responses was 91, showing that Luke's labeling vocabulary had become quite strong.

Phase 3: Conversational speech. By March 4, 1969, Luke had enough facility with imitative speech and labeling that he could begin learning to use speech to communicate. As indicated in Chapter 3, this involves teaching a child to use sentences, to answer and ask questions, to ask for things, and so forth. At the same time, it involves constantly increasing the child's vocabulary.

Luke's instruction on conversational speech began with a remarkable incident—considering that six months earlier Luke had been mute. In the first session, on March 4, I taught Luke to answer the question, "What do you want to do?" with the statement, "I want to

Figure 12: Cumulative Number of Functional Words Learned by
Luke Nash at Home

A word was defined as functional when it was an appropriate answer to a question, or when it could be used to elicit responses from others (e.g., "gimme"). Sessions were conducted by Mrs. Nash at home during lunch. She had had prior training in teaching functional words using the Risley-Wolf and Lovaas methods. She was not coached during the sessions. A word was considered learned when it was used appropriately, unprompted, ten consecutive times, and then was used appropriately, unprompted, five times in alternation with another word. From December 20 to January 13, there was a Christmas Break.

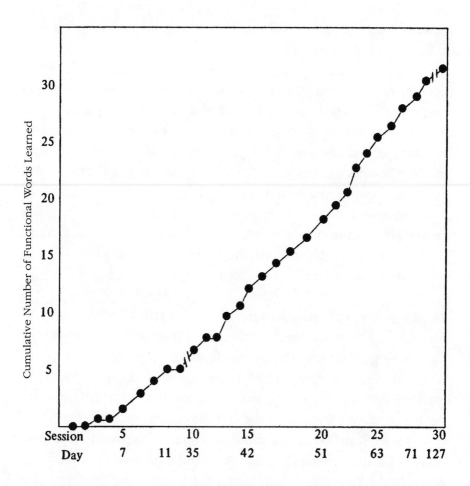

eat." During the second session, I reviewed this sentence with Luke. In addition, I held up bites of Luke's food and asked, "What is this?" to which Luke answered, as he had been taught, "Food." Then I asked Luke, *"What* do you want to *eat?"* Luke looked up at me with an intense look of concentration on his face, and very slowly and haltingly, as if he were a three-year-old learning a new sentence, said, "I want to eat *food."* He shrieked with delight when I shook his hand and gave him a huge bite of food. For the remainder of the session, I faded out the question, "What do you want to eat?" and taught Luke to *initiate* the exchange with his new sentence, "I want to eat food."

In essence, Luke had learned his first grammatical frame: "I want _____." And he had learned that the frame could be filled with at least two elements: "eat" and "eat food."

Mrs. Nash observed the first two sessions with Luke. On March 6, she was asked to concentrate on teaching Luke new sentences and new words during their language exchanges at home. She was coached at home for two days. In addition, she was given two general instructions: (1) teach Luke different grammatical frames and teach him to fill them with different words; and (2) prompt sentences from Luke throughout the day by asking him questions and giving him the appropriate answer, and by withholding from him things that he wanted until he asked for them with the appropriate word (at first) and then with a sentence. In other words, there was a transition from arbitrary exchanges (a bite of lunch for imitating "door") to natural exchanges (a sandwich for saying "I want a sandwich"). Recent research on these sorts of naturalistic language exchanges includes work on:

1. "Incidental teaching," in which a teacher waits for or sets up an opportunity for a child to communicate functionally, and then prompts the child to expand or improve an utterance: "Yes. That is blue. And what color is this one?" (Hart & Risley, 1975; Stowitschek, McConaughy, Peatross, Salzberg, & Lignugaris/Kraft, 1988).

2. The "mand-model technique," in which a teacher inserts a request into a child's ongoing activity, and then prompts the child to answer: "Very nice! ... What is the car DOING? ... Rolling." (Goetz & Sailor, 1988).

3. The "delay procedure," in which the teacher identifies a spot during interaction where, by waiting before providing a reinforcer, she can prompt the child to make a request: "Say, 'More milk'." (Halle, Baer, & Spradlin, 1981).

4. "Chain interruption," in which, for example, a teacher passively stands in a child's way and, if necessary, prompts the child to say, "Move, please" (Hunt & Goetz, 1988).

5. The "natural language paradigm," in which virtually all of a child's verbal attempts are reinforced; there is much turn-taking with materials; instruction is in the context of a variety of everyday tasks and with everyday materials; and a child is given much control over which materials to use and which activities to participate in with caregivers (Koegel, Bimbela, & Schreibman, 1996; Laski, Charlop, & Schreibman, 1988).

In 12 sessions, from March 6 to April 21 (there were no sessions from April 3 to April 20), Luke's mother taught him 12 sentences according to the same criteria as with labeling. They were:

> I am. (In answer to the question "Who is Luke?")
> I'm fine.
> I want to eat.
> I want food.
> I want a cookie.
> That's my eye.
> That's water.
> That's a chip.
> That's my hand.
> That's bread.
> That's a plate.
> That's a book.

Inter-observer reliability was computed as the percent of agreement between two observers for each response (whether the response was correct or incorrect, prompted or unprompted). The average percent of agreement for the two reliability checks was 89.

The above list underestimates the number of sentences Luke had learned to use in a consistent fashion. In sessions at the Laboratory, for instance, all of Luke's food was sometimes contingent upon his asking for it with a sentence. In this way, he learned to initiate natural verbal exchanges with "I want (*bacon, pancake, egg, sandwich, candy, biscuit, more, bread,* and *water*)."

Beginning March 11, 1969, Mr. Nash was also trained in teaching Luke to speak. A baseline was taken in the Laboratory for one week. Mr. Nash was given a list of words in Luke's imitative repertoire, and was asked to promote imitative responses from Luke. Luke's breakfast was available to Mr. Nash to use as a reinforcer. Although Mr. Nash had observed sessions between Luke and the researcher many times, he made a number of procedural errors. He presented models for Luke to imitate at an extremely high rate, repeating the same word over and over (as Mrs. Gordon had done before training) even though Luke was making errors. He rewarded correct responses only about 50% of the time, rewarded incorrect responses 14% of the time, and reinforced Luke about 75% of the time when Luke was not attending. By the end of the baseline, Luke's percent of correct responses in exchanges with Mr. Nash had fallen and stabilized at 31.

Mr. Nash was trained for two weeks. He was coached to present models at a slower rate, to switch to a different word when Luke made several mistakes in a row, to discriminate between correct and incorrect responses, and to ignore Luke when he was not attending. After the two weeks, he worked with Luke uncoached. Mr. Nash's rewarding of correct responses rose to approximately 100%, while his rewarding of both incorrect responses and inattention fell to approximately 0. At the same time, Luke's percent of correct imitations rose to 80.

There is much difference between learning to use sentences in the Laboratory or in the home during structured language sessions, when speaking is essentially a task for the child, and using sentences in spontaneous, natural exchanges during the day. The question remained whether Luke was using speech in the home *outside* of structured teaching sessions—i.e., whether he was using speech to communicate. This question will be answered shortly.

Building a Play Repertoire

On January 22, 1969, we decided to teach Mrs. Nash to manage play activities with Luke, and to assess the extent to which her training and Luke's playing generalized to other times of the day. The techniques used were the same as those learned by Mrs. Hare and Mrs. Gordon. Several times a week, for a little over a month, Luke's lunch at home centered on teaching him to play. Luke participated eagerly in the exchanges. During the month Mrs. Nash and he worked on plastic building blocks, simple and complex puzzles, snap-together beads, a pegboard landscape, a take-apart cash register, a peg-and-pull set (a large version of Tinkertoys), a take-apart porpoise, and a block box (wooden shapes to arrange in various patterns).

Data were taken during ten 20-minute play sessions. Variables included the frequency and type of Mrs. Nash's exchange initiations and the frequency of Luke's correct responses. Inter-observer reliability was checked once, and computed as the percent of agreement between the two observers on the frequencies recorded for each of the variables. The average agreement was 93%. The data can be summarized briefly. Mrs. Nash's use of questions fell from six to zero in two days. Contract statements were used but once. Directives rose in frequency and then fell off after three days as Luke learned to work both the toys and the exchange. Luke's frequency of correct responses remained at a fairly high and stable rate. For the first nine days he ranged between 45 and 64 correct responses, and on the last day he rose to 106 correct responses.

Like Mrs. Gordon, Mrs. Nash was asked to make the toys available during the day and to reward Luke if he initiated play with them. She also recorded how long and how often he played with each toy each day. The average duration of Luke's playing per day in the three months following the play sessions at home was, according to Mrs. Nash's logs, 25 minutes. This was too low, and it was decided to begin structured observations again.

Description of the Home After Training in Basic Techniques (B)

Baseline observations, it will be remembered, were made in early October 1968. From then until May 1969, the Nashes' only training was either in the Laboratory or at home during teaching sessions. The question remained whether the techniques the Nashes learned had generalized to other times of the day. How were they handling bizarre-disruptive behavior? Were language and play exchanges in effect? And as to Luke, how much bizarre-disruptive behavior in contrast to constructive behavior did he perform? How much speech was he using? Observations to check the degree of generalization were made from May 5–8, 1969, at the same time of day and for the same duration as the earlier baseline observations.

Progress and the Generalization of Training

The following is a summary of the findings:

1. Bizarre-disruptive behavior had decreased by a factor of four from the baseline. In addition, shrieking, playing in water, and destructiveness had been reduced to zero. Only "getting into things" remained much of a problem. Simultaneously, the Nashes' rewarding of bizarre-disruptive behavior had decreased from 72% to 20%.
2. As to speech, Luke was answering questions and using sentences. He answered an average of two questions and imitated an average of nine sentences per session, for a total of 11 appropriate verbal responses per session. The Nashes rewarded 62% of Luke's appropriate verbal responses.

3. Luke's increase in play over the baseline was slight. He played an average of seven minutes per session in contrast to four minutes during the baseline. However, in contrast to the baseline (when Luke's playing was never rewarded), 64% of his play episodes were rewarded.

There was, then, a general improvement in both the Nashes' management of exchanges and Luke's behavior, especially with respect to speech and bizarre-disruptive behavior.

Again, we were faced with the question of when to terminate the Training Program. Important gains had been made. But had the parents had enough practice to maintain the gains? Did they have enough skill to foster further improvement in Luke's behavior? We decided to continue.

Remaining Problems

The problems remaining in the exchanges in the Nash home, to be handled during the C period, are summarized in Table 12 on the next page. In summary, there was only a partial generalization of training to other times of day.

Training to Restructure the System of Exchanges (C_1, A_2, and C_2)

The duration of this period, including an experimental reversal, was a little over one month, from May 13 to June 25, 1969. The goals were to overcome the problems listed in Table 12, specifically teaching the Nashes how to (1) decelerate disruptive behaviors in which Luke still engaged; (2) strengthen Luke's functional speech; and (3) strengthen Luke's play behavior.

On May 12, I discussed the problems listed in Table 12 with Mr. and Mrs. Nash. Like the Hares, the Nashes helped write a prescription of techniques they should use to change the system of exchanges. The prescription is presented in Table 13 (p. 194). Observations be-

---

**Table 12: Basic Problems in the Nash Home Following Training in
the Laboratory and Home Teaching Sessions**

- Luke continued to receive a great deal of noncontingent reinforcement, including TV, music, food, and attention. He could get food, for instance, at almost any time without having to ask for it or earn it.

- The Nashes still rarely structured orthogenic exchanges with Luke, such as play exchanges. If he happened to play with a toy, he was likely to be rewarded, but the Nashes continued to let him sit idly listening to records or watching TV as long as he wished.

- The Nashes rarely attempted to evoke speech from Luke, either new verbal responses or responses he had already learned during the home speech training sessions.

- The Nashes did not seem to know how to restructure exchanges that Luke initiated with bizarre-disruptive behavior. When Luke attempted to get into food, for instance, the Nashes merely ignored him, rather than having him say what he wanted.

- In general, exchanges in the Nash home were not likely to strengthen bizarre-disruptive behavior, but were also unlikely to strengthen appropriate behavior. Luke was learning how to spend his days passively watching TV and listening to records.

---

gan May 13 and were conducted almost every day, except weekends, at the same time of day, for the same duration (90 minutes) and with respect to the same variables as in the A_1 and B periods. Inter-observer reliability was checked periodically, computed as the percent of agreement between the two observers on the frequencies recorded directly for the different variables. The agreement per variable was never below 90%; average agreement per session was 96%.

Training Sessions During C_1

Since Mr. Nash worked the night shift, he was present during the training sessions. The Nashes were coached in following the prescription for the first seven sessions of the C_1 period. Training sessions addressed all of the aforementioned problems. The organization of the training sessions was as follows.

Table 13: Tentative Prescription Given to the Nashes to Restructure the Exchange Patterns in the Home

Instructions:

To Ignore:	Do not look at or talk to Luke while he is engaging in inappropriate behavior. Do not yell at him, tell him to stop, go after him, scold him, or threaten him. Act as if you do not see him.
To Time Out:	Without speaking, take Luke quickly to the time out room. Leave him in one minute for the first offense, two minutes for the second offense, etc. Do not let him out if he is kicking the door, yelling, or throwing a tantrum.
To Reward:	Whenever Luke uses speech, cooperates with a request, or plays, immediately praise him *and* (whenever possible) give him a bite of food or let him hear records or watch the TV.

Luke's Behavior	Your Response
Playing with water in the bathroom	Immediately time him out. When you let him out, tell him, "If you want to play, play with your toys." Then lead him over to his toys and get him started playing. Reward him as soon as he gets started, and every minute or so while he is playing.
Getting into food in the refrigerator or pantries	Immediately time him out. When you let him out, ask him what he wants and prompt him to say, "I want food." Then get some food out for him and have him work for it. For instance, have him play with his toys, or have him do something for you such as a chore. Make absolutely certain that he never gets food without asking verbally.
Whenever he turns on TV or record player	Have him tell you what he wants before you let him watch or listen. Say to him, "What do you want?" and prompt him to say, "I want TV" or "I want music."
Shrieking or bizarre sounds	Ignore him.
Playing	If Luke starts to play with his toys, reward him with praise and food while he plays. After he has played 10 minutes or so, turn on the TV or record player for him and let him listen for a few minutes. Do not let him play with the same toy for more than 10 or 15 minutes. Get him started on a different one to prevent him from becoming bored.
Destructive or aggressive behavior	Immediately time him out.
Speech	Whenever he uses speech on his own, immediately reward him. Also, during the day, ask him questions about objects in the house or things that he or you are doing, and prompt him to answer. Then reward him. If, however, he begins to repeat a sentence over and over again like a parrot, ignore him.

First, the Nashes made available to Luke a number of toys in one area of the living room. Like Mrs. Hare, the Nashes were coached to structure play exchanges with Luke during the hour-and-a-half sessions and to try to maintain his playing as long as possible. They reinforced him intermittently with praise, small bites of food, music, or TV while he played; they taught him through prompts and models how to play with the toys; and they rotated the toys he was playing with *before* he began to lose interest (e.g., after ten minutes or so). In addition, they rotated the set of toys every few days.

Second, the Nashes prevented Luke from obtaining noncontingent reinforcement. He was not allowed to watch TV or turn on the record player unless he had played for at least ten minutes. When Luke tried to turn on the TV or record player, they stopped him and initiated an alternative exchange by saying, for instance, "As soon as you have (finished the puzzles, stacked the blocks, put the farm together, etc.), you can watch TV." If Luke cooperated with the contractual exchange signal, he was allowed to watch the TV or hear records for a few minutes.

The Nashes were asked to maintain these conditions throughout the day. In addition, they were asked to initiate play exchanges with Luke at other times of the day, and to reward him for initiating play with any of the toys. Moreover, to strengthen *cooperative* play, the Nashes were asked to encourage and help their other children play with Luke. As before, Mrs. Nash recorded how often Luke played throughout the day.

Third, the Nashes were coached to promote and strengthen Luke's verbal behavior. They were coached, for example, to ask questions while he played, to prompt appropriate answers when necessary, and to reward him on a *continuous* schedule for each appropriate answer. The questions concerned the names of objects with which he was playing (e.g., puzzle pieces or objects on the pegboard landscape), the colors of the objects, what he was *doing* with the objects or what he was making, and so forth. The emphasis was on building sentences, e.g., "What are you doing?"... "I'm playing" or "What do you want?"... "I want food."

Recall that Luke had learned to initiate exchanges with sentences such as "I want food," "I want a cookie," or "I want to eat." With respect to these self-initiated requests for food during sessions, the Nashes were coached to reward Luke on an intermittent schedule. It was felt that if he were rewarded every time he asked for food, his playing would soon decrease and he would be doing nothing but repeating the same request over and over. But if he found that he was not rewarded every time, he would have to continue playing to receive food reinforcement. In other words, appropriate verbal responses (answers) to parental initiations (questions) were to be rewarded continuously, while self-initiated requests for a food reinforcer were to be rewarded about half the time. Once Luke's play became stronger, the Nashes were coached to require Luke occasionally to ask for his food. For instance, when Luke completed a puzzle or a series of puzzles, his mother was coached to say, "What do you want?" and when Luke answered, "I want food," he was given a bite of food. Like the play exchanges, language exchanges were to be in effect throughout the day.

As to disruptive behavior, the Nashes needed coaching only in handling Luke's getting into food in the refrigerator or cabinets. The Nashes were coached to time him out immediately for this behavior. When he was let out of the time out room, they were to say to him, "What do you want?" When he answered, "I want (food, cookie, to eat, etc.)," they were to *restructure* the exchange by saying, "As soon as you have (worked your puzzles), you can have food." In this way, it was felt that getting into food would be weakened and playing and self-initiated requests for reinforcers would be strengthened.

Results During C_1

After seven days of coaching, the Nashes were uncoached for the remaining five days of the C_1 period. The results were dramatically successful. All of Luke's bizarre-disruptive behavior was replaced by the fourth session and remained at zero for the rest of the period. The average duration of constructive activity for the last five days of the period was 69 minutes out of the 90-minute sessions. And the average frequency of appropriate verbal responses was 91 per session. Of these, Luke responded correctly to questions with one- or two-word answers an average of 15 times, responded to parental initiations with sentences an average of 15 times, and emitted an average of 61 self-initiated sentences per session. At the same time, parental reinforcement of appropriate behavior was quite high, in contrast to the previous periods. Luke's constructive behavior was rewarded 100% of the time, while appropriate verbal responses were rewarded an average of 95% of the time.

Major Experimental Reversal in the Home (A_2 and C_2)

Toward the end of the C_1 period, the exchange behavior of Luke and his parents was in a steady state or equilibrium. It was decided to conduct an experimental reversal of the new system of exchanges. The A_2 period lasted for only three days, June 3–5. In the A_2 period, the parents were to make one change: they were asked not to reward Luke for constructive activity or speech. However, they were asked to continue to promote speech and to encourage Luke to play. Also, they were to handle his bizarre-disruptive behavior as they had been taught: to time him out for getting into food or for destructive behavior, and to ignore shrieking and bizarre sounds and gestures.

The effects of the reversal were immediate. On the first day, Luke began shrieking and getting into things. Shrieking increased to five episodes and getting into things stabilized at one episode by the third day. *Note that his disruptive behavior increased even though his parents were still either ignoring him or timing him out for it just as in C_1.* It is of interest that playing in water, destructive behavior, and bizarre sounds and gestures remained at zero. These results correspond to those obtained in experimental reversals in the Hare and Gordon families.

In addition, one- and two-word answers to questions fell to five; appropriate sentences in response to parental initiations fell to two; and self-initiated sentences fell to three by the third day of the reversal. And finally, constructive activity fell to 42 minutes by the third day. It is of interest, however, that in the last two days of the reversal, Luke began to initiate play, whereas previously all play episodes had been initiated by his parents. It was as if he were trying harder to produce reciprocation.

The productive system of exchanges was reinstituted in C_2 on June 6 and continued for several weeks. The Nashes were not coached during C_2, but were instructed to again reward Luke for speech and constructive activities, and to ask him more questions so as to teach new words.

As with C_1, the instituting of C_2 had dramatic effects on Luke's behavior. First, Luke's disruptive behavior immediately dropped to zero when play and language exchanges were again available. Disruptive behavior remained at zero for the rest of the sessions. Mrs. Nash also reported that he no longer engaged in the aforementioned forms of disruptive behavior during the day. Instead, Luke now engaged in a new disruptive behavior. He would soak large amounts of toilet paper in water and then play with the paper as if it were clay. This was handled by providing Play-doh as a substitute. Playing with water-soaked paper decreased immediately, according to Mrs. Nash.

In summary, in both the C_1 and C_2 periods, in which Luke was systematically ignored and/or timed out for bizarre-disruptive behavior and was encouraged and rewarded for constructive behavior, there was an almost immediate deceleration of bizarre-disruptive behavior which stabilized at zero disruptions per session.

The effects of the reversal on appropriate behaviors are summarized in Table 14 (on the next page), which presents the average of the last five days of the C_1 and C_2 periods with respect to the duration of constructive activity (mainly playing), the frequency of several types of verbal behavior, and the frequency of reinforcement for each class of appropriate behavior.

As Table 14 shows, there was in the C_2 period an increase in the duration of constructive activity and the frequency of appropriate verbal responses. Since the duration of Luke's constructive activity

Table 14: Constructive Activity and Appropriate Verbal Behavior During the C_1 and C_2 Periods

Item	C1 Period			C2 Period		
	Frequency	Number of Times Reinforced	Percent Reinforced	Frequency	Number of Times Reinforced	Percent Reinforced
Episodes of Constructive Activity	5 (69 minutes total)	5	100%	7 (74 minutes total)	7	100%
Appropriate Verbal Reponses	91	86	95%	98	84	84%
One- and Two-Word Answers to Questions	15	14	93%	51	44	86%
Sentences in Response to Parental Initiations	15	15	100%	18	15	83%
Self-Initiated Sentences	61	57	94%	29	24	83%

was in a steady state by the end of the C_1 and C_2 periods, the increase in constructive activity can be attributed to the reversal. There was, in other words, an intensification effect of 7%. The increase in the frequency of appropriate verbal responses, however, is attributed to a change in the way Mrs. Nash initiated verbal exchanges with Luke. In C_2, she asked Luke a large number of questions, prompting and rewarding his appropriate answers a high percentage of the time. Thus, in contrast to the C_1 period, Luke did not have to use self-initiated sentences as often to request food; he was receiving most of his food for answering questions, many of which involved new words. This accounts for the decrease in self-initiated sentences.

Although the frequency of sentences decreased about 38% in the C_2 period, there was an increase, not indicated by Table 14, in the number of *different* sentences Luke used. At the beginning of the C_1 period Luke used only two or three different sentences, all related to food, e.g., "I want food," "I want to eat," "I want a chip." Gradually, over both periods, there was an increase in the number of different sentences used, e.g., "Give me puzzle piece," "I am playing," "I am sweeping," "That's a house." The new words in these sentences were often words he learned from his parents' questions, e.g., "What are you doing? *Sweeping.*"

In addition to the quantitative changes in Luke's behavior summarized above, there were many unanticipated qualitative changes. First, as mentioned earlier, Luke was now initiating much of his play behavior—an average of two times per session during C_2. In addition, Mrs. Nash reported that Luke initiated play many other times during the day. Second, Luke was spending *most* of his day engaged in constructive activities, instead of idly sitting around the house as he had been doing for years. He played with toys that had been used during sessions. He was beginning to draw pictures with crayons and paper, something he had not done since the onset of his autistic behavior. He was learning, under his parents' instruction, how to draw the letters of the alphabet. And he was performing a number of small chores for his mother, such as sweeping, putting away toys, and stacking records and books.

Finally, and of special importance, Luke was playing coopera-
tively with his siblings. Mrs. Nash reported that Luke and his younger
brother often played outside together in the sandbox making sand
houses and walls; they worked complicated jigsaw puzzles together;
and they played together with plastic building blocks. In fact, before
one session I saw a whole toy town that Luke and his brother were
building, complete with houses, trees, cars, and a railroad.

Summary of the Results of the Training Program in the Nash Home

The results of the Parent Training Program with the Nash family are
summarized in Figures 13, 14, and 15 (pp. 202–204). The graphs
indicate changes in the exchanges between Luke and his parents
with respect to bizarre-disruptive behavior, speech, and constructive activity over the experimental training periods.

The graphs indicate clearly that changes in the structured exchanges managed by Mr. and Mrs. Nash produced favorable concomitant changes in Luke's behavior. His bizarre-disruptive behavior was all but eliminated. His speech developed from a baseline of
zero to a high rate of appropriate responses, including sentences
and answers to questions. And the duration of his constructive activity increased to the point where he spent most of the session time
playing and doing chores.

Follow-up Description of the Home

Observations during the C_2 period ended June 25, 1969. Follow-up
observations began two months later, on August 25, and lasted for
four days, until August 29. The four observations were made at the
same time of day and for the same duration as all previous observations. Inter-observer reliability was computed once, during the
second observation, by having two independent observers take data
on the various categories in question (e.g., the frequency of the several classes of verbal behavior, disruptive behavior, and reinforce-

Figure 13: Changing the Structure of Exchanges Involving Constructive and Disruptive Behavior in the Nash Home

The A_1 observations of the exchanges between parents and child were made before the parents were trained. The B observations were made after both parents were trained in running the language exchange and after the mother was trained in running the play exchange. For the first 7 days of C_1, the parents were coached in the home to change the pattern of exchanges observed in the A_1 and B periods. In the A_2 period the parents were asked to ignore constructive behavior and to continue to ignore and/or time out the child for disruptive behavior. In C_2 the parents were asked to again reward constructive behavior and to ignore and/or time out the child for disruptive behavior.

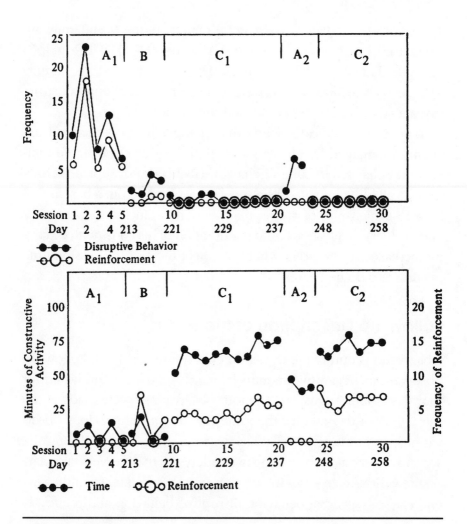

Figure 14: Frequency of Appropriate Verbal Responses in the Nash Home for Various Experimental Periods

The A_1 observations of the language exchange were made before the parents were trained. The B observations were made after the mother was trained to run speech training sessions. For the first 7 days of the C_1 period the mother was coached to evoke and reward appropriate verbal responses. In the A_2 period she was asked to ignore appropriate verbal responses. During the C_2 period she was instructed to again reward appropriate verbal responses.

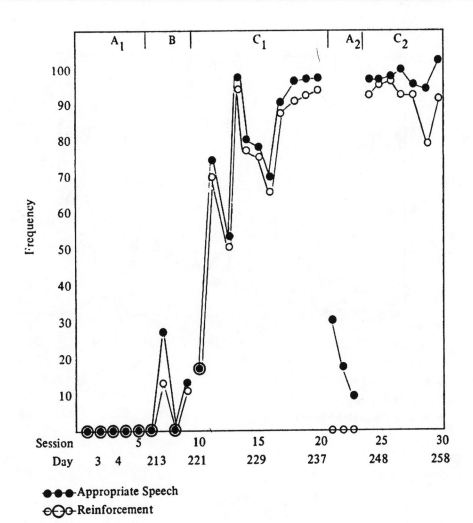

Figure 15: Topography of the Verbal Behavior of Luke Nash at Home for Various Experimental Periods

The A_1 observations of the child's language were made before his mother was trained. The B observations were made after the mother was trained to run speech training sessions. For the first 7 days of the C_1 period, the mother was coached to evoke and reward appropriate verbal responses. In the A_2 period she was asked to attempt to evoke but not to reward appropriate verbal responses. In the C_2 period she was instructed to again evoke and reward appropriate responses, but to focus on answers to questions.

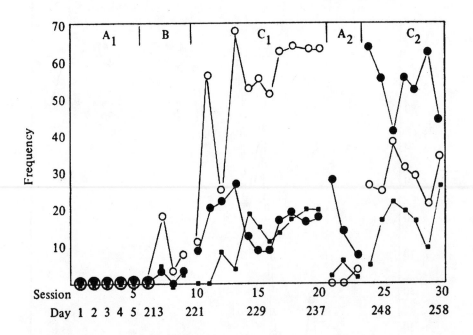

●–●–● 1- and 2-Word Responses
o–o–o Parent-Initiated Sentences
■–■–■ Self-Initiated Sentences

ment). The average agreement between the two observers was 88%.

The findings were more than satisfactory. First, the frequency of Luke's bizarre-disruptive behavior remained at zero. Second, the duration of constructive activity had increased slightly above the duration at the end of the C_2 period. At the end of the C_2 period Luke engaged in constructive activity an average of 74 minutes per 90-minute session; the average duration of constructive activity per session during the follow-up was 75 minutes. Simultaneously, Mrs. Nash rewarded Luke at the end of each play episode with praise and the opportunity to engage in other activities (e.g., television), and occasionally with food and praise while Luke was playing.

While Mrs. Nash rewarded Luke's episodes of constructive activity on a continuous schedule, as she had done during the C_1 and C_2 periods, during the follow-up she was increasing the length of time Luke worked or played before he was rewarded. The average duration of constructive activity by the end of the C_2 period was 11 minutes; during the follow-up, it was 15 minutes.

There was a substantial increase in Luke's cooperation between the end of C_2 and the follow-up. While the percentage of cooperative responses that were reinforced remained about the same (95% during the last five days of C_2 and 92% during the follow-up), Luke cooperated 85% of the time during the follow-up period, an increase of about 8%.

Finally, Luke continued to progress in speech training. Quantitatively, there was a 15% increase in Luke's total output of appropriate verbal responses between the last five days of the C_2 period and the follow-up. Both one- and two-word answers to questions and self-initiated sentences increased in frequency, while the frequency of sentences emitted in response to parental initiations remained about the same. In addition, Luke had learned several new grammatical frames: "I see _____" and "I eat _____"; he had learned about a dozen new functional words; and the length of time it took him to learn new functional words or even to imitate new words had decreased considerably.

In summary, it appeared that the Nashes had maintained a system of productive exchanges in their home between the C_2 and follow-up periods. Both Luke's and his parents' behavior indicated that the Nashes had not become lax in their teaching techniques. Indeed, Luke had progressed in all areas during the interim.

Conclusions

The research and training with the Nashes took approximately 11 months. From a theoretical standpoint, the results duplicated those obtained with the Hare family. Training the parents produced changes in exchanges in the home, followed quickly by beneficial changes in the children.

From an educational standpoint, the results were even more important. Luke was seven years old when his education at the Laboratory began. Moreover, he was mute. Past research had indicated that these two factors—age of the child and quality of speech—were important predictors of the success of instruction. There should have been little hope for Luke's making much progress. And yet he progressed a great deal in less than a year. He rarely engaged in bizarre-disruptive behavior; he no longer spent his waking hours passively watching TV or listening to music; and he was far from being mute. Not only did he spend a large amount of time playing (either alone, with his parents, or with his siblings), but he was learning to converse, to communicate his desires and his understanding of the world around him.

The results with the Nash family are an important lesson for anyone predicting a child's chances for improvement. Predictions will always be bound by current technologies and theories attempting to deal with the problem, and will reflect inadequacies of the various approaches more than the inherent capabilities of the child.

7 Kristen White

Description of the Child

Kristen White, a Caucasian female, was born on December 27, 1960, and began attending the Social Exchange Laboratory in late November, 1967. She had a brother, Stan, age 3. Kristen's mother, a housewife, had had some college education. Mr. White was an electrical engineer for a large aircraft corporation. Mrs. White indicated that the only instance of mental illness or retardation in the family had been a minor emotional problem of her younger brother regarding school.

Kristen's development is described in Appendices 1 and 2. The summary reveals that Kristen showed no clear evidence of autism before age 2. She smiled at and approached other people, reached out and prepared to be picked up, liked to be held, and imitated others. In addition, her motor and cognitive development were unexceptional. However, she may have begun to have problems communicating. Her parents indicated that she could repeat many nursery rhymes, recite the ABC'S, count to ten, and sing a few children's songs. But this speech was of a mechanical nature and may have been echolalic. In fact, the Whites indicated that Kristen seldom used speech to communicate her wants or experiences. She never used the words "mommy," "daddy," or "yes," and did not refer to herself when she spoke.

By age 3, Kristen began to develop a more obvious repertoire of autistic behaviors and impairments. She withdrew, stopped playing, began to scream, became destructive (throwing objects) and self-

destructive (striking and biting herself). She occupied herself by playing records, sitting quietly in a chair, ritualistically flapping wires,
belts, and hoses, or sniffing and chewing various objects. Her mother
described her as indifferent to her environment and "self-sufficient."

While it is not possible to determine the temporal priority of the
two events, Mrs. White reported that at the time Kristen was developing an autistic repertoire, she (Mrs. White) tended to be harsh
with Kristen. She yelled at her and spanked her for relatively minor
infractions, most of which were exploratory behaviors typical of children Kristen's age—for instance, handling certain objects. In conversations with me, Mrs. White admitted that she had been preoccupied
and overly concerned with orderliness in her house, which Kristen's
exploratory behavior disrupted. It is possible, then, that Mrs. White's
use of punishment weakened some of Kristen's appropriate behavior and her early positive feelings for others.

On the other hand, in the absence of support and training,
Kristen's screaming and bizarre behaviors may have been so stressful to Mrs. White that Mrs. White became disposed to punish Kristen,
or at least avoid her, thereby perhaps weakening some of Kristen's
appropriate behavior (Ferster, 1968). In either case, the exchanges
between Kristen and her mother were not conducive to strengthening appropriate behavior in Kristen, or to developing mutual sentiments of liking. However, it was clear from the way Mrs. White dressed
Kristen, spoke about her, prepared special snacks for her, and sought
help for her, that she loved Kristen deeply.

In an effort to help Kristen, the Whites sent her to two nursery
schools, and later to a school for emotionally disturbed children run on
Montessori principles. There was no improvement in Kristen's behavior. On the contrary, her screaming increased when she was in the
new surroundings or whenever demands were made on her. In addition, she remained aloof and withdrawn from the other children.

For several years Mrs. White tolerated Kristen's screaming and
other inappropriate behavior. Gradually, Kristen's screaming increased to the point that Mrs. White felt she could no longer live
with Kristen. The Whites took Kristen to a psychologist, who diag-

nosed her as autistic and instructed the Whites to punish Kristen for screaming. Each time Kristen screamed, the Whites were to yell "No!" and slap Kristen across the face. Mrs. White said she could not bring herself to slap Kristen's face. Instead, she spanked Kristen. The procedure was only temporarily effective in suppressing screaming. As Kristen's screaming decreased in frequency, the Whites reduced their rate of punishment for this behavior. As a result, Kristen's screaming eventually returned to its former level.

The psychologist also advised the Whites to have play sessions with Kristen. They did this for a time—but the fact that the psychologist did not teach them *how* to strengthen Kristen's playing, coupled with Kristen's indifference, resulted in the extinction of the Whites' efforts to play with Kristen.

By the time Kristen began her education at the Social Exchange Laboratory, her speech had improved somewhat. She used a number of one- and two-word "mands" to produce food or music, e.g., "peanut butter sandwich," "Land" (for the song "This Land is Mine"), and "ice cream cone." And she used several sentences. However, her speech was infrequent, garbled, and all but unintelligible. In addition, Kristen remained indifferent to others; she still screamed, bit and slapped herself, and stared intently at flapping belts; and she still performed little constructive activity at home.

During the six months that Kristen attended sessions at the Laboratory before I began to work with her family, the teacher worked with Kristen on simple manipulative tasks, such as puzzles and blocks, and on speech. The teacher taught Kristen the names for a number of objects and taught Kristen to use phrases and sentences to ask for food, toys, and activities.

The following is an outline of the stages of research and training with Kristen and her parents:

Dec. 4–8, 1967:	Baseline observation at the Laboratory on interaction between Kristen and her mother.
Apr. 9–10, 1968:	General observations at the White home.
Apr. 11–15, 1968:	Baseline observation at the White home (A_1).

May 1–7, 1968:	Mrs. White begins training in the Laboratory by recording observations of sessions.
May 8–17, 1968:	Mrs. White works with a child in the Laboratory.
May 30–31, 1968:	Observation at the White home to assess progress in applying techniques learned in the Laboratory and to locate remaining problems in the exchanges (B).
June 4–16, 1968:	Coaching at the White home to restructure exchanges during mealtime (beginning of C).
July 29–Aug. 21, 1968:	Follow-up observation of mealtime problems (continuation of C).
Oct. 14–Dec. 4, 1968:	Structured speech and play sessions at White home.
June 9–13, 1969:	Follow-up observation of exchanges in the White home.

Pre-Training Description of the Home (A₁)

Logs and Discussions with the Parents

Mrs. White's logs and my discussions with the Whites revealed little of the interaction between Kristen and her parents, but they did indicate the paucity of Kristen's social and constructive behavior. The degree to which Kristen was asocial, "self-sufficient," and engaged in bizarre and disruptive behavior can be seen by synthesizing a typical day in her life.

Kristen usually awoke around 9:00 A.M. She was able to dress herself, almost always without help, and to use the bathroom by herself. When called for breakfast, she was as likely to remain in her room as to come downstairs. When she did not come down for breakfast, she remained in her room, flapping and sniffing objects. When she finally came down, she took her own breakfast by rummaging through the refrigerator, taking bread off the counter, or sometimes asking for something with a one- or two-word mand (e.g., "milk," "jelly bread"). She spent the rest of the morning sitting in a chair, playing records, or standing quietly outside. She did not play with or near other children. In fact, she did not play at all. Instead, she flapped belts or hoses or sniffed various objects she had found.

After her teaching session at the Laboratory-school, Kristen spent the afternoon much as she had the morning. Sometimes Mrs. White took her shopping. During those outings, Kristen behaved perfectly by Mrs. White's standards—that is, she did not make a nuisance of herself by getting into things. She merely stood around, seemingly oblivious to the events around her.

Kristen screamed many times each day. She screamed whenever she was thwarted, e.g., if she were told that she could not have ice cream before dinner. She sometimes screamed in her own room when left to herself. And she screamed whenever she wanted something. For instance, Kristen often screamed at night, coercing her parents to come into her room. Then she would indicate (sometimes verbally) that she wanted water or that the air conditioner be turned on. In other words, screaming was an effective method of getting what she wanted.

At supper time, sometimes Kristen came downstairs and ate with the rest of the family. Sometimes she stayed in her room, and once everyone had left the table, she would come down and forage in the kitchen. And sometimes she merely stayed in her room and screamed.

General Home Observations

General home observations were made for two days, April 9–10, from 5:30 to 7:00 P.M. Observations were scheduled so as to allow me to observe Kristen before, during, and after supper. The observations verified Mrs. White's logs to the effect that Kristen's rates of constructive behavior were very low and bizarre behavior very high. The observations also revealed a number of problems at mealtimes that would require the restructuring of mealtime interaction.

Home Baseline

Baseline observations were made for five days, April 11–15, from 5:30 to 7:00 P.M. Raw data consisted of a flat description of ongoing interaction on a portable tape recorder. As with Michael Hare and

Luke Nash, the following variables were later measured: the overall structure of the exchanges, exchanges involving cooperation, bizarre-disruptive behavior, constructive activities, and speech.

Reliability was assessed once during the baseline. Two observers listening to the tape-recorded description of one baseline session chosen at random, independently scored exchanges in terms of the set of variables. Reliability was computed by comparing the agreement between the two observers on each *consecutive* scoring. The percent of agreement was 91.

Table 15 identifies exchanges that occurred repeatedly during the home baseline. Given the importance of communication in children's socialization, Kristen's speech during the baseline will be discussed in detail. During the baseline, Kristen's appropriate use of single-word utterances, phrases, and sentences, and her parents' rewarding her for speech were recorded. Over the 5-day period, Kristen

Table 15: Description of Typical Exchanges in the White Home Prior to Parent Training

Child's Behavior	Parents' Response
Self-destructive: slaps or bites herself.	Gives her attention about 60% of the time by telling her to stop or saying, "Kristen, that's no way to act."
Bizarre sounds and gestures: makes guttural sounds, stares at her hands, flaps belts and ropes.	Gives her attention only about 30% of the time. Usually ignores her.
Screams.	Gives her attention about 25% of the time, usually by asking what she wants.
Disrupts meal: leaves table and most often gets into food in the refrigerator.	Rewards her 100% of the time by allowing her to take and eat food other than what was prepared or telling her to come back and sit down.
Cooperates with parental exchange signals about 50% of the time.	Gives praise and/or attention for cooperating only about 65% of the time.
Uses speech to ask for something or answer a question.	Rewards (with praise or with what she asked for) only 65% of the time.

emitted an average of 26 single-word utterances and/or phrases and 2 sentences per session, a total of 28 appropriate verbal responses per session—about one utterance every three minutes. And, as shown in Table 15, her parents rewarded an average of 64% of Kristen's appropriate speech responses. Clearly, Kristen's verbal behavior was quite weak, and her parents were not using the continuous reinforcement necessary to accelerate her low rate of speech.

In addition to the exchanges listed in Table 15, a number of other problems were identified during the baseline sessions. First, during the evening meal, Mr. and Mrs. White directed a continual barrage of questions, comments, and advice to Kristen and her younger brother. Both children were constantly told to eat particular dishes being served or asked if they wanted more of anything, if they were enjoying the food, or if they were finished. At the same time, Kristen's brother, Stan, often disrupted meals. He spoke in a loud, high-pitched voice and often left his seat, yelling and running through the house between his toys, the dog, and the kitchen. The Whites invariably gave him attention for his disruptive behavior by yelling or threatening him. To the observer, mealtime at the White home was a chaotic and noisy affair. It was no wonder Kristen sometimes did not come downstairs for supper.

Second, many exchanges between Kristen and her parents were long *chains*. That is, if Kristen emitted an appropriate response, instead of rewarding her for it, her parents made additional demands on her, and rewarded her only after she complied with two or more of these. For instance, if Kristen initiated an exchange with the word "Potatoes," instead of praising her and giving her more potatoes, the Whites were likely to say, "Do you want potatoes?" To this Kristen was to reply, "Yes." If she did reply, "Yes," she was still not given any potatoes, but was then told to say, "More potatoes please" or "Yes, I do."

The Whites were trying to evoke more speech from Kristen with this system. Inadvertently, however, they were putting her on a schedule of intermittent reinforcement, when Kristen needed a schedule of continuous reinforcement that would accelerate her low rate of speech. Unfortunately, Kristen often did not respond properly to the additional requests. In fact, she often screamed or walked away.

A third problem was that Mr. and Mrs. White sometimes jointly initiated exchanges with Kristen, and sometimes their signals were contradictory. For example, one time Kristen wanted her daily vitamin pill. Mr. White said to her, "What color is this one?" and at the same time, Mrs. White said, "Do you want a green one?" Occasionally, both parents presented the same signal, e.g., "Do you want more cake?"

A fourth problem was friction between Mr. and Mrs. White regarding Kristen. They often seemed to hold each other responsible for her behavior. For example, once when Kristen was screaming Mrs. White said to her husband, "Can't you do anything to stop her screaming?" Mr. White's reply was, "Well, if you'd ever have dinner on time, maybe she wouldn't scream so much." Mutual blaming will be discussed in more detail later.

A fifth problem concerned constructive activities. The Whites seldom encouraged Kristen to engage in constructive activity, perhaps because their attempts had been all but extinguished by Kristen's indifference. During the 5-day baseline, only 11 attempts were made, and Kristen cooperated only 6 times.

Also, the Whites' method of initiating exchanges—again, using chains—fostered Kristen's resistance. For instance, Kristen was *allowed* to go outside and play after she first said that she wanted to, then answered the question, "Do you want to go out?" then put on her coat, finished her milk, or put on her shoes. If she refused to comply with any request in the chain, she missed the opportunity to play outside. It was as though the Whites, having located a reinforcer when Kristen asked to go outside, tried to get her to do many of the things she had not done during the day.

Moreover, when Kristen was engaged in a constructive exchange with her father, the exchange was frequently interrupted by her brother, who would tantrum and pull Mr. White away from Kristen. At these times, Kristen would hit her brother or scream.

A final problem, noted earlier, was the lack of expressed positive sentiments between Kristen and her mother. When Mrs. White praised Kristen, her praise sounded (to me, at least) as if it were given begrudgingly and without feeling. Likewise, Kristen did not seem to value her mother's praise—she never smiled when she got it—and usually tried to avoid contact with her mother. When Mrs. White entered a room where Kristen was sitting, Kristen left. She did value her father's attention and presence, however. She actively sought his presence and smiled when he spoke to and held her. But as mentioned before, exchanges between Kristen and her father were usually disrupted by her brother.

To summarize, the baseline observations revealed that Kristen had a number of behavioral deficits and performed several highly aversive bizarre-disruptive behaviors. At the same time, the Whites systematically but unwittingly reinforced these behaviors and seldom initiated exchanges involving appropriate, constructive behavior. In addition, several features of the White home hindered Kristen's education: Stan's disruptive behavior; the friction between the White parents; the excessive demands on Kristen; and the seeming lack of sentiments of liking between Kristen and her mother.

Training in Basic Techniques of Exchange Management

Training the Whites followed the stages described in Chapter 3. First, Mr. and Mrs. White were given introductory materials which they read and discussed with me. Next, from May 1–7, Mrs. White observed and recorded sessions in the Laboratory between Mrs. Hare and Michael. From May 8–17 she was taught to use the techniques of exchange management that she had been observing. She worked with Michael Hare, coached via the wireless intercom system by Mrs. Hare, who had just completed her Laboratory training. At the same time, I was coaching Mrs. Hare in how to coach Mrs. White.

Training in the Laboratory was quite successful. Mrs. White's use of questions ("Do you want to ... ?") to initiate exchanges was reduced to zero in six days. More dramatically, she increased Michael's rate of correct responding above his rate with his own mother. The reader will recall that by the end of her training in the Laboratory, Mrs. Hare maintained Michael's rate of about 85 correct responses per session. When Mrs. White took over, the rate dropped to 68 the first day, but eventually stabilized between 90 and 95. Mrs. White was coached to use both continuous and intermittent reinforcement schedules.

Michael's attention to tasks his first day with Mrs. White dropped from 90% of the time, the equilibrium attained with his mother, to 70%. By the end of her training, Mrs. White was also maintaining Michael's attention at 90%.

Finally, Mrs. White learned to ignore irrelevant behavior and time out a child for disruptive behavior. The increase in Michael's attending and working at tasks, for instance, was due in part to Mrs. White's ignoring him when he spun objects and timing him out when he left the table to climb on something.

Description of the Home After Training in Basic Techniques (B)

After two days observing in the White home (May 30–31), it was clear that little of the Whites' reading, discussions with me, and training in the Laboratory had generalized to the home. Nothing was done to handle Kristen's or Stan's meal disruptions; attempts to initiate and maintain constructive exchanges were few and ineffective; the Whites still chattered incessantly at Kristen during meals; and they continued to impose chains of additional demands. In addition, they did nothing to control her screaming—in fact, they now attended to screaming 33% of the time, in contrast to 25% during the baseline. The only improvement was an increase in the frequency with which they reinforced Kristen's speech. If, for instance, she asked for something during the meal, both Mr. and Mrs. White said, "Good girl." But as mentioned, she usually had to comply with several additional requests before she actually received the food (the reinforcer) she had asked for.

On the basis of these observations, the Whites and I chose three areas for the next period of training. First, the Whites would be helped to handle Kristen's screaming—an inappropriate substitute for functional speech, and an extremely aversive stimulus in itself. Second, Kristen's leaving the table and eating after everyone else was done would be replaced with appropriate mealtime behavior. And third, the Whites would be taught to initiate and maintain exchanges involving constructive behavior.

Training to Restructure the System of Exchanges (C)

The total duration of this period was six months, from June 4 to December 4, 1968.

Training to Handle Screaming and Restructure Mealtime

From June 4 to August 21, 1968, training with the Whites focused on Kristen's screaming and mealtime problems. On June 3, the Whites were given a written prescription specifying the techniques for handling the several problems to be worked on at that time. I spent the evening of June 3 discussing the prescription with the Whites, and instructed them to put a hook on the outside of the downstairs bathroom so it could be used as a time out room. The prescription is presented in Table 16 on the next page.

For the first four days of this period, I directly coached the Whites from another room during the evening meal via small wireless transceivers (Lloyd's Electronics, Model 7A17B-30A, 9-volt). Specifically, they were coached to reward Kristen for using speech, to time out Kristen and Stan for screaming or leaving the table, to have all of the food on the table before the meal began, and to remove all food from the table when they were finished eating. In addition, to help Mr. and Mrs. White change behaviors for which direct coaching did not appear feasible, such as their excessive questioning of the children, I had discussions with them before and after the meal.

Table 16: Prescription Given to the Whites to Restructure Several of the Exchange Patterns in the Home

To Ignore: Do not look at or talk to Kristen while she is engaging in inappropriate behavior. Especially you should not yell at her, tell her to stop, scold her, or threaten her; just act as if you do not see her.

To Time Out: Without speaking, and with some vigor, take Kristen to the time out room. Leave her in one minute for the first offense, two minutes for the second offense, etc. Do not let her out, however, if she is screaming or tantruming. Wait until she stops.

To Reward: Warmly give her praise and other things she likes such as music and candy. If you give her candy or music, make sure that you also give her praise before the other reinforcer.

Child's Behavior	Your Response
Not coming downstairs to supper	Before each meal, call Kristen (or Stan) once. Then sit down and eat your meal. If Kristen comes downstairs and sits at the supper table while you are still eating, allow her to eat, but do not say anything about her being late. When you are finished, remove all the food from the table, including Kristen's plate. Do not let her have any more to eat after your meal is over. If she does not come downstairs until after you have already eaten and cleared the table, do not let her have anything to eat until the next scheduled eating time.
Getting up from the table during the meal to get into food	Immediately time her out. At the same time, make sure that all of the food to be served during the meal is already on the table, so that she has no legitimate reason for getting up to get food. Furthermore, even if she asks for it, do not give Kristen any other food besides that which you have prepared for the meal.
Kristen's screaming; Stan's noise making	Immediately time out the offender for every offense.
Additional Comments	Do not ask the children if they want more food and do not tell them to eat more or to finish what they have on their plates. If Kristen asks for something on the table (whether or not she uses a whole sentence), praise her and give it to her. If she asks for something that is not on the menu, tell her, "We are not having that for supper tonight." If she then screams, time her out.

The effects of the training at home on Kristen's screaming and meal disruptions are presented in Table 17 on the next page. Table 17 indicates that there was a change in Kristen's behavior concomitant with changes in the behavior of her parents. When they began timing her out for screaming or leaving the table, these behaviors gradually weakened. Screaming was reduced to a consistent level of zero by the fifteenth home session (Day 57), and getting up from the table was eliminated by the twentieth session (Day 114).

Although the Program was generally successful, making mealtime more pleasant for all concerned, the results were not satisfactory. Even recognizing that we were dealing with disruptive behavior that had been part of Kristen's repertoire for years, it took far too long to change her behavior. In addition, as the table shows, by the last two days of the follow-up to this period, Kristen's screaming was beginning to increase in frequency. There are a number of reasons for this.

First, Mrs. White admitted that she had not been following the prescription at *other* times of day. She did not consistently time Kristen out for screaming or leaving the table. And in the morning she often let Kristen eat after breakfast was over, when Kristen had not come down for the meal. When asked why she did not follow the prescription, Mrs. White said it was "too much of a chore."

Second, when the coaching stopped, the Whites occasionally reverted to their old patterns of reinforcing Kristen when she left the table. Several additional days of coaching were required to strengthen their use of the techniques that they had helped design and had agreed to follow.

Third, Mr. White did not put a lock on the time-out room for several months, although he was repeatedly reminded. Each time he timed Kristen out, therefore, he had to stand at the door and hold it shut. This may have constituted inadvertent attention because Kristen was fully aware that her father was right outside the door.

Fourth, contrary to instructions, Mrs. White did not have meals ready at the same time each night. Supper was never at the same time on any two consecutive nights. In fact, meals were sometimes

Table 17: Exchange Patterns Involving Screaming and Meal Disruptions for Various Experimental Periods

Session	Baseline (A): April 11-15, 1968						(B): May 30-31			Coaching and Observing to Restructure Mealtime (C): June 4-16							Follow-Up Observations of Mealtime (Continuation of C): July 29-August 21						
Frequency	1	1			5		6	7	8					15	17	18	20			25			30
Screaming During Meals	10	10	2	0	7	8	7	6		5	1	1	1	0	0	0	2	0	0	0	0	1	2
Reinforced	6	0	0	0	1	3	5	1		0	0	0	0	0	0	0	0			0			0
Ignored	4	10	2	0	6	5	2	5		0	0	0	0	0	0	0	0			0			0
Timed Out	0	0	0	0	0	0	0	0		5	1	1	1	1	1	0	2			0			2
Getting Up From Table	3	3	4	3	5	4	5	4		3	3	1	2	1	2	2	1	0	0	0	0	0	0
Reinforced	3	3	4	3	5	4	5	0		0	0	1	0	1	0	2	0			0			0
Timed Out	0	0	0	0	0	0	0	4		3	3	0	1	1	1	0	1			0			0

* Kristen did not come downstairs to supper.

an hour and a half late. There was a basic inconsistency in Mrs. White's behavior. On one hand, she was preoccupied with the orderliness of her house (it was always arranged perfectly). Yet she was disorganized temporally, i.e., she did not organize the house according to time. The effect of this was that Kristen never knew when supper would be, and might even be called downstairs for supper and then have to wait at least half an hour before it was ready.

Fifth, the Whites did not handle Stan consistently or as the prescription suggested. They would sometimes time him out; sometimes argue with him; sometimes threaten him; and sometimes chase him. The exchanges between Stan and his parents showed Kristen that disruptive behavior would not always produce time out, but would sometimes still produce attention. There is evidence that Kristen observed the exchanges between Stan and his parents, for whenever Stan became disruptive and the Whites tried to control him by threatening, yelling at, or spanking him, Kristen would giggle, flap her hands, and dance about the room.

And finally, although I discussed it with them repeatedly, the Whites continued to make much of trivial matters during the meal, and by doing so made the meal an unpleasant experience for Kristen. They continued to ask irrelevant and unnecessary questions ("Are you finished?"); they persisted in coaxing or telling her to eat more ("As soon as you finish your dessert, you can hear 'This Land is Mine'."); and they were sometimes arbitrary in their handling of Kristen's verbal requests for food. During one meal, Kristen asked for more butter and Mrs. White refused, telling her she had already had some. Kristen screamed as a consequence and was timed out for screaming. Yet her request seemed legitimate enough.

Because the training had been generally successful in decelerating Kristen's screaming and meal disruptions, and because many problems remained, an experimental reversal would have been both risky and unnecessary.

When follow-up observations to the C period were completed, I stopped observing in the White home. Periodically, however, I discussed Kristen's behavior with Mrs. White. She indicated that Kristen seldom screamed and that mealtimes were running smoothly. A final series of observations was made nearly a year later to learn how well the Whites were managing the mealtime exchange and how Kristen was behaving. The results will be reported later.

Structured Play and Speech Sessions

It will be recalled that Kristen seldom "played," that her speech was weak, and that her mother did not seem to be a positive reinforcer for her. It was hoped that these problems might be remedied in part by teaching Mrs. White to run exchanges with Kristen involving speech and play. Thus, from October 14 to December 4, 1968, speech and play sessions were held at the White home, beginning at approximately 3:00 P.M. The conditions were as follows. All sessions were 15 minutes long. Mrs. White sat next to Kristen on a couch and read her a story. Every few lines, Mrs. White asked Kristen questions about the names of objects in the pictures or about the content of the story. She reinforced Kristen with praise and bites of candy or sips of soda for correct answers. Kristen was prompted if she did not give the correct answer on her own. The schedule of reinforcement was continuous for the first several days and gradually changed to a variable schedule, not to exceed about one reinforcement for three correct answers. Mrs. White ignored irrelevant behavior and timed Kristen out for screaming. She read and asked questions only while Kristen was sitting on the couch and attending. The storybook was changed every few days.

After the reading sessions, Kristen and her mother went downstairs to the play area of the basement. A table and two chairs were set up. Every few days, a different play object was brought into the house; Mrs. White taught Kristen to play with the object and reinforced her while she played.

The reader will recall that Mrs. White had already learned basic techniques for running the speech and play sessions during her training in the Laboratory. Only a few days of direct coaching were needed for the speech sessions. Mrs. White was soon quite effective at maintaining Kristen's attention, rewarding her, and asking questions and prompting correct answers. Closer supervision was required in the play exchanges, for Mrs. White needed practice in the techniques (e.g., modeling and prompting) for teaching Kristen *how* to play with different toys.

Data were taken during speech sessions on prompted and unprompted correct answers. After 15 sessions, Kristen's rate of correct answers stabilized. An experimental reversal was conducted to assess the extent to which Kristen's correct responses to questions were affected by the structure of the exchange and whether the reversal would increase her rate of responding. The data, presented in Figure 16 on the next page, show that Kristen's rate of correct answers *was* a function of the structure of the exchanges managed by Mrs. White. In addition, the reversal produced an intensification of her rate of correct responses. The data on Kristen's unprompted correct answers are also interesting. They indicate either that she was learning functional words to use in answering questions, or that her interest in the stories (or motivation to participate in the exchange) was increasing.

As to the play sessions, data consisted merely of the observer's judgment of Kristen's skill at playing with the toys. In some sessions, Kristen played with toys she had already learned to use in the Laboratory, such as puzzles and pasting. She also learned to play with several new toys—for instance, to use finger paints; to draw circles, squares, and parallel lines; to play with Play-doh, roll it out flat, and cut it with cookie cutters; and to operate several mechanical toys such as a tape recorder and a battery-operated bank.

Mrs. White was asked to make the toys available to Kristen at all times, to reward her for initiating play with them, and to reward her intermittently while she played. Mrs. White was also asked to record the number of times Kristen initiated play and the amount of time she played during the day. Mrs. White did not keep a record of Kristen's playing as asked. In discussions with her, however, she noted that Kristen was initiating play with the toys, particularly with finger paints and the toy tape recorder, several times a day and was playing from fifteen minutes to half an hour. If true, this would indi-

Figure 16: Building Functional Speech in an Autistic Girl

The mother was asked to read stories to the girl and to ask her questions about the story every few lines. Sessions were 15 minutes long. In A_1, the mother was asked to reward the child with praise and food on a schedule of continuous reinforcement for several days and then intermittently for correct answers. In B_1, the mother was asked not to reward the child for correct answers. And in A_2, the mother was asked to again reward the child intermittently for correct answers.

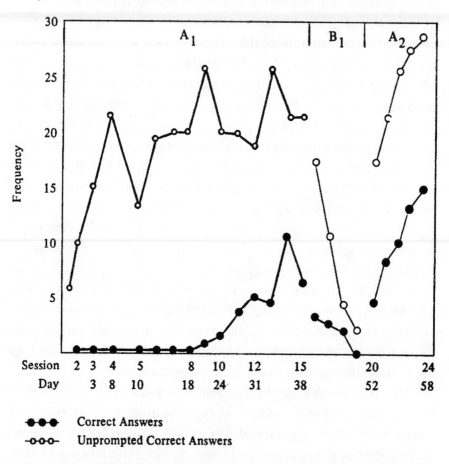

cate at least a beginning in Kristen's substituting constructive activity for inactivity or self-stimulation—for, prior to the structured play sessions, she did not play with toys at all.

Except for the final series of observations, training with the Whites and the structured speech and play sessions ended December 4, 1968. The reason for stopping was my conclusion that I simply did not have control of the variables that might have increased the Whites' willingness and ability to more effectively work with Kristen.

First, after only three consecutive speech and play sessions, Mrs. White began to complain that working with Kristen was too much of a burden on her. At first she repeatedly remarked, "Working with Kristen is a full-time job." Then she began cancelling sessions, sometimes for as long as a week. Toward the end she remarked several times, "There are many other things I would rather be doing. Other women get to go shopping, but not me." The sessions, it will be remembered, were only about half an hour in duration. In other words, Mrs. White seemed to have repertoires "prepotent" over the child (Ferster, 1968). While she desperately wanted Kristen to be like "other" little girls, the amount of work required to help educate Kristen (added to the strain and work involved in just living with Kristen) seemed to be too much for her.

Second, Mrs. White simply did not comply with the prescriptions she had helped write. A case in point was her son Stan. Although he was three years old, Stan was not even beginning to be toilet trained. The reason, perhaps, was Mrs. White's continually making an issue of his mishaps. At any rate, I gave her an article on toilet training, and she helped write a prescription of instructions to follow. Her prescription was to keep track for a week of the times of day that Stan had bowel movements. After that, Mrs. White was to put Stan on the toilet at the likely times and reward him just for sitting there. Later, she was to reward him if he had a bowel movement while on the toilet. Though she was asked several times to keep the list, and although I went so far as to make a chart which only required her to place check marks on it, she did not comply. And Stan continued to have bowel movements in his pants.

Although in retrospect there may have been alternatives to the decision to terminate, at the time I was simply overwhelmed by a feeling of inability to help.

Follow-Up Description of the Home

Three follow-up observations were made in the White home from June 9–13, 1969, six months after the last observations. The observations were at the same time of day (suppertime) and for the same duration as the previous A_1, B, and C observations. One reliability check was made; the agreement between the two observers on their scoring of interactions was 100%.

The follow-up observations yielded interesting and encouraging findings. First, although I had not worked with the Whites since December, 1968, the Whites were almost completely successful in applying the techniques they had been taught regarding mealtime problems. Mr. or Mrs. White called Kristen to the table only once; all food was put on the table ahead of time; and Kristen's plate was removed when she indicated that she was finished. Moreover, Kristen *never* got up from the table during the meal and she *never* screamed, either before, during, or after the meal. Indeed, the Whites indicated that Kristen rarely screamed at all anymore, and then only when pestered by Stan. The Whites still asked unnecessary questions, but less than during the previous periods.

Second, the Whites seldom made excessive or serial requests of Kristen. The effect of this was to increase the probability that Kristen's speech would be reinforced. In contrast to the baseline, in which Kristen's speech was reinforced an average of 64% of the time, during the follow-up the Whites reinforced Kristen's appropriate speech an average of 88% of the time.

By asking fewer questions, the Whites were, in effect, requiring Kristen to initiate speech if she wanted something. Consequently, whereas during the baseline Kristen's appropriate speech was self-initiated only 31% of the time on the average, during the follow-up her speech was self-initiated 80% of the time. Kristen's rate of self-initiated speech had more than doubled. In addition, although her overall rate of speech had not increased (she emitted 28 verbal responses per session on the average during the baseline, and 27 per session during the follow-up), her rate of sentences had increased.

She used an average of two sentences per session in the baseline period and an average of five sentences per session during the follow-ups—a slight but notable increase.

As to playing, a qualitative change was observed in the follow-up. Play was still of short duration. However, Kristen now initiated play outside on the swings and on the climber, and for this she received praise from her parents. More importantly, both Mr. and Mrs. White indicated that Kristen spent *most* of her time playing outside, near and sometimes with other children in the neighborhood. During the baseline, she rarely went outside on her own, and when she did go out she merely stood around flapping wires or sniffing things. Now she followed other children around to different yards in the neighborhood and seemed to enjoy being with them. In this respect, the Whites felt, and had been told by the neighbors, that Kristen had become a different child.

Conclusions

The work with the White family may be the most important of the four cases in terms of future research and training with families of autistic children. On one hand, the research demonstrated that Kristen's disruptive behavior could be all but eliminated and appropriate behavior could be strengthened as long as her parents were willing to structure and manage educational exchanges consistently and continuously. However, the research also indicated that the Training Program's effectiveness with the White family had its limits. Mr. and Mrs. White were not always willing to structure and manage educational exchanges with Kristen. They were often inconsistent in using the exchange management procedures. And they did not apply the procedures on a continuous basis. In summary, the research showed that Kristen's behavior was changed by the systematic application of prescribed techniques, but the Training Program had only modest effects on the *parents'* behavior so that they would and could apply the techniques.

A number of factors in the White home have been mentioned

which limited the effectiveness of the Training Program. A full discussion of these factors and others is found in the next chapter. Both the limits of the Training Program in general and suggestions for modifying it will be considered.

8

Summary of Results and Implications for the Future

The program of teaching and research described in this book represents the application of sociological theory, applied behavior analysis and experimental design to the problem of human suffering. The researcher hoped that the program would reduce the frustration and desperation of parents and demonstrate clearly that they can be effective agents of their children's educations and psychosocial development. Guided by three hypotheses stated at the beginning of Chapter 3, this chapter addresses:

1. new exchanges and features of exchanges discovered during the research;
2. effects of training parents at the Laboratory-school;
3. generalization of change from the Laboratory-school to the homes;
4. changes in children; and
5. implications for designing programs with families.

Kinds of Productive and Counterproductive Exchanges

Chapter 2 provided a beginning formulation of child-caregiver exchanges drawing on the work of Blau (1964), Homans (1961), Patterson and Reid (1970), and Simmel (1971). However, interviews with parents and observations in homes and in the Laboratory-school during the research and training yielded a richer description of exchanges and how they work.

Social interaction (exchange) is the means by which members of a group accomplish activities such as play, chores, conversations, lessons, arguments, and efforts to resolve disagreements. Some exchanges are performed *singly*. For example, a mother walks toward her little boy playing in the living room; she smiles at him and says, "Oh, you are building a BIG tower"; he looks up, smiles and continues playing; the mother walks into the next room. Typically, however, exchanges are performed in *sequences*, such as lessons and family meals. With repetition (practice) single exchanges and sequences crystallize into script-like *forms*, and are performed so fluently that they become almost invisible to participants—they are seen but not noticed.

The research makes clear that there are two sorts of exchanges. One is *counterproductive exchanges*. These involve *conflict* and/or *incongruity*. For example, one or both persons perform behaviors that are aversive to the other person; or one person engages in desirable behavior but receives nothing in return; or one person wants what the other person does not give. In *productive exchanges*, each person performs behaviors that are reinforcers for the other person. From the standpoint of participants, the other person's behavior is "desirable." This section discusses features of exchanges discovered during the research and identifies additional exchanges that were not anticipated. Exchanges are examined in pairs—a counterproductive exchange is followed by a productive alternative.

1a. Rewarded Coercion

In one version of rewarded coercion, a child engages in behavior that is aversive to a parent (e.g., Kristen's screaming or Luke's making messes). The behavior may be so intense, of such long standing, so embarrassing, so disruptive, so strange, or so frightening that it feels coercive to the parent: "I have to make it stop!" The parent tries to stop the behavior—i.e., reciprocates the child's initiation—by ex-pressing shock or anger; asking ineffectual questions ("Are we supposed to make messes?"); stating rules ("We don't scream."); trying to distract the child (e.g., "Here's your favorite toy."); or removing events (e.g., difficult tasks, leaving a store) that may be signals or occasions for the child's aversive/coercive behavior. Some of these reactions or reciprocations reinforce the child's aversive/coercive behavior. And because the child is temporarily distracted by the reinforcing consequence, the child temporarily stops the behavior. This *negatively* reinforces the parent for unwittingly reinforcing the child's aversive/coercive behavior. The reader no doubt sees the vicious circle. *The parent reinforces precisely the behavior that the parent is trying to decrease* (Bijou, 1967; Patterson & Reid, 1984; Patterson, Reid, & Dishion, 1989).

Both persons are reinforced for their actions in this exchange. Elementary principles of respondent and operant learning discussed in Chapter Two—as well as data collected through interviews and direct observations in this research—suggest changes that are therefore likely to occur.

1. Since each person is reinforced for his or her actions in this exchange, each person is *increasingly likely* to perform his or her respective actions (coercing and giving in to coercion) when the next occasion arises.
2. This means that the rewarded coercion exchange will be performed *more often.*
3. As the rate of rewarded coercion exchanges increases, there will be *less opportunity* (and energy) for parents and child to learn and perform productive alternative exchanges.
4. With repetition of the exchange (as a script) and with repetition (practice) of their respective actions ("parts"), parent and child become *more skillful.* For example, a parent may find that merely asking her child to stop whining during a task does not work—the child whines longer or louder. In other words, the parent's asking is on extinction or is punished. The parent then tries making the task easier. The child whines even louder and begins to

flap her hands. Finally, the parent lets the child out of the task. The whining stops. Letting the child out of the task when the child escalates the loudness of whining and flaps her hands accidentally *shapes* the child's undesirable behavior in a worse direction. Reciprocally, when the child stops whining right after (but *only* after) the parent lets her out of the task, the child negatively reinforces (and shapes) the parent's "giving-in" escape behavior. Ironically, each person's reactions to the other person's actions teach the other person the more skillful way to produce reinforcement. In other words, parent and child are getting better at doing what is contrary to their best interests.

5. A further change is that the child and parent perform this exchange in *more settings*. For example, the child will whine at home, in stores, and in restaurants "in order to" get out of other tasks. Likewise, the parent will "give in" to coercive behavior in these new settings. In other words, the exchange (and each person's behavior in it) becomes more *generalized*.

6. The child will also learn to use the same aversive behaviors to serve other *functions*. For example, Michael Hare's whining coerced his parents not only to *remove* tasks or to leave stores but to *give* him positive reinforcers (e.g., a different meal).

7. It is also likely that the child will learn *new* aversive/coercive behaviors. For example, a parent may get used to (*habituate* to) a child's whining and hand flapping. Therefore, when the child whines and flaps her hands, the parent barely notices it, or notices it but does nothing to stop it. In effect, the child's whining and flapping are now on extinction. We can predict that the child will *escalate* whining to the level of screaming—an *"extinction burst."* Or perhaps she will throw herself to the floor and tantrum. If the parent is frightened by this ("Oh, no, it's getting worse!"), the parent may accidentally reinforce this new or more intense behavior. In summary, the child is gradually learning a repertoire of aversive/coercive behavior.

8. In time, parents and other persons may see the child as an *adversary* and a major source of stress with whom they therefore avoid

interacting. These two changes—in how others perceive the child and in their willingness to interact with the child—amount to *degrading* the child's identity and social place. This further decreases the child's opportunities to learn desirable behavior, leaving the child even fewer alternative prosocial ways to produce reinforcers. Consequently, the child's aversive/coercive behaviors may increase in rate, the number of settings where these behaviors are performed, and in severity—possibly straining or exhausting parents' teaching and coping repertoires (van de Rijt–Plooij & Plooij, 1993). At this point, the process of "placing" the child in a special environment may begin.

In another version of rewarded coercion, a parent engages in behavior that is aversive to a child (e.g., rough handling). The child then engages in escape behavior that is reinforcing to the parent (e.g., the child is quiet). The parent's aversive behavior therefore increases in frequency and skill, as does the child's coerced quiet behavior. This exchange (characteristic of abusive families) *was not seen* in the research. Nor is it suggested that this version of rewarded coercion is likely to be found in families of autistic children. However, it is certainly seen in some schools and treatment facilities (Sobsey, 1994).

1b. Unrewarded Coercion

In unrewarded coercion, a parent tries to remain outwardly calm and does not give in to a child's aversive/coercive behavior. Instead, the parent provides opportunities and reinforces desirable alternative behaviors, less intense or shorter episodes of undesirable behavior (e.g., milder tantrums), or undesirable behaviors performed in an appropriate place (Carr, Levin, McConnachie, Carlson, Kemp, & Smith, 1994). This alternative productive exchange works best if it is combined with 3b, "cooperation training," described below.

2a. Rewarded Threat

This research suggests that the rewarded threat exchange often and easily develops out of the rewarded coercion exchange. For example, parents eventually notice that if their child screams for more than a minute or so, she will perform even worse behavior; e.g., self-injury. Or, parents know that a child's coercive behavior is likely in certain environments; e.g., during lessons on speech or during interaction with another child. When presented with these signals (perceived threats), parents express shock, fear, or anger; try to soothe or distract their child; allow the child to receive reinforcers for inadequate performances; or remove tasks or requests that seem to upset the child. These reciprocations probably reinforce the child's threatening ("leading up to...") behavior. When the placated child temporarily stops the threatening behavior, and does not go on to perform the more coercive behavior, parents feel relief and are negatively reinforced for reinforcing their child's threats.

The child's threat behaviors then increase in frequency, and the child commands a great deal of reinforcement by performing threats. The price the child pays for this reinforcement is minimal psychosocial development; the price parents pay for a little piece and quiet is an increasingly heavy load trying to placate their child and chronic fear of their child "getting worse." This fear helps to sustain parents' placating responses.

In a second version of the rewarded threat exchange, a child learns signals (e.g., a parent's moodiness) that predict that the parent will soon engage in aversive behavior (e.g., yelling). The child learns to placate the parent by performing tasks for the parent, remaining quiet, or hugging the parent. This exchange strengthens the parent's threatening behavior and the child's placating behavior. The increasing frequency of the exchange may keep the child in a state of chronic anxiety and/or depression, which inhibits the child's attention and learning more complex behaviors (Culp, Little, Letts, & Lawrence, 1991). Several parents reported that they had engaged in a mild form of this exchange before the Training Program (e.g., Mrs.

Nash threatened to spank Luke if he did not stop playing with water in the bathroom), but it was rarely seen even during baseline observations.

2b. Unrewarded Threat

Instead of reinforcing a child's threatening behavior, parents remain outwardly calm; ignore mild problem behaviors; and require at least a small amount of desirable behavior before giving reinforcers: "As soon as you ___, you can ___." If repeated, this exchange teaches children that threatening behavior does not work; children become more skillful at performing desirable behaviors; parents develop tolerance of milder problem behaviors and become more skilled at teaching desirable behavior. Again, this alternative exchange works best if it is combined with 3b, "cooperation training."

3a. Rewarded Noncompliance (or Nagging)

In one version of this exchange, a child does not cooperate with a parent's initiation; e.g., requests or questions. Perhaps the child walks away, whines, acts as if she did not hear, or does the opposite of what was asked. The parent repeats the initiation—perhaps louder and/or with extra signals (e.g., facial expressions and hand gestures signifying impatience). These repetitions probably reinforce the uncooperative behavior (i.e., whatever else the child did following the parental signals). Uncooperative behavior therefore increases in strength. The vicious cycle is completed whenever the child finally cooperates, for then the parent is reinforced for nagging on a variable ratio (once-in-a-while reinforcement) schedule. This schedule sustains the parent's nagging. "If you ask her enough times she will finally do it—maybe."

At some point, the combination of a low probability of being reinforced for making requests and a higher probability of being reinforced for other activities (e.g., doing household chores or playing with the child) results in the parent making fewer requests of the child. "It's not worth the trouble to ask her," or "She may not under-stand what we want." In this case, the child has fewer chances to learn to cooperate and take part in family or school, and the child is unwittingly assigned the role of a person who is "here but not really with us." However, parents may find a child's increasing or contin-ued noncompliance highly provocative, and they may begin to pun-ish the child. This often sets the occasion for the child to use counter-aggression (Schindler & Arkowitz, 1986).

In a second version of rewarded noncompliance, a parent does not cooperate with a child's initiations—e.g., Kristen's expressions of activity preference. The child repeats the initiations, which may reinforce the parent's disattention and "noncompliance." Then, ei-ther the child's initiating behaviors weaken (and the frequency of child-parent interaction decreases) or the parent finally cooperates (which teaches the child to nag).

3b. Single Cues or Cooperation Training

Instead of repeating requests again and again, a parent: (1) makes sure that a child is paying attention before presenting signals; (2) gives clear simple signals; (3) at first focuses on tasks that are easy for the child (Ducharme, 1996); (4) provides prompts to help the child to perform the requested task; (5) immediately reinforces im-provements in cooperation; and (6) responds to obvious noncom-pliance by consistently *manually prompting a child through the motions*—so that the child learns exactly what actions the signal speci-fies and learns that he or she must respond to the signal in that way (Engelmann & Colvin, 1983).

4a. Aversive Methods

Mutually aversive interaction is another logical possibility that was not seen in the research. However, it is important to describe this sort of interaction. In one version, a child does something that is aversive to a caregiver (e.g., noncompliance or hitting). The caregiver reacts by delivering aversive consequences (e.g., insults or spank-ing--type 1 punishment) or taking away positive reinforcers (e.g., toys—type 2 punishment). Sometimes this exchange is performed as a *single episode.* That is, the child reacts to punishment by ex-pressing fear or pain, and temporarily stops the behavior. This rein-forces the caregiver for using punishment.

Sometimes, however, the first punishment exchange calls forth another. In this case, there is a fight, or mutual punishment. For in-stance, instead of stopping his or her aversive behavior, the child escalates (hits harder) and/or adds another aversive behavior (bit-ing). The caregiver then punishes the child for returning the punish-ment, and another episode of mutual punishment begins. Gradually, each person learns *new and more skillful aversive/aggressive meth-ods* to punish (usually to escape from) the other person's aversive behavior and presence (Patterson, 1982). In addition, caregivers may begin to punish *indiscriminately* (if they do not do so already). That is, they punish both undesirable and desirable behaviors (Dumas, LaFreniere, Beaudin, & Verlaan, 1992). Therefore, the child may be-come anxious, depressed, and withdrawn; and the child's learning prosocial and instrumental competencies is hindered. Moreover, the child may come to use aggression in other environments and with other persons (siblings, parents, and peers). This may result in the child being socially rejected, and sometimes victimized when other children begin to retaliate. In addition, a child may come to be seen as having an emotional disorder or sociopathic personality (Cole, Lochman, Terry, & Hyman, 1992; Downey & Walker, 1989; McGonigle, Smith, Benjamin, & Turner, 1993; Olson, 1992; Straasberg, Dodge, Bates, & Pettit, 1992; Volling & Belsky, 1992; Walker, Colvin, & Ramsey, 1995; Weiss, Dodge, Bates, & Pettit, 1992).

4b. Mutual Reward Alternatives to Aversive Methods

Instead of responding to a child's undesirable behavior with aver-sive methods, a parent remains outwardly calm and encourages or waits for desirable behaviors to reinforce; e.g., milder forms of a problem behavior; performance of an undesirable behavior in a more desirable place; or performance of desirable alternative behavior.

5a. Lack of Opportunities for Desirable Behavior

In a situation where a child would benefit by an opportunity to respond (e.g., helping to prepare a meal), the parent does not notice opportunities, or the parent notices but does not signal or prompt the child to respond. The child's interest and proximity to activities is, therefore, on extinction and weakens. As the child's competencies fail to improve, parents regard their child as incapable of more skill, and may spend even less effort finding opportunities for the child to participate. This stabilizes the child's role as "an incompetent."

5b. Plenty of Opportunities for Desirable Behavior

In a situation where a child would benefit by an opportunity to respond, a parent notices learning opportunities and gives the child clear signals to respond. For example, Michael Hare indicates that he wants to stir the soup. Mrs. Hare quickly involves him in the activity. As the child's interest and competence increase, parents are reinforced for their efforts to find and provide learning opportunities. This completes a productive cycle; parents find and provide even more opportunities, and their child's psychosocial development procedes.

6a. Improper Prompting

When a child makes or is about to make an incorrect or inadequate response, a parent either provides no prompts or prompts ineffectively. Consequently, the child makes (in effect *practices*) errors; the child's competencies increase slowly; the parent is minimally reinforced for teaching efforts (which therefore weaken); and the child comes to be seen as less capable than he or she is.

6b. Proper Prompting

When a child makes or is about to make an incorrect or inadequate response, a parent provides an effective prompt. Both the child and the parent become more competent at teaching and learning. The parent's estimation of the child's capacities increases.

7a. Lack of Rewards for Desirable Behavior

When a child performs a desirable behavior—either a new one or an improved one (e.g., with more skill or in a new place)—a parent does not notice the desirable behavior and/or does not provide adequate reinforcement. Consequently, the child's desirable behaviors weaken or fail to increase. This further decreases the child's opportunities for social participation and reinforcement, which therefore increases the value of any reinforcing consequences the child receives for disruptive behavior—as in the rewarded coercion, reward threat, and nagging exchanges.

7b. Plenty of Rewards for Desirable Behavior

When a child performs a desirable behavior, a parent notices and properly reinforces the behavior (that is, quickly, enthusiastically, and with events that are known reinforcers). The child's desirable behaviors increase, as does the parent's attention and reinforcement of desirable behaviors.

The training and research helped the researcher and parents to more fully describe different exchanges. The research also suggested how *one type of exchange facilitates or hinders the development of other exchanges.* For example, as rewarded coercion increases in frequency, the family environment becomes more stressful, and parents live in a state of chronic sensitization and anticipation of "something bad" happening. Therefore, they are more likely to accidentally reinforce their child's threatening behavior. The family now has two counterproductive exchanges—rewarded coercion and rewarded threat. At some point, the rates and severity of the child's coercive and threatening behaviors are so high that parents' capacities to improve the situation are exhausted. Some parents then may begin using aversive methods in a desperate effort to stop their child's disruptive or self-injurious behavior. This often provokes fights and leaves parents feeling guilty, but with no idea of what else to do.

However, introducing a mutal reward exchange (e.g., increasing reinforcement for desirable behavior combined with cooperation training) can begin a productive spiral. As a child's desirable behaviors (e.g., attention, performing tasks) increase, parents have more opportunities to reinforce their child's desirable behaviors, and they form more valorizing images of their child: "She's a lot easier to live with." This results in a further increase in reinforcement for the child's desirable behavior and a decrease in aversive or inattentive responses from parents. With a decrease in their child's incentive to obtain reinforcers through coercive or threatening behavior, the rate of mutual reward exchanges increases, thus completing a positive cycle.

This section discussed productive and counterproductive exchanges identified in the research. The next sections discuss the results of the Training Program.

Changing Parental Behavior Patterns

Results of Laboratory Training

Several parents were taught basic methods for structuring and managing simple play or task exchanges. In brief, the parents were taught to initiate or structure exchanges with directives or contract statements instead of with questions; to spot appropriate responses versus inappropriate and/or disruptive ones; to reward a child using both continuous and intermittent schedules for appropriate responses; to shape and prompt appropriate responses; and to ignore and time out a child contingent upon bizarre-disruptive behavior.

This training was quite successful, as revealed by comparing the behavior of the parents and child before and during/after training.

Before training, Michael Hare's rate of constructive task responses was very low (12 per 20-minute session on the average), and Mrs. Hare seldom reinforced his actions. At the same time, Mrs. Hare attended to Michael's bizarre-disruptive and inattentive behavior at a high frequency, and often initiated exchanges with questions. After she and Mrs. White were trained, they were able, independently, to accelerate and maintain Michael's task responses to between 85 and 95 per session and maintain his attention to tasks at 90% of session time. They learned to reinforce appropriate responses systematically and to ignore and/or time out Michael for bizarre-disruptive behavior; and in a few days, questions to initiate exchanges were replaced by directives and contract statements. Mrs. Hare's training was so successful that she effectively trained three other persons (her two daughters and Mrs. White) to maintain Michael's task behavior at a high level.

In addition, three parents were taught advanced speech training techniques in the Laboratory. Mrs. Hare, for instance, learned how to prompt and reward Michael for correct imitative responses, maintaining his correct imitations at about 78% per session. After five days of training, Mrs. Nash increased Luke's imitative vocabulary by 24 words in 17 days. Mr. Nash was also trained. During the baseline he made a number of procedural errors, e.g., rewarding correct imitations only 50% of the time, rewarding incorrect imitations, and rewarding inattention. Consequently, though Luke's imitative speech had become strong, correct imitations fell to and stabilized at 31% with his father. After two weeks of coaching, Mr. Nash learned to reward nearly 100% of Luke's correct responses and to ignore inattention and incorrect responses. Concomitantly, Luke's correct verbal responses rose to 80% per session.

Changes in the Systems of Structured Exchanges in the Homes

After parents were trained in the Laboratory, observations were made in the homes to assess the extent of generalization, to note any changes resulting from the training, and to locate problems requiring further training. These observations constituted the B period. It was found that by itself, Laboratory training was partially effective in teaching parents how to modify exchanges in the home. In particular, parents at home after training rewarded their child much less often for bizarre-disruptive behavior and rewarded their child more often for appropriate speech, cooperation, and constructive activity than they had before training.

Nevertheless, parents continued to reward bizarre-disruptive behavior too often, did not reward speech, constructive activity, and cooperation often enough, and had trouble initiating productive exchanges. Thus, the children still engaged in too much bizarre-disruptive behavior, and their speech, constructive activity, and cooperation had increased only slightly. Consequently, during the C period, parents were trained at home to handle the problems identified during the B period.

Initial training in the homes lasted from one to two weeks. Observations were made on training days and on subsequent days to assess changes in family exchanges. When new problems arose, or when the child's progress indicated that he or she was ready for the next stage, the parents received additional training sessions. Follow-up observations in the homes were conducted from at least one to six months after the end of the C period.

Table 18 on the next page summarizes changes in one component of exchanges in the homes, namely parental *reciprocation,* resulting from training during the C period. This table presents the percentage of times the children were rewarded for various behaviors. The percentages are based on an average of the last three to five days in each of three periods: A_1 (pre-training), C, and follow-up. The data represent the behavior of the parents when they were "on their own," not during coached sessions.

As indicated in Table 18, the Training Program during the C period was quite successful in helping parents increase productive exchanges and replace counterproductive exchanges. Prior to the Training Program, the parents rewarded a high percentage of bizarre-dis-

Table 18: Patterns of Exchange Reciprocation by Parents for Various Experimental Periods

Response Class	Hare Family			Nash Family			White Family		
	Prior to Training	End of C Period	Follow-Up	Prior to Training	End of C Period	Follow-Up	Prior to Training	End of C Period	Follow-Up
Bizarre-Disruptive	73%			72%			54%		
Episodes of Constructive Activity	54%	100%	100%		100%	100%	50%	None Occurred	100%
Appropriate Speech	No Speech Present	100%	100%	No Speech Present	84%	85%	64%	88%	88%
Cooperation	60%	100%	96%		95%	92%	69%	100%	94%

Percentage of Reinforcement

ruptive responses and a low percentage of appropriate responses. By the end of the C period, however, the patterns had dramatically reversed. Bizarre-disruptive behavior was almost never rewarded (the parents, instead, were either ignoring or timing out the children), and appropriate behavior was rewarded almost 100% of the time. Of great importance is the finding that changes produced during the C period were maintained months after the Training Program had ended.

Data on the Gordon family are not presented in Table 18 because the design of the Training Program with the Gordons was different from the program with the other three families. The results of the Training Program with the Gordons will be presented later.

In addition to parents' exchange reciprocation, the Training Program also produced changes in the parents' structuring or initiating exchanges. Of concern here are the *new* exchanges that the parents initiated and managed in the homes. These new exchanges constituted the condition under which the parents could teach their children constructive behavior as alternatives to autistic patterns.

Before the Parent Training Program, none of the parents systematically managed educational exchanges involving language, play, cooperation, and the like. During the C period, the parents were taught how to structure and manage such exchanges in the home, and observations were made to determine the parents' success. Table 19 on the next page summarizes the new, educational exchanges that the parents instituted. Considering Tables 18 and 19 together, it is evident that the homes were becoming environments in which the children could begin learning new patterns of behavior.

Behavioral Changes in the Children

Many experimental reversals were conducted during the Training Program. The reversals demonstrated that the children's undesirable and desirable behaviors were functionally related to the structured exchanges managed by their parents. For example, the rates of different behaviors were strongly affected by children's opportunities to earn reinforcers, the kinds of signals parents used, and the prob-

Table 19: Socializing Exchanges Instituted and Managed in the Homes by the Parents

Educational Exchanges	Hare Family	Nash Family	Gordon Family	White Family
Speech	Imitative speech and beginnings of functional speech. Taught phonemes and many words by imitation, and several functional words. Worked on verbal discrimination (colors and objects).	Imitative and functional speech. Taught many words by imitation; built fairly large labeling vocabulary; taught a number of sentences. Worked on verbal discrimination: numbers, colors, and objects.	Imitative speech, beginnings of functional speech. Greatly strengthened imitative pattern; taught several phrases and sentences to use in answering questions and asking for things.	Imitative speech and beginnings of functional speech. Taught child to answer questions and ask for things with phrases and several sentences.
Constructive Activity	Play and chores. Built a very large play repertoire with toys and activities involving various skills (color-form discrimination, gross and fine motor coordination, increased attentiveness, and attention span). Taught a fairly large number of chores, ranging from small tasks to complex response sequences. Built pattern of generalized imitation.	Play and chores. Built a very large play repertoire with toys involving various skills (color-form discrimination, gross and fine motor coordination, increased attentiveness, and attention span). Built pattern of cooperative play and beginnings of competitive play. Taught several simple chores.	Play. Built a fairly large play repertoire with toys involving various skills (color-form discrimination, fine motor coordination, increased attentiveness, and attention span). Strengthened pattern of self-initiated play.	Play. Built a small play repertoire with toys involving various skills (color-form discrimination, fine motor coordination). Structured story sessions increased child's interest, attentiveness, and attention span.
Cooperation	Systematic differential reinforcement of constructive responses.	Systematic differential reinforcement of constructive responses.		Systematic differential reinforcement of constructive responses.
Counter Exchanges	Systematically structured counter exchanges to weaken disruptive behavior.			

ability of reinforcement. These functional relationships were found within and across behaviors and families. Therefore, we are able at least to suggest that these relationships are likely to be found with other children and families.

In all cases, beneficial behavioral changes in the children occurred concomitantly with changes in the exchanges with their parents. In particular, bizarre-disruptive behavior and autistic aloneness were dramatically reduced or replaced, while speech and constructive activity were markedly strengthened. Tables 20 through 23 (pp. 247-250) summarize the changes in the children. The data are based on an average of the last three to five days in two experimental periods: A_1 (pre-training) and follow-up.

As Tables 20 through 23 show, by follow-up there was marked improvement in the behavior of all of the children, and—with the possible exception of Peter Gordon, the oldest of the children—their socialization was underway. Though the children reached different levels of improvement, this does not mean we had reached the limits of their abilities to learn. A longer period of time, different procedures, or more effective use of procedures may have been required.

An interesting finding is the differences in the children's rates of improvement in various areas. The acceleration of constructive activity and deceleration of bizarre-disruptive behavior were the fastest in all cases. This may be because these two classes of behavior are incompatible: acceleration of constructive behavior reduces the time the child has for bizarre-disruptive behavior. Constructive behavior is also an alternative means by which the child can obtain the rewards he used to obtain through bizarre-disruptive behavior (Durand, 1990). The improvement in speech, however, was slower.

The children also differed in their overall rates of improvement. Luke Nash improved the fastest in all areas; Kristen White improved the slowest in all areas. Michael Hare and Peter Gordon were somewhere in between, with Michael Hare improving the faster of the two children. A number of factors may account for these differences, such as the age of the child, the severity of behavioral retardation, organic impairment, and the details of the parents' teaching meth-

Table 20: Behavioral Changes in Michael Hare

Behavior	Prior to Training Program	During Follow-Up
Bizarre-Disruptive	Average of 45 disruptions per session, including crying/whining, playing in water, getting into food, pulling/pushing, playing with stove, climbing, disrupting meals, spinning objects.	Average of 1 disruption per session. All but getting into food, crying/whining, playing in water, and climbing eliminated.
Constructive Activity	Average duration 5 minutes per session. Play repertoire limited to simple puzzles and stacking blocks. No chores. Manual dexterity poor.	Average duration 55 minutes per session, an increase by a factor of 11. Play repertoire included complex puzzles, Play-doh, Tinkertoys, swing & climber sets, pegboard landscape, coloring with crayons, sewing cards, riding tricycle, "Lite-Brite," musical toys, etc. Chore repertoire included setting/clearing table, loading/ starting washer and dryer, scouring toilet, taking out trash, packing lunch box, washing dishes, dressing. Development of generalized motor imitation. Plays and works with mother several hours per day.
Speech	Mute. No words.	Rate of acquisition of imitative speech positively accelerating. Repertoire included at least 37 words. Beginning to develop labeling vocabulary, including words "mama," "daddy," "food." Object discrimination (pointing to or picking up objects named) quite developed (89% unprompted correct responses).
Autistic Aloneness	Values presence and attention of others, but cooperates with parental exchange signals only 49% of the time and does not engage in cooperative play.	Cooperates with parental exchange signals an average of 95% of the time and engages in games requiring attentiveness to others, such as hide and seek, imitation.

Table 21: Behavioral Changes in Peter Gordon

Behavior	Prior to Training Program	During Follow-Up
Bizarre-Disruptive	No data available before training, but mother indicated high frequency. Average of 4 disruptions per day during first experimental period, including tantrums, removing clothes, disarranging house.	Only 1 disruption during last 5 days of the follow-up. Tantrums and removal of clothing eliminated.
Constructive Activity	Mother indicated that play was rare and sporadic. Less than 2 play initiations per day with available toys. No chores.	Average duration 75 minutes per day. Play repertoire included complex puzzles, pegboard landscape, large version of Tinkertoys, Play-doh, pasting, building with plastic blocks, simple mechanical toys, etc. Several simple chores such as bringing milk in from garage, carrying out empty soda bottles.
Speech	Though capable of imitative speech, response refusal was predominant. Average of only 4 appropriate verbal responses during structured, 20-minute speech sessions. Little or no functional speech.	Imitative speech quite strong, i.e., imitates almost any verbal stimulus. Average of 79 appropriate verbal responses during structured, 20-minute speech sessions. Functional speech developing, i.e., answers questions (often unprompted) about names for things and past and future events. Uses one- and two-word mands and sometimes phrases and sentences to ask for things.
Autistic Aloneness	Values presence and attention of others, but cooperation is sporadic, displays marked indifference to environment, and has no cooperative play pattern.	Cooperation much improved, according to mother. Performs almost any small task he is given. Interested in and enjoys going places with others. Engages in some cooperative play with father and brother (playing catch, wrestling, chasing one another).

Table 22: Behavioral Changes in Luke Nash

Behavior	Prior to Training Program	During Follow-Up
Bizarre-Disruptive	Average of 10 disruptions per 90-minute session, including shrieking, playing in water, getting into things, destructiveness, bizarre sounds/gestures, jumping on beds.	No disruptions. All but getting into things was decelerated to zero immediately after parents were coached in the home.
Constructive Activity	Average duration 4 mins. per session. Rarely plays during day. Usually sits watching TV or listening to records. However, has much manual dexterity: can dress self, work complicated puzzles, perform small chores (wipe off table), ride bicycle, build sand castles.	Average duration 75 mins. per session, an increase by a factor of 19. Plays about 4 hours a day, according to mother. Play repertoire included jigsaw puzzles, Play-doh, building with plastic blocks, pegboard landscape, simple mechanical and musical toys, drawing houses and people, swing and climber sets, large version of Tinkertoys, circus toy, block design box. Several new chores: sweeping floor, cleaning up living room.
Speech	Mute. No words.	Progressed through all stages of speech training and into the stage of conversational speech. Imitation of words quite strong; imitates almost any verbal stimulus. Imitative repertoire of at least 75 words. Labeling vocabulary of at least 50 words. Uses at least 20 different sentences (both mands and tacts). During 90-minute observation sessions, emitted an average of 115 appropriate verbal responses, 60 one- and two-word answers to questions, 17 sentences in response to parental initiations, 38 self-initiated sentences.
Autistic Aloneness	Values presence and attention of others, but is often aloof and indifferent and does not engage in cooperative play. Cooperates with 66% of parental exchange signals.	Much less aloof and indifferent. Often initiates exchanges with others with speech. Engages in cooperative play with siblings, working puzzles and building elaborate constructions with blocks. Cooperates with 92% of parental exchange signals.

Table 23: Behavioral Changes in Kristen White

Behavior	Prior to Training Program	During Follow-Up
Bizarre-Disruptive	Average of 9 disruptions per 90-minute session, including extremely loud and aversive screaming and meal disruptions. According to parents, screaming occurred with high frequency at all hours of day and night.	No screaming or meal disruptions during the observation periods. Parents indicated, moreover, that meal disruptions were almost nonexistent and that screaming rarely ever occurred anymore during the day.
Constructive Activity	Average duration 1 minute per 90-minute session. As observed during baseline, mother indicated that Kristen spent most of her time sitting in a chair, flapping belts and wires, or sniffing things. Rarely wanted to go outside, and seldom played on swing set when she did go out. Never played with available toys. Only chore was feeding dog.	Average duration 9 minutes per 90-minute session. Mother indicated that Kristen was spending at least several hours per day playing outside on swing and climber sets and was occasionally playing with available toys inside.
Speech	Functional speech present but very weak. Average of 28 appropriate verbal responses per 90-minute session (31% of which were self-initiated), including 2 sentences. Speech limited mainly to one- and two-word mands and tacts.	Self-initiated speech greatly strengthened. Average of 27 appropriate verbal responses per 90-min. session (80% of which were self-initiated), including 5 sentences. Average of 24 appropriate answers to questions (45% of which were unprompted) during structured 20-min. reading sessions. Asks mother to read her stories during the day and, as in structured reading sessions, answers questions about the stories.
Autistic Aloneness	Aloof and indifferent. Occupied most of the time in self-stimulation. Avoids presence of and physical contact with mother. Enjoys physical contact with father. Does not value praise or approval from either parent. No cooperative play. Cooperates with average of 46% of parental exchange signals.	Autistic aloneness markedly reduced. Initiates exchanges with mother (for stories). Self-stimulatory behavior present, but spends much time outside playing. Cooperative play beginning to develop. Seeks presence of other children and follows them around neighborhood as they play. Sometimes makes physical contact with them, e.g., holding hands. Cooperates with average of 85% of parental exchange signals.

ods and the researcher's consulting style. While the first three factors cannot readily be controlled, the last two can be. Suggestions will be discussed below.

Limitations of the Parent Training Program

Time Involved

The first major shortcoming of the Parent Training Program was the large amount of time spent training each family. Although the Training Program was quite effective in dealing with many targets of change, especially in the Hare and Nash families, the amount of time involved limits the number of families one consultant can work with. Also, the cost of that time would likely be prohibitive for most families or training facilities. During the year in which the Training Program was carried out, I spent approximately 480 hours (not including driving time) training these four families. If parent training programs are to made more widely available to families of autistic children and children with related disorders, the time factor will have to be reduced. Promising modifications will be discussed more fully later.

Application of Techniques

The Parent Training Program was quite successful overall in changing exchanges in the homes and thus fostering positive changes in the behavior of the children. However, a second limitation of the Training Program was its effectiveness in motivating and teaching some parents to apply the techniques in a consistent and wholehearted way. For example, the Whites were at times unwilling to apply the techniques at all. And with all the parents, in varying degrees, applying the techniques consistently and continuously was a problem. In fact, this was one of the main reasons why so much time was spent with the parents at home.

Three factors may account for the above problems. First, training sessions in the homes were, at most, two hours long. This may not have been enough time to replace the counterproductive patterns of behavior that had been in existence for years with new ones.

Second, other problems in the families inhibited the effectiveness of the training in more quickly replacing old patterns. Examples of such underlying problems are as follows:

1. The parents may have other behaviors "prepotent" over the child, lessening their willingness to apply the techniques, learn the techniques, or even work with the child on constructive behavior. For example, Mrs. White was torn between her wish to see Kristen lead a normal life, which would require much time and effort on her part, and her wish to lead a normal life herself.

2. There may be friction or hostility between the parents which prevents them from supporting one another in tense situations with the child and from accepting coaching from one another when they are working with the child. For example, when Kristen was screaming, Mr. White blamed Mrs. White for Kristen's screaming, instead of comforting Mrs. White or helping her to handle Kristen.

3. Other children's disruptive behavior may interfere with the parents' effective application of the techniques they have learned. Kristen's younger brother, for instance, invariably threw a tantrum whenever Mr. White played with Kristen.

4. The parents themselves may have strong behavior patterns that interfere with learning or applying the techniques. One parent was very literal-minded, and this prevented her from generalizing techniques to other situations or behavior problems of her child. Another parent was disorganized in scheduling family activities, and this prevented her from running sessions with her child on a continuous basis.

5. There may be negative sentiments, or at least a lack of positive sentiments, between the parents and the child. The implications of this are twofold: not only may the parents be less willing to work with their child, but the parents' praise and approval will not be rewarding to the child. Thus, an important source of reinforcement for appropriate behavior is absent.

6. Finally, the parents' methods for coping with their child's problem behaviors and behavior deficits may have been used for so
   many years that the two-hour training sessions at home were not
   sufficient to modify them for very long. Some parents are very
   solicitous to their child: they cannot do enough for the child, and
   constantly talk to and cuddle him or her. In sum, they give the
   child a great deal of noncontingent reinforcement, and thus waste
   reinforcers that they could use to strengthen appropriate behavior. Some parents, on the other hand, have learned to control
   their child's disruptive behavior in the short run with the threat
   of punishment. It was difficult at first to teach these parents to
   simply ignore disruptive behavior and to structure productive
   exchanges instead of spanking the child.

The third limitation may have been the contingencies of reinforcement affecting the parents. Many training programs are based
on the assumption that a powerful reinforcer for the parents is beneficial change in their child. Theoretically, the appearance of these
changes, coupled with praise from the consultant, should strengthen
and maintain the parents' application of teaching procedures in the
home. However, the situation is not that simple.

The rapid changes in the child's behavior which follow the parents' use of basic procedures (ignoring or timing out the child for
bizarre-disruptive behavior and immediately reinforcing even gross
approximations to appropriate behavior) at the start of training do
seem to strengthen parents' use of those procedures, increase their
interest in learning more procedures, and produce optimistic statements from them regarding their child's future. As mentioned, most
parent training programs end at that point. However, if, as in the
program reported here, the training is extended to include a wide
range of behaviors (eye contact, play, chores, motor and verbal imitation, functional speech), the contingencies of reinforcement on the
parents change. They are asked to spend more time teaching their
child, and when they begin to work on complex skills such as verbal
imitation and functional speech, teaching becomes even more pains-

taking and has many ups and downs. The parents go through many extinction trials for precious little reinforcement from their child. In sum, when they are working on many skills and harder skills, the relative amount of reinforcement decreases, while the cost (in terms of time and effort that could have been spent on other opportunities, such as a job, recreation, and rest) increases. Clearly, if parent training programs are to be comprehensive (that is, teach parents the large number of skills needed to foster an entire behavioral repertoire in their child), larger and more even amounts of reinforcement must be built in.

Implications for the Future

Suggested Modifications in Parent Training Programs

There are several ways to modify parent training programs in light of the above limitations. First, parents might spend the initial phases of training learning the skills that will help them manage home programs more on their own. Specifically, parents should be taught to assess their children in each of the skill areas they will later work on, for instance:

- social skills (eye contact, approaching others);
- small and gross motor skills;
- vocalizing (the frequency of vocalizations and the size of the phonemic repertoire);
- motor imitation;
- verbal imitation (sounds, words, phrases);
- functional speech;
- chores and
- self-help skills.

Once the parents have learned to assess their children's strengths and behavioral deficits, they could be taught how to design home programs for each skill area. This would involve specifying behavioral objectives, suggesting a possible series of successive approximations to or steps toward the objective, planning contingencies of reinforcement and special teaching methods to use at each step, taking data on the child's progress, and designing alternate programs in light of the data (Kozloff, 1994b).

Second, parents must have available to them, and must be helped to use, resources that can perform the same support and instruction functions performed by consultants. Examples are written and videotape materials, or Internet listservs and Web sites that contain papers, assessment instruments, and e-mail from other parents and services providers.

Parent groups should serve some of the functions performed by a consultant (Kozloff, 1979; Kozloff et al., 1988; Neef, 1995). For example, parents who have already worked on verbal imitation can be models and coaches for those who are just starting on it. Similarly, through videotape presentations or hearing parents describe their home programs, other families can both reinforce and serve as consultants for the parents. Continued contact between families would also help provide parents with the support and reinforcement they need when their child's progress is slow.

Finally, with respect to underlying problems in a family that interfere with the parents' training and effectively applying teaching procedures in the home, a feasible suggestion is to first teach parents how to manage the behavior of one of their typically developing children before they design and conduct home programs for their autistic child. Since a typically developing child will initiate and reciprocate exchanges more readily than an autistic child, this may help make parents more competent and confident in their use of the techniques before they try to tackle the problems of their autistic child.

Alternative Productive Exchanges and Bizarre-Disruptive Behavior

One of the more important findings of this research was that ignoring and/or timing out a child contingent upon bizarre-disruptive behavior are *not* effective *by themselves* in markedly reducing those behaviors. Although certain bizarre-disruptive behaviors may have been maintained by attention, merely removing that attention by ignoring or timing out the child does not greatly weaken, much less eliminate, the bizarre-disruptive behavior. Actually, using the ignoring and time-out techniques alone would, in effect, make the home a custodial environment. And it is clear from research on mental hospitals which serve a custodial function that patients not only do not lose their bizarre-disruptive behavior, but usually become worse.

Stated more positively, to greatly weaken bizarre-disruptive behavior, exchanges in the home have to be structured so that the child is both (1) ignored and/or timed out for bizarre-disruptive behavior *and* (2) given the opportunity to be reinforced for working exchanges involving constructive behavior. It should be pointed out that it is not enough merely to make productive (mutually rewarding) exchanges available to the child. The parents at the start have to initiate the alternative exchanges, and prompt the child to engage in the exchanges, before a child will begin to learn the constructive behavior.

Alternative exchanges were necessary, in other words, to build repertoires of constructive behavior that the child learned to use as an alternate way to obtain rewards. Gradually, as constructive behaviors (e.g., play and speech) became more fluent and perhaps more rewarding in themselves, extrinsic reinforcement was needed less often to maintain the constructive behavior.

The above statements are documented dramatically in the experimental reversals conducted in the Gordon, Hare, and Nash families. In the Gordon home, for example, when Peter was provided with toys and was rewarded for playing with them, and timed out for disruptive behavior, the frequency of disruptions fell to two per day.

During the three-day reversal, however, when all toys were removed and only the time-out contingency or exchange was in effect, Peter's disruptions increased to eight per day by the second day. And when he was again provided with toys and rewarded for playing, the frequency of his disruptions immediately decreased again. In other words, time out alone was not effective.

In the Hare and Nash families, during the C_1 period, Michael and Luke were systematically rewarded for playing and performing chores and ignored and/or timed out for disruptive behavior. As the duration of constructive activities increased, the frequency of bizarre-disruptive behavior decreased (to near zero in Michael's case, and immediately and consistently to zero in Luke's case). During the reversal (A_2), the parents stopped rewarding Michael and Luke for constructive behavior, but continued to ignore them or time them out contingent upon bizarre-disruptive behavior. In both cases, the duration of constructive behavior decreased and the frequency of bizarre-disruptive behavior rapidly increased. In Michael Hare's case, the frequency of bizarre-disruptive behavior increased above the frequency in A_1. Finally, when the alternative exchange was again made available (C_2), constructive behavior increased at least as high as during the C_1 period (in Michael's case there was an intensification of 25% in the duration of constructive activity) and a simultaneous decrease in bizarre-disruptive behavior (in Michael's case, the frequency after the reversal was even lower than in C_1). Again, ignoring and time out in the absence of alternative exchanges was ineffective in weakening bizarre-disruptive behavior.

Methods for Strengthening Self-Initiated Play

As was indicated earlier, during the A_1 period, the duration of appropriate play for all of the children was nearly zero. None played for more than ten minutes per day. By the end of the follow-up periods, however, all of the children were engaging in appropriate play—from approximately one hour per day (Peter Gordon) to four hours per day (Luke Nash). It is significant that the duration of playing initiated by the parents increased; it is of greater importance that the duration of self-initiated play increased, for self-initiated play is more like the play of typically developing children.

Two methods were effective in increasing the frequency and duration of self-initiated play. One method involved the following procedures. First, the parents ran play sessions each day, lasting from 20 minutes (Michael Hare, Peter Gordon, and Kristen White) to 90 minutes (Luke Nash). The parents were coached for approximately one week in procedures for:

1. *initiating* the play exchange (establishing a setting for teaching, encouraging the child's participation);
2. *teaching* the child to play through prompting, modeling, and shaping; and
3. *rewarding* the child intermittently with praise and, if needed, food while he or she played, and with backup reinforcers—music, TV, a car ride, etc.—at the conclusion of the session.

In addition, the parents made the play exchange available throughout the day. They were asked and coached to occasionally initiate the play exchange or encourage the child to play during the day, and to reward the child at those times as they had during the structured play sessions. Of special importance, they structured exchanges so that things the child indicated she wanted (e.g., music) were made contingent upon the child's playing for a brief period of time. For instance, if a child indicated that she wanted to hear music, the parent would say, "As soon as you _____, you can hear a record." If the child cooperated with the contractual signal by playing, the parent would praise the child and reward her after a few minutes with the thing she wanted. And, finally, if the child initiated play, the parents rewarded her with praise and a backup reinforcer after a few minutes of self-initiated play.

It was found that over time, the children initiated play more and more. At first, they would initiate play with some toy, play for a while, and then come to their parents for a reward. Later they began to initiate play seemingly for the enjoyment of playing, and did not come to their parents for a reward. They began to go outside and play on the swings or climber sets, work puzzles, play with Play-doh, or draw without signals from their parents and without coming to their parents for a reward.

The second method focused on strengthening self-initiated play as a class of behavior. This method, used with Peter Gordon, involved the following steps:

1. making several new toys available to Peter by placing them on a table;
2. waiting for Peter to make contact with any of the toys and immediately rewarding him with praise and a bite of food;
3. sitting at the table with Peter and teaching him to play with the toy, rewarding him intermittently as he played;
4. removing the toy he was playing with after a few minutes and waiting for him to make contact with another of the available toys, and repeating Step 3 if and when he made contact; and
5. leaving the toys available to Peter for the rest of the day, repeating the above steps if and when he initiated play with any of them.

As indicated in Chapter 5, this method was somewhat effective at first in strengthening Peter's self-initiated play. On Day 1, the duration of Peter's self-initiated play was 87 minutes. By Day 9, it had increased to 130 minutes. By Day 17, however, the duration of self-initiated play as well as the frequency of initiations began to decrease. By Day 35, Peter engaged in self-initiated play for only 25 minutes. Despite the gradual weakening of Peter's self-initiated play, this second method may have promise for strengthening play in autistic children, because it increases the frequency of the child's contacts with play objects.

Multiple Questions

In the families studied, parents often used multiple questions (also known as nagging) to promote speech or cooperation from their child. For instance, if a parent asked the child a question, and the child either did not answer or did not answer appropriately, the parent was likely to repeat the same question over and over until either the child finally answered correctly or the parent gave up.

An important finding from an ABAB experiment with Peter Gordon and his mother as reported in Chapter 5 is that instead of promoting appropriate verbal responses from the child, multiple questions *inhibit* appropriate verbal responses. In the A_1 and A_2 periods, in which Mrs. Gordon predominantly used multiple questions when asking Peter about objects in a storybook or on picture cards, his rate of appropriate answers either remained at a very low level (A_1) or decreased sharply (A_2). In the B_1 and B_2 periods, on the other hand, Mrs. Gordon used only single questions—i.e., went on to another question if Peter made no response or gave an inappropriate response. Under this condition, Peter's rate of appropriate answers rapidly increased to and remained at a high level. Future parent training programs will have to focus from the very beginning on changing parents' use of multiple questions to initiate exchanges, and teach parents to use only single questions.

Experimental Reversals and Reinforcement Control

The findings of the short-term experimental reversals conducted with each family cut with a two-edged sword. The reversals showed that the rewarding exchanges managed by the parents seemed to control the behavior of their children. When reinforcement for playing and talking was no longer available, playing and talking decreased. And when reinforcement was again available, playing and talking quickly accelerated to the previous high levels or higher.

In a very strong sense, I would have preferred to see those reversals fail. For while they indicated strong reinforcement control, they also indicated how easily those behaviors—worked on so painstakingly by the parents—could deteriorate.

The task for future work, then, is not to teach parents merely to reinforce their autistic children more often. Rather, the task is to teach parents how to give their child the kind of practice that leads to fluency, endurance, and retention of performance (Binder, 1996), and how to teach using more "natural" contingencies (Ferster, 1967) as described in the recent work of Koegel, Bimbela, and Schreibman (1996).

Summary

The implications for further work concern extensive analyses of structured exchanges of progressive complexity, and the development of sophisticated techniques for identifying complex exchange signals and reciprocations, however weak or subtle they may be. In addition, we need to develop accessible and affordable services to families as early as possible, when their children's socialization is less difficult. There is indeed a quality of urgency in the implications for further research outlined here. For if such research can be undertaken soon, it might be possible for many of the present generation of autistic and other severely impaired children to bridge the behavioral gaps which hinder their entry into the larger community.

Appendices: Developmental Histories of the Children

Appendix I*: Infantile Syndrome (to Age 2)

Item	Michael Hare 1-31-60	Luke Nash 5-10-61	Peter Gordon 5-19-60	Kristen White 12-27-60
Conditions Surrounding Birth				
1. Pregnancy and delivery	Both normal	Pregnancy troubled; delivery routine	—	Both normal
2. Premature birth	No	No	—	No
3. Oxygen given in first week	No	No	No	No
4. Appearance during first week	Average, don't know, or other	Average, don't know, or other	Unusually healthy looking	Unusually healthy looking
5. Health in first three months	Constipation	Excellent	Excellent	Excellent
Autistic Aloneness				
6. Reaction to bright lights, colors, unusual sounds	Unusually unresponsive	Average, or don't know	Average, or don't know	Average

* From Bernard Rimland's Diagnostic Check List for Behavior-Disturbed Children (E-2).

Item	Michael Hare	Luke Nash	Peter Gordon	Kristen White
7. Reaching out or preparing to be picked up upon mother's approach	No	Yes	Yes	Yes
8. Did child like to be held?	Only when and how he preferred	Yes	Yes	Yes
9. Imitate another person	No, or not sure	—	No, or not sure	Waved bye-bye, pat-a-cake, peek-a-boo, etc.
10. Did parent suspect deafness?	No	Yes	No	No
Speech				
11. Age child said first word	Never used words	8-12 months	16-24 months	13-15 months
12. Did child start to talk and then become silent?	Never began talking	Yes, at 16 months	Never began talking	Yes, at 2 years
13. Quality of pronounciation of first words	No words	Average or below average	Too little speech to tell	Too little speech to tell
14. Did child refer to himself on first learning to talk?	No, or too little speech to tell	No, or too little speech to tell	No, or too little speech to tell	No, or too little speech to tell
15. When child talked, did he understand what he was saying?	Never talked	Didn't talk enough to tell	Didn't talk enough to tell	No doubt that child understood
16. Has child used the word "Yes"?	No speech	Other words or phrases but not "yes"	No speech	Other words or phrases but not "yes"
17. Did child imitate "yes" by repeating the question?	No speech	Too little speech to tell	Too little speech to tell	Yes, does not say "yes" directly
Bizarre-Disruptive Behavior				
18. Did child rock in crib?	No, or very little	Yes, quite a lot	No, or very little	No

Item	Michael Hare	Luke Nash	Peter Gordon	Kristen White
Motor Skills				
19. Age child learned to walk alone	19-24 months	8-12 months	13-15 months	13-16 months
20. Transition from crawling to walking	Prolonged crawling	Normal	Normal	Normal
Cognitive Skills				
21. Did child seem intelligent during first year?	Looked somewhat dull	Suspected high intelligence	Suspected average intelligence	Suspected average intelligence
22. Memory before age 3	Remarkable memory for songs, routes, etc.	No evidence for remarkable memory	Remarkable memory for music (humming only)	Remarkable memory for songs (in words and humming), places, routes, etc.
From Present Perspective, at What Age Did Abnormal Behavior Begin?	First 3 months (father); 7-12 months (mother)	16 months	2-3 years	2-3 years

Appendix 2: Early Childhood Syndrome (2-5 Years)

Item	Michael Hare	Luke Nash	Peter Gordon	Kristen White
Overall Description of Child				
1. Parent's description of child	Hyperactive, aloof, indifferent, remote, self-contented	Hyperactive, watches TV for long periods, confused, self-concerned, worried, perplexed, dependent	Hyperactive, aloof, indifferent, remote, self-contented	Sits for long periods, staring into space or playing aimlessly and repetitively with objects; aloof, indifferent, remote, self-contented

Item	Michael Hare	Luke Nash	Peter Gordon	Kristen White
Autistic Aloneness				
2. Is child "deaf" to some sounds but hears others?	Yes	No	No	No
3. Looks or "walks" through people as though they weren't there	No	Yes, I think so	No	No
4. Was child unreachable, "in a shell," distant?	Once in awhile	Yes, an accurate description	Yes, an accurate description	Yes, an accurate description
5. Can you direct child's attention to distant objects?	Rarely	Yes	Rarely	Rarely
6. Does child look at the eyes of those who talk to him?	Usually	Never or rarely	Rarely	Never or rarely
7. Is child cuddly?	Average	Definitely likes to cling to adults	No, rather stiff and awkward to hold	No, rather stiff and awkward to hold
8. Physically pliable (led easily; melts into your arms)?	Normal	Normal	Definitely not pliable	Definitely not pliable
9. Does child seem to want to be liked?	Just normally so	Unusually so	Indifferent to being liked	Indifferent to being liked
10. Sensitive and/or affectionate	Not sensitive to criticism, but affectionate	Sensitive to criticism and affectionate	Sensitive to criticism and sometimes affectionate	Neither sensitive to criticism nor affectionate
11. Gleeful when pleased	No or rarely	Yes, typically	No or rarely	Yes, typically
12. Strong insistence on listening to music or records	Yes, on certain records	Liked but did not demand music	Liked but did not demand music	Yes, on certain records
Speech				
13. Is child's naming or pointing vocabulary out of proportion to his ability to communicate?	Doesn't use or understand words	Can point to many objects, but does not speak	Doesn't use or understand words	Can correctly name many objects, but not communicate

Item	Michael Hare	Luke Nash	Peter Gordon	Kristen White
14. Does child repeat, echo, or parrot words or phrases he has heard?	No speech	No speech	No speech	Some speech, but not echolalic
15. Can child answer a single question?	Too little speech to tell	Too little speech to tell	Too little speech to tell	Too little speech to tell
16. Can child understand what is said to him judging by his ability to follow instructions?	Understands a little if you repeat and repeat	Yes, very well	Yes, fairly well	Yes, very well
17. Takes adult's hand to get things for him	Yes	Yes	Yes	Yes
18. How does child usually say "No" or refuse something?	Other, or too little speech to tell	Would ignore you	Other, or too little speech to tell	Would just say "No"
Bizarre-Disruptive Behavior				
19. Strange hand postures	Yes	No	Yes	No
20. Rhythmic or rocking for long periods	No	Yes	Yes, only for short periods	Yes
21. Unusual craving for things to eat or chew	Certain foods, as well as plastics, leather	No	Yes, spicy food	Yes, chews many objects
22. Hits own head	Never or rarely	Never or rarely	Yes, slapping with hand	Yes, slapping with hand
23. Is child destructive?	Not deliberately or severely	Not deliberately or severely	Not especially	Not especially
24. Child hits, pinches, bites, or otherwise injures self or others	No	Yes, others only	Yes	Yes, self and sometimes others
25. Child whirls himself	Yes, sometimes	Yes, often	No	No

Item	Michael Hare	Luke Nash	Peter Gordon	Kristen White
26. Child spins objects	Yes, often and for long periods	Very seldom or never	Very seldom or never	Very seldom or never
27. Interest in mechanical objects	Average	Average	Below average	Little or no interest
Motor Skills				
28. Physical coordination	Below average or poor	Unusually graceful	About average	Unusually graceful
29. Skill in doing fine work with fingers	A little or very awkward	Average for age	A little or very awkward	Average to exceptional for age
30. Any skills above average for age	None	Puzzles, perfect musical pitch	Perfect musical pitch	Perfect musical pitch
31. Refusal to use hands for extended periods	No	No	Yes	No
32. Falling while running or climbing	Never or almost never	Average	Never or almost never	Never or almost never
Preservation of Sameness				
33. Lining things precisely	No	Yes	Not sure	No
34. Reaction to being interrupted	Sometimes mildly but rarely very upset	Sometimes mildly but rarely very upset	Sometimes mildly but rarely very upset	Rarely or never upset
35. Complicated rituals which if not followed upset him	No	Yes	No	No
36. Gets upset if certain usual arrangements are changed	No	No	Yes, definitely	No
37. Extreme fearfulness	Only normal	Only normal	Only normal	Ignores or is unaware of fearsome objects

Item	Michael Hare	Luke Nash	Peter Gordon	Kristen White
Other				
38. EEG	No, or don't know	Normal	Normal	Normal
39. Diagnoses made of child in order of occurrence	Noncommittal (family physician); Aphasia (State Univ. Medical Center); Aphasia (now confirmed by family physician); Exceptional child (psychiatrist)	Autistic (Child Guidance Clinic)	Autistic (neurologist); Retarded (psychologist); Noncommittal (physician); Noncommittal (nursery school); Autistic, Retarded (hospital staff); Hyperkinetic (special school district); Hyperkinetic (neurologist); Autistic (psychologist); Noncommittal (psychologist)	Autistic (psychologist); Not Aphasic (second psychologist)
*40. Punishment history	Rarely or never either before or after onset	Many threats and occasional strappings after onset	Rare, mild spanking contingent upon specific classes of disruptive behavior, only after onset	Much verbal abuse & some spanking contingent on minor infractions (spilling milk, touching certain objects) prior to onset. Severe slapping contingent on screaming (on the advice of a psychologist) after onset.
41. Evidence of early social isolation or sensory deprivation	None available	None available	None available	None available

* Item not included on Rimland form.

References

Abidin, R.R., Jenkins, C.L., & McGaughey, M.C. (1992). The relationship of early family variables to children's subsequent behavioral adjustment. *Journal of Clinical Child Psychology, 21*(1), 60-69.

Allen, K.E., & Harris, F.R. (1966). Elimination of a child's excessive scratching by training the mother in reinforcement procedures. *Behaviour Research and Therapy, 4,* 79-84.

Anderson, S.R., Avery, D.L., DiPietro, E.K., Edwards, G.L., & Christian, W.P. (1987). Intensive home-based early intervention with autistic children. *Education and Treatment of Children, 10,* 352-366.

Arnstein, H.S. (1965). An approach to the severely disturbed child. In P.T.B. Weston (Ed.), *Some approaches to teaching autistic children* (pp. 1-7). Oxford: Pergamon Press.

Axelrod, S., & Apsche, J. (1983). *The effects of punishment on human behavior.* New York: Academic Press.

Ayllon, T. (1965a). Intensive treatment of psychotic behavior by stimulus satiation and food reinforcement. In L.P. Ullmann & L. Krasner (Eds.), *Case studies in behavior modification* (pp. 77-83). New York: Holt, Rinehart & Winston.

Ayllon, T. (1965b). Some behavioral problems associated with eating in chronic schizophrenic patients. In L.P. Ullmann & L. Krasner (Eds.), *Case studies in behavior modification* (pp. 73-77). New York: Holt, Rinehart & Winston.

Ayllon, T., & Azrin, N. (1968). *The token economy.* New York: Appleton-Century-Crofts.

Ayllon, T., & Michael, J. (1959). The psychiatric nurse as a behavioral engineer. *Journal of the Experimental Analysis of Behavior, 2,* 323-334.

Baer, D.M. (1968). Some remedial uses of the reinforcement contingency. In J.M. Shlien (Ed.), *Research in psychotherapy: Vol. III* (pp. 3-21). Washington, DC: American Psychological Association.

Baer, D., & Sherman, J. (1964). Reinforcement control of generalized imitation in young children. *Journal of Experimental Child Psychology, 1,* 37-49.

Baer, D., & Wolf, M.M. (1967). *The entry into natural communities of reinforcement.* Paper presented at the annual meeting of the American Psychological Association.

Bailey, A., Phillips, W., & Rutter, M. (1996). Autism: Towards an integration of clinical, genetic, neuropsychological, and neurobiological perspectives. *Journal of Child Psychology and Psychiatry, 37,* 89-126.

Bandura, A., & Walters, R.H. (1959). *Adolescent aggression.* New York: Ronald Press Co.

Bandura, A., & Walters, R.H. (1963). *Social learning and personality development.* New York: Holt, Rinehart & Winston.

Barker, R. (Ed.) (1963). *The stream of behavior.* New York: Appleton-Century-Crofts.

Barker, R. (1968). *Ecological psychology.* Stanford, CA: Stanford University Press.

Baron-Cohen, S. (1990). Autism: A specific cognitive disorder of "mind blindness." *International Journal of Psychiatry, 2,* 81-90.

Bart, D.S. (1984). The differential diagnosis of special education: Managing social pathology as individual disability. In L. Barton & S. Tomlinson (Eds.), *Special education and social interests* (pp. 81-121). New York: Nichols Publishing Company.

Bateson, G., Jackson, D., Haley, J., & Weakland, J. (1956). Toward a theory of schizophrenia. *Behavioral Science, 1,* 251-264.

Becker, W., Engelmann, S., & Thomas, D. (1971). *Teaching: A course in applied psychology.* Chicago: SRA Associates.

Becker, W.C., & Carnine, D.W. (1981). Direct instruction: A behavior theory model for comprehensive educational intervention with the disadvantaged. In S.W. Bijou & R. Ruiz (Eds.), *Behavior modification: Contributions to education* (pp. 145-210). Hillsdale, NJ: Lawrence Erlbaum Associates.

Becker, W.C., Engelmann, S., & Thomas, D. (1971). *Teaching: A course in applied psychology.* Chicago, IL: SRA Associates.

Bender, L. (1953). Childhood schizophrenia. *Psychiatric Quarterly, 27,* 663-681.

Bender, L. (1960). Autism in children with mental deficiency. *American Journal of Mental Deficiency, 63,* 81-86.

Bender, L., & Grugett, A.E. (1956). A study of certain epidemiological factors in a group of children with childhood schizophrenia. *American Journal of Orthopsychiatry, 26,* 131-145.

Bettelheim, B. (1967). *The empty fortress.* Toronto: Collier-Macmillan.

Bijou, S.W. (1967). Experimental studies of child behavior, normal and deviant. In L. Krasner & L.P. Ullmann (Eds.), *Research in behavior modification* (pp. 56-82). New York: Holt, Rinehart & Winston.

Bijou, S.W., Peterson, R.F., & Ault, M.H. (1968). A method to investigate descriptive and experimental field studies at the level of data and empirical concepts. *Journal of Applied Behavior Analysis, 1,* 175-191.

Binder, C. (1996). Behavioral fluency: Evolution of a new paradigm. *The Behavior Analyst, 19,* 163-197.

Binder, C., Haughton, E., & Van Eyk, D. (1990). Precision teaching attention span. *Teaching Exceptional Children, Spring,* 24-27.

Binder, C., & Watkins, C.L. (1990). Precision teaching and direct instruction: Mea-

surably superior instructional technology in schools. *Performance Improvement Quarterly, 3,* 74-95.

Blau, P.M. (1964). *Exchange and power in social life.* New York: John Wiley & Sons.

Bornstein, M.H., & Ludemann, P.M. (1989). Habituation at home. *Infant Behavior and Development, 12,* 25-29.

Boullin, D.J., Coleman, M., O'Brien, R.A., & Rimland, B. (1971). Laboratory predictions of infantile autism based on 5-hydroxytryptamine efflux from blood platelets and their correlation with the Rimland E-2 score. *Journal of Autism and Childhood Schizophrenia, 1,* 63-71.

Brazelton, T., Koslowski, B., & Main, M. (1974). The origins of reciprocity: The early mother-infant interaction. In M. Lewis & L.A. Rosenblum (Eds.), *The effect of the infant on its caregiver* (pp. 49-76). New York: John Wiley & Sons.

Brazelton, T.B., Tronick, E., Adamson, L., Als, H., & Wise, S. (1975). Early mother-infant reciprocity. In M.A. Hofer (Ed.), *The parent-infant relationship* (pp. 137-155). London: Ciba.

Brewer, H.A., & Kakalik, J.S. (1979). *Handicapped children: Strategies for improving services.* New York: McGraw-Hill.

Bricker, D., & Casuso, V. (1979). Family involvement: A critical component of early intervention. *Exceptional Children, 46*(2), 108-116.

Bromwich, R.M. (1976). Focus on maternal behavior in infant interaction. *American Journal of Orthopsychiatry, 46,* 439-446.

Bronfenbrenner, U. (1979). *The ecology of human development.* Cambridge, MA: Harvard University Press.

Brotherson, M.J., & Goldstein, B.L. (1992). Time as a resource and constraint for parents of young children with disabilities: Implications for early intervention services. *Topics in Early Childhood Special Education, 12*(4), 508-527.

Brown, J. (1960). Prognosis from presenting symptoms of preschool children with atypical development. *American Journal of Orthopsychiatry, 30,* 382-390.

Bruner, J.S. (1983). *Child talk: Learning to use language.* New York: Norton.

Bryson, S.E. (1996). Brief report: Epidemiology of autism. *Journal of Autism and Developmental Disorders, 26,* 165-167.

Campbell, M., Perry, R., Small, A.M., & Green, W.H. (1987). Overview of drug treatment in autism. In E. Schopler & G. Mesibov (Eds.), *Neurobiological issues in autism* (pp. 341-356). New York: Plenum Press.

Canter, L., & Canter, M. (1991). *Parents on your side: A comprehensive parent involvement program for teachers.* Santa Monica, CA: Lee Canter & Associates.

Carlson, C.F. (1967). *A neurological model of early infantile autism and its therapeutic implications.* Paper presented at the APA Symposium on Early Infantile Autism, Columbia, MO.

Carlson, C.S., Arnold, C.R., Becker, W.C., & Madsen, C.H. (1968). The elimination of tantrum behavior of a child in an elementary classroom. *Behaviour Research and Therapy, 6,* 117-119.

Carr, E.G., Levin, L., McConnachie, G., Carlson, J.I., Kemp, D.C., & Smith, C.E. (1994). *Communication-based intervention for problem behavior.* Baltimore, MD: Paul H. Brookes Publishing Co.

Cohn, J.F., & Tronick, E.Z. (1987). Mother-infant face-to-face interaction: The sequence of dyadic states at 3, 6, and 9 months. *Developmental Psychology, 23*(1), 68-77.

Cole, J.D., Lochman, J.E., Terry, R., & Hyman, C. (1992). Predicting early adolescent disorder from childhood aggression and peer rejection. *Journal of Consulting and Clinical Psychology, 60*(5), 783-792.

Coleman, M. (1987). The search for neurological subgroups in autism. In E. Schopler & G. Mesibov (Eds.), *Neurobiological issues in autism* (pp. 163-178). New York: Plenum Press.

Coleman, M., & Gillberg, C. (1985). *The biology of the autistic syndromes.* New York: Praeger.

Connolly, K., & Dalgleish, M. (1989). The emergence of tool-using in infancy. *Developmental Psychology, 25*(6), 894-912.

Courchesne, E. (1989). Neuroanatomical systems involved in infantile autism. In G. Dawson (Ed.), *Autism: Nature, diagnosis, and treatment* (pp. 119-143). New York: Guilford Press.

Creak, M., & Ini, S. (1960). Families of psychotic children. *Journal of Child Psychology and Psychiatry, 2,* 156-175.

Culp, R.E., Little, V., Letts, D., & Lawrence, H. (1991). Maltreated children's self-concept: Effects of a comprehensive treatment program. *American Journal of Orthopsychiatry, 61*(6), 114-121.

Cutler, B.C. (1991). *Families and services in autism: Promises to keep.* Unpublished doctoral dissertation, School of Education, Boston University, Boston, MA.

Cutler, B.C., & Kozloff, M.A. (1987). Living with autism: Effects on families and family needs. In D.J. Cohen, A. Donnellan, & R. Paul (Eds.), *Handbook of autism and pervasive developmental disorders* (pp. 513-527). New York: John Wiley & Sons.

Darling, R.B. (1979). *Families against society: A study of reactions to children with birth defects.* Beverly Hills, CA: Sage Publications.

Davison, G.C. (1964). A social learning therapy program with an autistic child. *Behaviour Research and Therapy, 2,* 149.

Dawson, G. (1996). Brief report: Neuropsychology of autism: A report on the state of the science. *Journal of Autism and Developmental Disorders, 26,* 179-183

Dawson, G., & Lewy, A. (1989a). Arousal, attention, and socioemotional impairments of individuals with autism. In G. Dawson (Ed.), *Autism: Nature, diagnosis, and treatment* (pp. 49-74). New York: Guilford Press.

Dawson, G., & Lewy, A. (1989b). Reciprocal subcortical-cortical influences in autism. In G. Dawson (Ed.), *Autism: Nature, diagnosis, and treatment* (pp. 144-173). New York: Guilford Press.

Dawson, M.M., Catania, J.J., Schell, A.M., & Grings, W.W. (1979). Autonomic classical conditioning as a function of awareness of stimulus contingencies. *Biological Psychology, 9,* 23-40.

Demchack, M. (1989). A comparison of graduated guidance and increasing assistance in teaching adults with severe handicaps leisure skills. *Education and Training in Mental Retardation, 24*(1), 45-55.

DeMyer, M.K. (1979). *Parents and children in autism.* Washington, DC: Winston.

DeMyer, M.K., Barton, S., DeMyer, W.E., Norton, J.A., Allen, J., & Steele, R. (1973). Prognosis in autism: A follow-up study. *Journal of Autism and Childhood Schizophrenia, 3,* 199-246.

DesLauriers, A.M., & Carlson, C.F. (1969). *Your child is asleep.* Homewood, IL: Dorsey Press.

Didden, R., de Moor, J., & Bruyns, W. (1997). Effectiveness of DRO tokens in decreasing disruptive behavior in the classroom with five multiply handicapped children. *Behavioral Interventions, 2,* 65-75.

Dishion, T.J., Spracklen, K.M., Andrews, D.W., & Patterson, G.R. (1996). Deviancy training in male adolescent friendships. *Behavior Therapy, 27*(3), 373-390.

Donnellan, A.M., Mirenda, P.L., Mesaros, R.A., & Fassbender, L.L. (1984). Analyzing the communicative functions of aberrant behavior. *Journal of the Association for Persons with Severe Handicaps, 3,* 201-212.

Dougherty, K.M., & Johnston, J.M. (1996). Overlearning, fluency, and automaticity. *The Behavior Analyst, 19,* 289-292.

Downey, G., & Walker, E. (1989). Social cognition and adjustment in children at risk for psychopathology. *Developmental Psychology, 25*(5), 835-845.

Ducharme, J.M. (1996). Errorless compliance training: Optimizing clinical efficacy. *Behavior Modification, 20,* 259-280.

Ducharme, J., & Van Houten, R. (1994). Operant extinction in the treatment of severe maladaptive behavior: Adapting research to practice. *Behavior Modification, 18,* 139-170.

Dumas, J., LaFreniere, P.J., Beaudin, L., & Verlaan, P. (1992). Mother-child interactions in competent and aggressive dyads: Implications of relationship stress for behavior therapy with families. *New Zealand Journal of Psychology, 21*(1), 3-13.

Dunlap, K. (1932). *Habits: Their making and unmaking.* New York: Liveright.

Durand, M.V. (1990). *Severe behavior problems: A functional communication training approach.* New York: Guilford Press.

Durand, V.M., & Carr, E.G. (1987). Social influences on "self-stimulatory" behavior: Analysis and treatment application. *Journal of Applied Behavior Analysis, 20,* 119-132.

Durand, V.M., & Carr, E.G. (1992). An analysis of maintenance following functional communication training. *Journal of Applied Behavior Analysis, 25,* 777-794.

Eisenberg, L. (1956). The autistic child in adolescence. *American Journal of Psychiatry, 112,* 607-612.

Eisenberg, L., & Kanner, L. (1956). Early infantile autism, 1943-1955. *American Journal of Orthopsychiatry, 26,* 556-566.

Emerson, R.M. (1969). Operant psychology and exchange theory. In R.L. Burgess & D. Bushell, Jr. (Eds.), *Behavioral sociology* (pp. 379-405). New York: Columbia University Press.

Engelmann, S., & Carnine, D. (1991). *Theory of instruction: Principles and applications (Revised edition).* Eugene, OR: ADI Press.

Engelmann, S., & Colvin, S. (1983). *Generalized compliance training: A direct instruction program for managing severe behavior problems.* Austin, TX: Pro-Ed.

Engeln, R., Knutson, J., Laughy, L., & Garlington, W. (1968). Behavior modification techniques applied to a family unit: A case study. *Journal of Child Psychology and Psychiatry, 9,* 245-252.

Featherstone, H. (1980). *A difference in the family.* New York: Basic Books.

Fenske, E.C., Zalenski, S., Krantz, P.J., & McClannahan, L.E. (1985). Age at intervention and treatment outcome for autistic children in a comprehensive intervention program. *Analysis and Intervention in Developmental Disabilities, 5,* 7-31.

Ferritor, D. (1969). *Modifying interaction patterns: An experimental training program for families of autistic children.* Unpublished doctoral dissertation, Washington University, St. Louis, MO.

Ferster, C.B. (1958). Reinforcement and punishment in the control of human behavior by social *agencies. Psychiatric Research Reports, 10,* 101-118.

Ferster, C.B. (1967). Arbitrary and natural reinforcement. *Psychological Review, 17,* 341-347.

Ferster, C.B. (1968). Positive reinforcement and behavioral deficits of autistic children. In H.C. Quay (Ed.), *Children's behavior disorders* (pp. 107-132). Princeton, NJ: D. Van Nostrand.

Ferster, C.B., & DeMyer, M.K. (1961). The development of performances of autistic children in an automatically controlled environment. *Journal of Chronic Diseases, 13,* 312-345.

Ferster, C.B., & DeMyer, M.K. (1965). A method for the experimental analysis of autistic children. In L.P. Ullmann & L. Krasner (Eds.), *Case studies in behavior*

modification (pp. 121-130). New York: Holt, Rinehart & Winston.

Ferster, C.B., & Perrott, M.C. (1968). *Behavior principles.* New York: Meredith Corporation.

Field, T. (1989). Individual and maturational differences in infant expressivity. *New Directions for Child Development, 44*(Summer), 9-23.

Fischer, S.M., Iwata, B.A., & Mazaleski, J.L. (1997). Noncontingent delivery of arbitrary reinforcers as treatment for self-injurious behavior. *Journal of Applied Behavior Analysis, 30,* 239-249.

Fogel, A. (1992). Movement and communication in infancy: The social dynamics of development. *Human Movement Science, 11*(4), 387-423.

Fogon, J., & Schor, D. (1993). Mothers of children with spina bifida: Factors related to maternal psychosocial functioning. *American Journal of Orthopsychiatry, 63,* 1, 146-152.

Folstein, S.E., & Rutter, M. (1987). Familial aggregation and genetic implications. In E. Schopler & G. Mesibov (Eds.), *Neurobiological issues in autism* (pp. 83-105). New York: Plenum Press.

Fox, L., Dunlap, G., & Philbrick, L.A. (1997). Providing individual supports to young children with autism and their families. *Journal of Early Intervention, 21*(1), 1-14.

Frank, G. (1965). The role of the family in the development of psychopathology. *Psychological Bulletin, 64,* 191-205.

Frank, J. (1961). *Persuasion and healing.* New York: Schocken Books.

Frankenberg, W.K., & Dodd, J.B. (1967). The Denver developmental screening test. *Journal of Pediatrics, 71*(2), 181 191.

Fuller, P.R. (1949). Operant conditioning of a vegetative human organism. *American Journal of Psychology, 62,* 587-590.

Gagné, R.M., Briggs, L.J., & Wager, W.W. (1992). *Principles of instructional design* (4th ed.). Fort Worth, TX: Harcourt Brace Jovanovich.

Gast, D.L., Ault, M.J., Wolery, M., Doyle,

P.M., & Belanger, S. (1988). Comparison of constant time delay and the system of least prompts in teaching sight word reading to students with moderate mental retardation. *Education and Training in Mental Retardation, 23*(2), 117-128.

Gaultieri, T., Evans, R.W., & Patterson, D.R. (1987). The medical treatment of autistic people. In E. Schopler & G. Mesibov (Eds.), *Neurobiological issues in autism* (pp. 373-388). New York: Plenum Press.

Gaylord-Ross, R., & Holvoet, J. (1985). *Strategies of educating students with severe handicaps.* Boston: Little, Brown, & Co.

Gelfand, D.M., & Hartmann, D.P. (1968). Behavior therapy with children: A review and evaluation of research methodology. *Psychological Bulletin, 69*(3), 204-215.

Gelfand, D.M., & Hartman, D.P. (1984). *Child behavior analysis and therapy* (2nd ed.). New York: Pergamon.

Goetz, L., & Sailor, W. (1988). New directions: Communication development in persons with severe disabilities. *Topics in Language Disorders, 8*(4), 41-54.

Goffman, E. (1963). *Stigma: Notes on the management of spoiled identity.* New York: Simon & Schuster.

Goldfarb, W. (1955). Emotional and intellectual consequences of psychologic deprivation in infancy: A revaluation. In P.H. Hoch & J. Zubin (Eds.), *Psychopathology of childhood* (pp. 105-119). New York: Grune & Stratton.

Goldstein, K. (1959). Abnormal conditions in infancy. *Journal of Nervous and Mental Diseases, 128,* 538-557.

Goode, D.A. (1984). Socially produced identities, intimacy, and the problem of competence among the retarded. In L. Barton & S. Tomlinson (Eds.), *Special education and social interests* (pp. 228-249). New York: Nichols Publishing Co.

Goodwin, M.S., Cowen, M.A., & Goodwin, T.C. (1971). Malabsorption and cerebral dysfunction: A multivariate and comparative study of autistic children. *Journal of*

Autism and Childhood Schizophrenia, 1(1), 48-62.

Green, L., Fein, D., Joy, S., & Waterhouse, L. (1995). Cognitive functioning in autism. In E. Schopler & G. Mesibov (Eds.), *Learning and cognition in autism* (pp. 13-31). New York: Plenum Press.

Guess, D., Helmstetter, E., Turnbull, H.R., & Knowlton, S. (1987). *Use of aversive procedures with persons who are disabled: An historical review and critical analysis.* Seattle, WA: The Association for Persons with Severe Handicaps.

Haley, J. (1959). The family of the schizophrenic: A model system. *Journal of Nervous and Mental Diseases, 129,* 357-374.

Halle, J.W., Baer, D.M., & Spradlin, J.E. (1981). An analysis of teachers' generalized use of delay in helping children: A stimulus control procedure to increase language use in handicapped children. *Journal of Applied Behavior Analysis, 14,* 389-409.

Hamblin, R.L, Buckholdt, D., Ferritor, D., Kozloff, M., & Blackwell, L. (1971). *The humanization processes.* New York: John Wiley & Sons.

Hamblin, R.L., Ferritor, D.E., Blackwell, L.J., & Kozloff, M.A. (1968). *Structured exchange and childhood learning: The severely retarded child.* Technical Report No. 3. St. Ann, MO: Central Midwestern Regional Educational Laboratory, Inc.

Hammock, R.G., Schroeder, S.R., & Levine, W.R. (1995). The effect of Clozapine on self-injurious behavior. *Journal of Autism and Developmental Disorders, 25,* 611ff.

Hanley, G.P., Piazza, C.C., & Fisher, W.W. (1997). Noncontingent presentation of attention and alternative stimuli in the treatment of attention-maintained destructive behavior. *Journal of Applied Behavior Analysis, 2,* 229-237.

Haring, N.G. (1988). *Generalization for students with severe handicaps: Strategies and solutions.* Seattle: University of Washington Press.

Haring, N.G., White, O.R., & Liberty, K.A. (1978). *An investigation of phases of learning and facilitating instructional events for the severely handicapped. An annual progress report, 1977-78.* Bureau of Education of the Handicapped, Project No. 443CH70564. Seattle, WA: University of Washington, College of Education.

Harlow, H.F. (1949). The formation of learning sets. *Psychological Review, 56,* 51-65.

Harris, S., Handleman, J.S., Kristoff, B., Bass, L., & Gordon, R. (1990). Changes in language development among autistic and peer children in segregated and integrated preschool settings. *Journal of Autism and Developmental Disorders, 20,* 23-32.

Harris, S.L., Handleman, J.S., Gordon, R., Kristoff, B., & Fuentes, F. (1991). Changes in cognitive and language functioning of preschool children with autism. *Journal of Autism and Developmental Disorders, 21*(3), 281-290.

Hart, B.M., Allen, K.E., Buell, J.S., Harris, F.R., & Wolf, M.M. (1965). Effects of social reinforcement on operant crying. In L.P. Ullmann & L. Krasner (Eds.), *Case studies in behavior modification* (pp. 320-325). New York: Holt, Rinehart & Winston.

Hart, B., & Risley, T. (1975). Incidental teaching of language in the preschool. *Journal of Applied Behavior Analysis, 8,* 411-420.

Hashimoto, T., Tayama, M., Murakawa, K., Yoshimoto, T., Miyazaki, M., Harada, M., & Kurado, Y. (1995). Development of the brainstem and cerebellum in autistic patients. *Journal of Autism and Developmental Disorders, 25,* 1-18.

Hauck, M., Fein, D., Waterhouse, L., & Feinstein, C. (1995). Social initiations by autistic children to adults and other children. *Journal of Autism and Developmental Disorders, 25,* 579-595.

Haughton, E.C. (1980). Practicing practices: Learning by activity. *The Behavior Analyst, 1,* 3-20.

Hawkins, R.P., Peterson, R.F., Schweid, E., & Bijou, S. (1966). Behavior therapy in the home: Amelioration of problem parent-child relations with the parent in a therapeutic role. *Journal of Experimental Child Psychology, 4,* 99-107.

Hemsley, R., Howlin, P., Berger, M., Hersov, L., Holbrook, D., Rutter, M., & Yule, W. (1978). Treating autistic children in a family context. In M. Rutter & E. Schopler (Eds.), *Autism: A reappraisal of concepts and treatment* (pp. 379-411). New York: Plenum Press.

Henry, J. (1966). Personality and aging—with special reference to hospitals for the aged poor. In J.C. McKinney & F.T. DeVyver (Eds.), *Aging and social policy* (pp. 281-301). New York: Meredith.

Henry, J. (1967). My life with families of psychotic children. In G. Handel (Ed.), *The psychosocial interior of the family: A sourcebook for the study of whole families* (pp. 30-46). Chicago: Aldine.

Herrnstein, R.J. (1961). Relative and absolute strength of response as a function of frequency of reinforcement. *Journal of the Experimental Analysis of Behavior, 4,* 267-272

Hewett, F.M. (1965). Teaching speech to an autistic child through operant conditioning. *American Journal of Orthopsychiatry, 35,* 927-936.

Hill, B.K., & Bruininks, R.H. (1984). Maladaptive behavior of mentally retarded individuals in residential settings. *American Journal of Mental Deficiency, 88,* 380-387.

Hingtgen, J.N., Coulter, S.K., & Churchill, D.W. (1967). Intensive reinforcement of imitative behavior in mute autistic children. *Archives of General Psychiatry, 17,* 36-43.

Hittner, J.B. (1994). Case study: The combined use of imipramine and behavior modification to reduce aggression in an adult male diagnosed as having autistic disorder. *Behavioral Interventions, 9, 123-139.*

Holmes, D.L. (1998). *Autism through the*

lifespan: The Eden model. Bethesda, MD: Woodbine House.

Homans, G.C. (1961). *Social behavior: Its elementary forms.* New York: Harcourt, Brace & World.

Homme, L. (1967). *A behavior technology exists—here and now.* Paper presented at the Aerospace Education Foundation's "Education for the 1970s" Seminar, Washington, DC.

Howlin, P., & Rutter, M. (1987). *Treatment of autistic children.* Chichester, England: Wiley.

Howard, O. (1970). *Teaching a class of parents as reinforcement therapists to treat their own children.* Paper presented at the annual meeting of the Southeastern Psychological Association, Louisville, KY.

Hoyson, M., Jamieson, B., & Strain, P.S. (1984). Individualized group instruction of normally developing and autistic-like children: A description and evaluation of the LEAP curriculum model. *Journal of the Division of Early Childhood, 8,* 157-171.

Hudson, E., & DeMyer, M.K. (1968). Food as a reinforcer in educational therapy of autistic children. *Behaviour Research and Therapy, 6,* 37-43.

Hunt, P., & Goetz, L. (1988). Teaching spontaneous communication in natural settings through interrupted behavior chains. *Topics in Language Disorders, 9*(1), 58-71.

Hutt, C. (1967). Effects of stimulus novelty on manipulatory exploration in an infant. *Journal of Child Psychology and Psychiatry and Allied Disciplines, 8,* 3-4, 241-247.

Hutt, S.J., Hutt, C., Lee, D., & Ounsted, C. (1964). Stereotypy, arousal, and autism. *Nature, 204,* 908-909.

Hutt, S.J., & Ounsted, C. (1966). The biological significance of gaze aversion with particular reference to the syndrome of childhood autism. *Behavioral Science, 11*(6), 346-356.

Huynen, K.B., Lutzker, J.R., Bigelow, K.M.,

Touchette, P.E., & Campbell, R.V. (1996). Planned activity training for mothers of children with developmental disabilities. *Behavior Modification, 20,* 406-427.

Ilg, F.F., & Ames, L.B. (1955). *Child behavior.* New York: Harper & Row.

Jennings, S.E. (1990). *Understanding differences in families with developmentally disabled children: A stress and coping approach.* Unpublished doctoral dissertation. Boston University, Boston, MA.

Johnson, K.R., & Layng, T.V.J. (1992). Breaking the structuralist barrier: Literacy and numeracy with fluency. *American Psychologist, 47,* 1475-1490.

Johnson, K.R., & Layng, T.V.J. (1996). On terms and procedures: Fluency. *The Behavior Analyst, 19,* 281-288.

Jones, E.E., & Gerard, H.B. (1967). *Foundations of social psychology.* New York: John Wiley & Sons.

Jones, O.H.M. (1977). Mother-child communication with pre-linguistic Down's syndrome and normal infants. In H.R. Schaffer (Ed.), *Studies in mother-infant interaction* (pp. 379-401). New York: Academic Press.

Jones, O.M.H. (1980). Prelinguistic communication skills in Down's syndrome and normal infants. In T.M. Fields, S. Goldberg, D. Stern, & A.M. Sostek (Eds.), *High-risk infants and children* (pp. 205-255). New York: Academic Press.

Jones, R.N., McDonnell, J.J., & Houlihan, D.D. (1994). The generalized control of excessive behaviors. *Behavioral Interventions, 9,* 177-190.

Jordon, J.B., & Robbins, L.S. (1971). *Let's try doing something else kind of thing.* Arlington, VA: Council for Exceptional Children.

Kallmann, F.J. (1946). The genetic theory of schizophrenia. *Archives of Neurology and Psychiatry, November,* 309-322.

Kallmann, F.J., & Roth, B. (1956). Genetic aspects of preadolescent schizophrenia. *American Journal of Psychiatry, 112,* 599-606.

Kanner, L. (1943). Autistic disturbances of affective contact. *Nervous Child, 2,* 217-250.

Kanner, L. (1948). *Child psychiatry* (2nd ed.). Springfield, IL: Charles C. Thomas.

Kanner, L., & Eisenberg, L. (1955). Notes on the follow-up studies of autistic children. In P.H. Hoch & J. Zubin (Eds.), *Psychopathology of childhood* (pp. 227-239). New York: Grune & Stratton.

Kaufman, K. (1977). New directions in comprehensive programming for parents of autistic children. In *Proceedings of the Annual Meeting and Conference of the National Society for Autistic Children.* Albany, NY: National Society for Autistic Children.

Kaufman, K.F., Prinz, R.J., Bakalor, J., Tyson, R., & Paradise, B. (1978, November). *Comprehensive training for parents of autistic children: A controlled comparison study.* Presented at the Association for the Advancement of Behavior Therapy.

Kaufman, K. (1976). Teaching parents to teach their children: The behavior modification approach. In B. Feingold & C. Banks (Eds.), *Developmental disabilities of early childhood.* Springfield, IL: Charles C Thomas.

Kennedy, C.H., & Shulka, S. (1995). Social interaction research for people with autism as a set of past, current, and emerging propositions. *Behavior Disorders, 21,* 21-35.

Kety, S.S. (1959). Biochemical theories of schizophrenia. *Science, 129,* 1528-1532, 1590-1596.

Kinsbourne, M. (1987). Cerebral-brainstem relations in infantile autism. In E. Schopler & G. Mesibov (Eds.), *Neurobiological issues in autism* (pp. 107-125). New York: Plenum Press.

Koegel, R.L., Schreibman, L., Good, A., Cerniglia, L., Murphy, C., & Koegel, L.K. (1989). *How to teach pivotal behaviors to children with autism: A training manual.* Santa Barbara: University of California at Santa Barbara.

Koegel, L.K., Koegel, R.L., Hurley, C., & Frae, W.D. (1992). Improving social skills and disruptive behavior in children with autism through self-management. *Journal of Applied Behavior Analysis, 25,* 341-353.

Koegel, R.L., Bimbela, A., & Schreibman, L. (1996). Collateral effects of parent training on family interactions. *Journal of Autism and Developmental Disorders, 26,* 3, 347-359.

Koegel, R.L., & Johnson, J. (1989). Motivating language use in autistic children. In G. Dawson (Ed.), *Autism: Nature, diagnosis, and treatment* (pp. 310-325). New York: Guilford Press.

Koegel, R.L., & Koegel, L.K. (1996). *Teaching children with autism: Strategies for initiating positive interactions and improving learning opportunities.* Baltimore, MD: Paul H. Brookes.

Koegel, R.L., Rincover, A., & Egel, A.L. (1982). *Educating and understanding autistic children.* San Diego, CA: College-Hill Press.

Kogan, K.L., Tylor, N., & Turner, P. (1974). The process of interpersonal adaptation between mothers and their cerebral palsied children. *Developmental Medicine and Child Neurology, 16,* 518-527.

Kozloff, M.A. (1974). *Educating children with learning and behavior problems.* New York: John Wiley & Sons.

Kozloff, M.A. (1979). *A program for families of children with learning and behavior problems.* New York: John Wiley & Sons.

Kozloff, M.A. (1988). *Productive interaction with students, children, and clients.* Springfield, IL: Charles C Thomas.

Kozloff, M.A. (1994a). *Improving educational outcomes for children with disabilities: Principles for assessment, program planning, and evaluation.* Baltimore, MD: Paul H. Brookes.

Kozloff, M.A. (1994b). *Improving educational outcomes for children with disabilities: Guidelines and protocols for practice*. Baltimore, MD: Paul H. Brookes.

Kozloff, M.A., Helm, D.T., Cutler, B.C., Douglas-Steele, D., Wells, A., & Scampini, L. (1988). Training programs for families of children with autism or other handicaps. In R.D. Peters & R.J. McMahon (Eds.), *Social learning and systems approaches to marriage and the family* (pp. 217-250). New York: Brunner/Mazel.

Kringlen, E. (1970). Schizophrenia in twins: An epidemiological-clinical study. In H. Wechler, L. Solomon, & B.M. Kramer *(Eds.), Social psychology and mental health* (pp. 272-286). New York: Holt, Rinehart & Winston.

Kunzelmann, H.P. (1970). *Precision teaching: An initial training sequence*. Seattle, WA: Special Child Publications.

Laski, K.E., Charlop, M.H., & Schreibman, L. (1988). Training parents to use the Natural Language Paradigm to increase their autistic children's speech. *Journal of Applied Behavior Analysis, 21*, 391-400.

Laufer, M.W., & Gair, D.S. (1969). Childhood schizophrenia. In L. Bellak & L. Loeb (Eds.), *The schizophrenic syndrome* (pp. 378-461). New York: Grune & Stratton.

LaVigna, G.W., & Donnellan, A.M. (1986). *Alternatives to punishment: Solving behavior problems with non-aversive strategies*. New York: Irvington.

Leff, R. (1968). Behavior modification and the psychoses of childhood: A review. *Psychological Bulletin, 69,* 396-409.

Lerman, D.C., Iwata, B.A., Shore, B.A., & DeLeon, I.G. (1997). Effect of intermittent punishment on self-injurious behavior: An evaluation of schedule thinning. *Journal of Applied Behavior Analysis, 30*, 187-201.

Levitt, E.E. (1957). The results of psychotherapy with children: An evaluation. *Journal of Consulting Psychology, 21,* 189-196.

Levitt, E.E. (1963). Psychotherapy with children: A further evaluation. *Behaviour Research and Therapy, 1,* 45-51.

Lewis, M.H. (1996). Brief report: Psychopharmacology of autism spectrum disorders. *Journal of Autism and Developmental Disorders, 26*, 231-235

Lewis, V., & Boucher, J. (1995). Generativity in the play of young people with autism. *Journal of Autism and Developmental Disorders, 25*, 105-121.

Lichstein, K.L., & Schreibman, L. (1976). Employing electric shock with autistic children: A review of the side effects. *Journal of Autism and Childhood Schizophrenia, 6*, 163-173.

Lindsley, O.R. (1956). Operant conditioning methods applied to research in chronic schizophrenia. *Psychiatric Research Reports, 5,* 118-139.

Lindsley, O.R. (1964). Direct measurement and prosthesis of retarded behavior. *Journal of Education, 147,* 62-81.

Lindsley, O.R. (1966). An experiment with parents handling behavior at home. *Johnstone Bulletin, 9,* 27-36.

Lindsley, O.R. (1990). Precision teaching: By teachers for children. *Teaching Exceptional Children, Spring,* 10-15.

Lindsley, O.R. (1992). Precision teaching: Discoveries and effects. *Journal of Applied Behavior Analysis, 25,* 51-57.

Lindsley, O.R. (1996). Is fluency free-operant response-response chaining? *The Behavior Analyst, 19,* 211-224.

Linscheid, T.R., Iwata, B.A., Ricketts, R.W., Williams, D.E., & Griffin, J.C. (1990). Clinical evaluation of the Self-Injurious Behavior Inhibiting System (SIBIS). *Journal of Applied Behavior Analysis, 23,* 53-78.

Lord, C. (1993). Early social development in autism. In E. Schopler, M.E. Van Bourgondien, & M.M. Bristol (Eds.), *Preschool issues in autism* (pp. 61-94). New York: Plenum Press.

Lord, C., Bristol, M., & Schopler, E. (1993). Early intervention for children with autism and related developmental disorders. In E. Schopler, M.E. Van Bourgondien, & M.M. Bristol (Eds.), *Preschool issues in autism* (pp. 199-221). New York: Plenum Press.

Lotter, V. (1966). Epidemiology of autistic conditions in young children—Part 1: Prevalence. *Social Psychiatry, 1*(3), 124-137.

Lotter, V. (1967). Epidemiology of autistic conditions in young children—Part 2: Some characteristics of the parents and children. *Social Psychiatry, 1*(4), 163-173.

Lotter, V. (1974). Factors related to outcome in autistic children. *Journal of Autism and Childhood Schizophrenia, 4*, 263-277.

Lovaas, O.I. (1966a). Acquisition of imitative speech by psychotic children. *Science, 151*(11), 705-707.

Lovaas, O.I. (1966b). A program for the establishment of speech in psychotic children. In J.K. Wing (Ed.), *Early childhood autism* (pp. 115-144). London: Pergamon Press.

Lovaas, O.I. (1967). A behavior therapy approach to the treatment of childhood schizophrenia. In J. Hill (Ed.), *Minnesota symposium on child psychology*. Minneapolis: University of Minnesota Press.

Lovaas, O.I. (1968). Some studies on the treatment of childhood schizophrenia. In J.M. Shlien (Ed.), *Research in psychotherapy: Vol. III* (pp. 103-122). Washington, D. C.: American Psychological Association.

Lovaas, O.I. (1977). *The autistic child: Language development through behavior modification*. New York: Irvington.

Lovaas, O.I. (1987). Behavioral treatment and normal educational and intellectual functioning of young autistic children. *Journal of Consulting and Clinical Psychology, 55*, 3-9.

Lovaas, O.I., Freitag, G., Gold, V., & Kassorla, I. (1965). Experimental studies in childhood schizophrenia: Analysis of self-destructive behavior. *Journal of Experimental Child Psychology, 2*, 67-84.

Lovaas, O.I., Freitas, L., Nelson, K., & Whalen, C. (1967). The establishment of imitation and its use for the development of complex behavior in schizophrenic children. *Behaviour Research and Therapy, 5*, 171-181.

Lovaas, O.I., & Kassorla, I. (1966). *Reinforcement control of psychotic speech in an autistic child*. Unpublished manuscript.

Luiselli, J.K., Suskin, L., & Slocumb, P.R. (1984). Application of immobilization time-out in management programming with developmentally disabled children. *Child and Family Behavior Therapy, 6*, 1-15.

Luria, A.R., & Yudovich, F.I. (1968). *Speech and the development of mental processes in the child*. London: Staples Press.

Marcus, L.M., & Schopler, E. (1989). Parents as co-therapists with autistic children. In C.E. Schaefer & J.M. Briesmeister (Eds.), *Handbook of parent training: Parents as co-therapists for children's behavior problems* (pp. 337-360). New York: John Wiley & Sons.

Martens, B.K., & Hiralall, A.S. (1997). Scripted sequences of teacher interaction: A versatile, low-impact procedure for increasing appropriate behavior in a nursery school. *Behavior Modification, 21*, 308-323.

Mattaini, M.A. (1996). Envisioning cultural practices. *The Behavior Analyst, 19*, 257-272.

Maurice, C., Green, G., & Luce, S.C. (1996). *Behavioral intervention for young children with autism*. Austin, TX: Pro-Ed.

McDowell, J.J. (1988). Matching theory in natural human environments. *The Behavior Analyst, 11*, 95-109.

McEachlin, J.J., Smith, T., & Lovaas, O.I. (1993). Long-term outcome for children with autism who received early intensive behavioral treatment. *American Journal on Mental Retardation, 97*, 359-372.

McGonigle, M.M., Smith, T. W., Benjamin, L.S., & Turner, C.W. (1993). Hostility and nonshared family environment: A study of monozygotic twins. *Journal of Research in Personality, 27*(1), 23-34.

McWilliams, R., Nietupski, J., & Hamre-Nietupski, S. (1990). Teaching complex activities to students with moderate handicaps through the forward chaining of shorter total cycle response sequences. *Education and Training in Mental Retardation, 25*(3), 292-298.

Mesibov, G.B. (1983). Current perspectives and issues in autism and adolescence. In E. Schopler & G.B. Mesibov (Eds.), *Autism in adolescents and adults* (pp. 37-53). New York: Plenum Press.

Metz, J.R. (1965). Conditioning generalized imitation in autistic children. *Journal of Experimental Child Psychology, 2,* 389-399.

Mill, J.S. (1949). *A system of logic.* London: Longmans, Green and Company. (First published in 1844.)

Miller, U.C., & Test, D.W. (1989). A comparison of constant time delay and most-to-least prompting in teaching laundry skills to students with moderate retardation. *Education and Training in Mental Retardation, 24*(4), 363-370.

Mira, M. (1970). Results of a behavior modification training program for parents and teachers. *Behaviour Research and Therapy, 8,* 309-311.

Mirenda, P.L., Donnellan, A.M., & Yoder, D.E. (1983). Gaze behavior: A new look at an old problem. *Journal of Autism and Developmental Disorders, 13,* 397-409.

Mischler, E.G., & Waxler, N E. (1970). Family interaction processes and schizophrenia: A review of current theories. In H. Wechler, L. Solomon, & B.M. Kramer (Eds.), *Social psychology and mental health* (pp. 235-271). New York: Holt, Rinehart and Winston.

Mosher, L.R., Feinsilver, D., Katz, M.M., & Wienckowski, L.A. (1970, April). *Special report on schizophrenia.* U.S. Department of Health, Education and Welfare.

Mundschenk, N.A., & Sasso, G.M. (1995).

Assessing sufficient social exemplars for students with autism. *Behavioral Disorders, 21,* 62-78.

Mundy, P., & Sigman, M. (1989). Specifying the nature of social impairment in autism. In G. Dawson (Ed.), *Autism: Nature, diagnosis, and treatment* (pp. 3-21). New York: Guilford Press.

Myklebust, H.R. (1995). Verbal and nonverbal cognitive processes: A comparison of learning disability and autistic children. In E. Schopler & G. Mesibov (Eds.), *Learning and cognition in autism* (pp. 33-55). New York: Plenum Press.

Napalkov, A.V. (1962). Chains of motor conditioned reactions in pigeons. *Zh. vyssh. nervn. Deiatel, 1959,* 9, 615-630. Cited in R.T. Kelleher & L.R. Gollub, A review of positive conditioned reinforcement. *Journal of the Experimental Analysis of Behavior,* Supplement to 5(4), 561.

Naylor, J.C., & Briggs, G.E. (1963). Effect of task complexity and task organization on the relative efficiency of part and whole training methods. *Journal of Experimental Psychology, 65,* 217-224.

Neef, N.A. (1995). Pyramidal parent training by peers. *Journal of Applied Behavior Analysis, 28,* 333-337.

Newman, B., Buffington, D.M., O'Grady, M.A., McDonald, M.E., Poulson, C.L., & Hemmes, N.S. (1995). Self-management of schedule following in three teenagers with autism. *Behavioral Disorders, 20,* 190-196.

Oliver, M. (1996). *Understanding disability: From theory to practice.* New York: St. Martin's Press.

Olson, S.L. (1992). Development of conduct problems and peer rejection in preschool children: A social systems analysis. *Journal of Abnormal Child Psychology, 20*(3), 327-350.

Ornitz, E.M., & Ritvo, E.R. (1968). Neurophysiological mechanisms underlying perceptual inconstancy in autistic and schizophrenic children. *Archives of General Psychiatry, 19*(1), 22-27.

Ornitz, E.M., & Ritvo, E.R. (1969). Perceptual inconstancy in early infantile autism. In S. Chess & A. Thomas (Eds.), *Annual progress in child psychiatry and child development: 1969* (pp. 411-446). New York: Brunner/Mazel, Inc.

Ornitz, E.M. (1989). Autism at the interface between sensory and information processing. In G. Dawson (Ed.), *Autism: Nature, diagnosis, and treatment* (pp. 174-207). New York: Guilford Press.

Pace, G.M., Iwata, B.A., Edwards, G.L., & McCosh, K.C. (1986). Stimulus fading and transfer of treatment of self-restraint and self-injurious behaviors. *Journal of Applied Behavior Analysis, 19,* 381-389.

Paisey, T.J.H., Whitney, R.B., & Hislop, P.M. (1990). Client characteristics and treatment selection: Legitimate influences and misleading inferences. In A.C. Repp & N.N. Singh (Eds.), *Perspectives on the use of nonaversive and aversive interventions for persons with developmental disabilities* (pp. 175-197). Sycamore, IL: Sycamore Publishing Co.

Patterson, G.R. (1982). *Coercive family processes.* Eugene, OR: Castaglia.

Patterson, G.R., & Brodsky, G. (1966). A behavior modification programme for a child with multiple problem behaviors. *Journal of Child Psychology and Psychiatry, 7,* 277-295.

Patterson, G.R., & Gullion, M.E. (1968). *Living with children: New methods for parents and teachers.* Champaign, IL: Research Press.

Patterson, G.R., McNeal, S.M., Hawkins, N., & Phelps, R. (1967). Reprogramming the social environment. *Journal of Child Psychology and Psychiatry, 8,* 181-195.

Patterson, G.R., & Reid, J.B. (1970). Reciprocity and coercion: Two facets of social systems. In J. Michaels & C. Neuringer (Eds.), *Behavior modification in clinical psychology* (pp. 133-177). New York: Appleton-Century-Crofts.

Patterson, G.R., & Reid, J.B. (1984). Social interaction processes within the family: The study of the moment-by-moment family transactions in which human development is embedded. *Journal of Applied Developmental Psychology, 5,* 237-262.

Patterson, G.R., Reid, J.B., & Dishion, T.J. (1989). *Antisocial boys.* Eugene, OR: Cataglia.

Pavlov, I.P. (1927). *Conditioned reflexes.* Oxford, UK: Oxford University Press.

Peck, H.B., Rabinovitch, R.D., & Cramer, J.B. (1949). A treatment program for parents of schizophrenic children. *American Journal of Orthopsychiatry, 19,* 592-598.

Peine, H.A. (1971). *Effects of training models on the modification of parent behavior.* Unpublished manuscript, Department of Psychology, Western Michigan University.

Pfeiffer, S.I., Norton, J., Nelson, L., & Shott, S. (1995). Efficacy of vitamin B6 and magnesium in the treatment of autism: A methodology review and summary of outcomes. *Journal of Autism and Developmental Disorders, 25,* 481ff.

Piazza, C.C., Fisher, W.W., Hanley, G.P., Remick, M.L., Contrucci, S.A., & Aitken, T.L. (1997). The use of positive and negative reinforcement in the treatment of escape-maintained destructive behavior. *Journal of Applied Behavior Analysis, 30,* 279-298.

Piaget, J. (1954). *The construction of reality in the child.* New York: Basic Books.

Plaud, J.J., & Gaither, G.A. (1996). Behavioral momentum: Implications and development from reinforcement theories. *Behavior Modification, 2,* 183-201.

Premack, D. (1965). Reinforcement theory. In D. Levine (Ed.), *Nebraska symposium on motivation* (pp. 123-180). Lincoln, NE: University of Nebraska Press.

Prizant, B.M. (1996). Brief report: Communication, language, social, and emotional development. *Journal of Autism and Developmental Disorders, 26,* 173-178.

Prizant, B.M., & Wetherby, A.M. (1989). Enhancing language and communication in autism. In G. Dawson (Ed.), *Autism: Nature, diagnosis, and treatment* (pp. 282-309). New York: Guilford Press.

Prizant, B.M., & Wetherby, A.M. (1993). Communication in preschool autistic children. In E. Schopler, M.E. Van Bourgondien, & M.M. Bristol (Eds.), *Preschool issues in autism* (pp. 95-128). New York: Plenum Press.

Quintana, H., Birmaher, B., Stedge, D., Lennon, S., Freed, J., Bridge, J., & Greenhill, L. (1995). *Journal of Autism and Developmental Disorders, 25,* 283-294.

Rast, J., Johnson, J., Drum, C., & Cronin, J. (1981). The relation of food quantity to rumination behavior. *Journal of Applied Behavior Analysis, 14,* 121-130.

Reichler, R.J., & Lee, E.M.C. (1987). Overview of biomedical issues in autism. In E. Schopler & G. Mesibov (Eds.), *Neurobiological issues in autism* (pp. 13-41). New York: Plenum Press.

Reid, J.B., Hawkins, N., Keutzer, C., McNeal, S.A., Phelps, R.E., Reid, K.M., & Mees, H.L. (1967). A marathon behaviour modification of a selectively mute child. *Journal of Child Psychology and Psychiatry, 8,* 27-30.

Repp, A.C., & Singh, N.N. (Eds.) (1990). *Perspectives on the use of nonaversive and aversive interventions for persons with developmental disabilities.* Sycamore, IL: Sycamore Publishing.

Rice, H.K., & McDaniel, M.W. (1966). Operant behavior in vegetative patients. *Psychological Record, 16,* 279-281.

Rimland, B. (1964). *Infantile autism.* New York: Appleton-Century-Crofts.

Rimland, B. (1968). On the objective diagnosis of infantile autism. *Acta Paedopsychiatrica* (Basel), *35,* 146-161.

Rimland, B. (1969). Psychogenesis versus biogenesis: The issues and the evidence. In S.C. Plog & R.E. Edgerton (Eds.), *Changing perspectives in mental illness* (pp. 702-735). New York: Holt, Rinehart and Winston.

Rimland, B. (1997, October). *Historical perspectives and techniques that work.* Presented at the International Symposium on Autism, Illinois Center for Autism, McKendry College, Lebanon, IL.

Ringdahl, J.E., Vollmer, T.R., Marcus, B.A., & Roane, H.S. (1997). An analogue evaluation of environmental enrichment: The role of stimulus preference. *Journal of Applied Behavior Analysis, 30,* 203-216.

Risley, T.R. (1968). The effects and side effects of punishing the autistic behaviors of a deviant child. *Journal of Applied Behavior Analysis, 1*(Spring), 21-35.

Risley, T.R., & Wolf, M.M. (1966). Experimental manipulation of autistic behavior and generalization into the home. In R. Ulrich, T. Stachnik, & J. Mabry (Eds.), *Control of human behavior* (pp. 193-199). Glenview, IL: Scott, Foresman & Co.

Risley, T.R., & Wolf, M.M. (1967). Establishing functional speech in echolalic children. *Behaviour Research and Therapy, 5,* 73-88.

Ritvo, E.R., Ornitz, E.M., & LaFranchi, S. (1968). Frequency of repetitive behaviors in early infantile autism and its variants. *Archives of General Psychiatry, 19*(3), 341-347.

Rogers, S.J. (1996). Brief report: Early intervention in autism. *Journal of Autism and Developmental Disorders, 26,* 243-246.

Rogers, S.J., & DiLalla, D.L. (1991). A comparative study of the effects of a developmentally based preschool curriculum on young children with autism and young children with other disorders of behavior development. *Topics in Early Childhood Special Education, 11,* 29-47.

Rogers, S.J., & Lewis, H.C. (1989). An effective day treatment model for young children with pervasive developmental disorders. *Journal of the American Academy of Child and Adolescent Psychiatry, 28,* 207-214.

Rolider, A., & Van Houten, R. (1990). The role of reinforcement in reducing inappropriate behavior: Some myths and misconceptions. In A.C. Repp & N.N. Singh (Eds.), *Perspectives on the use of nonaversive and aversive interventions for persons with developmental disabilities* (pp. 119-127). Sycamore, IL: Sycamore Publishing Company.

Russo, D.C., Cataldo, M.F., & Cushing, P.J. (1981). Compliance training and behavioral covariation in the treatment of multiple behavior problems. *Journal of Applied Behavior Analysis, 14,* 209-222.

Russo, S. (1964). Adaptations of behavioral therapy with children. *Behaviour Research and Therapy, 2,* 43-47.

Rutter, M. (1965). Medical aspects of the education of psychotic (autistic) children. In P.T.B. Westen (Ed.), *Some approaches to teaching autistic children* (pp. 61-74). Oxford, UK: Pergamon Press.

Rutter, M. (1969). Concepts of autism: A review of the research. In S. Chess & A. Thomas (Eds.), *Annual progress in child psychiatry and child development: 1969* (pp. 379-410). New York: Brunner/Mazel, Inc.

Rutter, M. (1978). Diagnosis and definition. In M. Rutter & E. Schopler (Eds.), *Autism: A reappraisal of concepts and treatment* (pp. 1-25). New York: Plenum Press.

Rutter, M. (1983). Cognitive deficits in the pathogenesis of autism. *Journal of Child Psychology and Psychiatry, 24,* 513-531.

Rutter, M. (1996). Autism research: Prospects and priorities. *Journal of Autism and Developmental Disorders, 26,* 257-275.

Rutter, M., & Bartak, L. (1971). Causes of infantile autism: Some considerations from recent research. *Journal of Autism and Childhood Schizophrenia, 1*(1), 20-32.

Rutter, M., Bartak, L., & Newman, S. (1971) Autism: A central disorder of cognition and language? In M. Rutter (Ed.), *Infantile autism: Concepts, characteristics and treatment* (pp. 148-171). London: Churchill.

Rutter, M., Greenfeld, D., & Lockyer, L.

(1967). A five to fifteen year follow-up study of infantile psychosis. *British Journal of Psychiatry, 113,* 1183-1199.

Schaffer, H.R. (1984). *The child's entry into a social world.* London: Academic Press.

Schaffer, H.R., Collis, G.M., & Parsons, G. (1977). Vocal interchange and visual regard in verbal and pre-verbal children. In H.R. Schaffer (Ed.), *Studies in mother-infant interaction* (pp. 291-324). New York: Academic Press.

Schell, R.E., & Adams, W.P. (1968). Training parents of a young child with profound behavior deficits to be teacher-therapists. *Journal of Special Education, 2*(4), 439-454.

Schlinger, H.D., & Blakely, E. (1994). A descriptive taxonomy of environmental operations and its implications for behavior analysis. *The Behavior Analyst, 17,* 43-57.

Schindler, F., & Arkowitz, H. (1986). The assessment of mother-child interactions in physically abusive and nonabusive families. *Journal of Family Violence, 1*(3), 247-257.

Schoen, S.F., & Ogden, S. (1995). Impact of time delay, observational learning, and attentional cuing upon word recognition during integrated small-group instruction. *Journal of Autism and Developmental Disorders, 25,* 503-519.

Schopler, E. (1969, September). *Parents of psychotic children as scapegoats.* Paper presented at the Symposium of the American Psychological Association, Washington, DC.

Schopler, E. (1995). *Parent survival manual.* New York: Plenum Press.

Schopler, E., Lansing, M., & Waters, L. (1983). *Individualized assessment and treatment for autistic and developmentally disabled children: Volume 3. Teaching activities for autistic children.* Austin, TX: Pro-Ed.

Schopler, E., & Loftin, J. (1969). Thinking disorders in parents of young psychotic children. *Journal of Abnormal Psychology, 74*, 3281-3287.

Schopler, E., & Reichler, R.J. (1971). Parents as cotherapists in the treatment of psychotic children. *Journal of Autism and Childhood Schizophrenia, 1*(1), 87-102.

Schopler, E., & Mesibov, G. (1995). Introduction to learning and cognition in autism. In E. Schopler & G. Mesibov (Eds.), *Learning and cognition in autism* (pp. 3-11). New York: Plenum.

Schreibman, L., Koegel, R.L., Mills, D.L., & Burke, J.C. (1984). Training parent-child interactions. In E. Schopler & G. Mesibov (Eds.), *The effects of autism on the family* (pp. 187-205). New York: Plenum Press.

Schroeder, S.R., & LeBlanc, J.M. (1996). Brief report: A life-span perspective on the development of individuals with autism. *Journal of Autism and Developmental Disorders, 26*, 251-255.

Schuham, A.I. (1967). The double-bind hypothesis a decade later. *Psychological Bulletin, 68*, 409-416.

Schwartz, D.B. (1992). *Crossing the river: Creating a conceptual revolution in community and disability*. Cambridge, MA: Brookline Books.

Sears, R.R., Maccoby, E.R., & Levin, H. (1957). *Patterns of child rearing*. New York: Harper.

Shodell, M.J., & Reiter, H.H. (1968). Self-mutilative behavior in verbal and nonverbal schizophrenic children. *Archives of General Psychiatry, 19*, 4, 453-455.

Sidman, M. (1960). *Tactics of scientific research*. New York: Basic Books.

Sigafoos, J., & Meikle, B. (1996). Functional communication training for the treatment of multiply determined challenging behavior in two boys with autism. *Behavior Modification, 20*, 60-84.

Silliman, E.R., Campbell, M., & Mitchell, R.S. (1989). Genetic influences in autism and assessment of metalinguistic performance in siblings of autistic children. In

G. Dawson (Ed.), *Autism: Nature, diagnosis, and treatment* (pp. 225-259). New York: Guilford Press.

Simmel, G. (1971). *On individuality and social forms*. Chicago: University of Chicago Press.

Singh, N.N., Watson, J.E., & Winton, A.S. (1986). Treating self-injury: Water mist versus facial screening or forced arm exercise. *Journal of Applied Behavior Analysis, 19*, 403-410.

Slater, E. (1953). *Psychotic and neurotic illnesses in twins*. London: H.M. Stationery Office.

Sloane, H.N., Jr., & MacAulay, B.D. (1968). *Operant procedures in remedial speech and language training*. Boston: Houghton Mifflin Co.

Smith, J.M., & Smith, D.E.P. (1966). *Child management: A program for parents*. Ann Arbor, MI: Ann Arbor.

Smith, T., Eikeseth, S., Klevstrand, M., & Lovaas, O.I. (1997). Intensive behavioral treatment for preschoolers with severe mental retardation and pervasive developmental disorder. *American Journal on Mental Retardation, 102*(3), 238-249.

Sobsey, D. (1994). *Violence and abuse in the lives of people with disabilities*. Baltimore: Paul H. Brookes.

Spitz, R.A. (1945). Hospitalism: An inquiry into the genesis of psychiatric conditions in early childhood. *Psychoanalytic Study of the Child, 1*, 53-74.

Stahmer, A.C. (1995). Teaching symbolic play skills to children with autism using pivotal response training. *Journal of Autism and Developmental Disorders, 25*, 123-141.

Stahmer, A.C., & Schreibman, L. (1992). Teaching children with autism appropriate play in unsupervised environments using a self-management treatment package. *Journal of Applied Behavior Analysis, 25*, 447-459.

Stowitschek, J.J., McConaughy, E.K., Peatross, D., Salzberg, C.L., & Lignugaris/ Kraft, B. (1988). Effects of group incidental training on the use of social amenities by adults with mental retardation in work settings. *Education and Training in Mental Retardation, 23*(3), 202-212.

Straasberg, Z., Dodge, K.A., Bates, J.E., & Pettit, G.S. (1992). The longitudinal relation between parental conflict strategies and children's sociometric standing in kindergarten. *Merrill-Palmer Quarterly, 38*(4), 477-493.

Straughan, J.H. (1964). Treatment with child and mother in the playroom. *Behaviour Research and Therapy, 2,* 37-41.

Tager-Flusberg, H. (1989). A psycholinguistic perspective on language development in the autistic child. In G. Dawson (Ed.), *Autism: Nature, diagnosis, and treatment* (pp. 92-115). New York: Guilford Press.

Thompson, G.G. (1962). *Child psychology: Growth trends in psychological adjustment.* Boston: Houghton Mifflin.

Tilton, J.R., & Ottinger, D.R. (1964). Comparison of the toy play behavior of autistic, retarded, and normal children. *Psychological Reports, 15,* 967-975.

Tobias, M. (1959). The disturbed child—A concept: Usefulness of Deanol in management. *Amer. Practit. Dig. Treat.,* 10, 1759-1766.

Touchette, P.E., & Howard, J.S. (1984). Errorless learning: Reinforcement contingencies and stimulus control transfer in delayed prompting. *Journal of Applied Behavior Analysis, 17,* 175-188.

Trachtenberg, W., & Goldblatt, M. (1968). *From mutism to conversational language in autism using operant conditioning in an out patient clinic.* Paper read at the annual convention of the American Speech and Hearing Association.

Trevarthen, C. (1977). Descriptive analysis of infant communicative behavior. In H.R. Schaffer (Ed.), *Studies in mother-infant interaction* (pp. 227-270). New York: Academic Press.

Turnbull, A.P., & Turnbull, J.A. (1990).

Families, professionals, and exceptionality: A special partnership. Columbus, OH: Merrill.

Ullmann, L.P., & Krasner, L. (1965). *Case studies in behavior modification.* New York: Holt, Rinehart and Winston.

Ulrich, R., Stachnik, T., & Mabry, J. (1966). *Control of human behavior.* Glenview, IL: Scott, Foresman and Co.

Valsiner, J. (1987). *Culture and the development of children's action.* New York: John Wiley & Sons.

van de Rijt–Plooij, H.H.C., & Plooij, F.X. (1993). Distinct periods of mother-infant conflict in normal development: Sources of progress and germs of pathology. *Journal of Child Psychology and Psychiatry, 34*(2), 229-245.

Volkmar, F.R., & Anderson, G.M. (1989). Neurochemical perspectives on infantile autism. In G. Dawson (Ed.), *Autism: Nature, diagnosis, and treatment* (pp. 208-224). New York: Guilford Press.

Volling, B.L., & Belsky, J. (1992). The contribution of mother-child and father-child relationships to the quality of sibling interaction: A longitudinal study. *Child Development, 63*(5), 1209-1222.

Vollmer, T.R., Northup, J., Ringdahl, J.E., LeBlanc, L.A., & Chauvin, T.M. (1996). Functional analysis of severe tantrums displayed by children with language delays. *Behavior Modification, 20,* 97-115.

Vygotsky, L. (1978). *Mind in society.* Cambridge, MA: Harvard University Press.

Wahler, R.G., Winkel, G.H., Peterson, R.F., & Morrison, D.C. (1965). Mothers as behavior therapists for their own children. *Behaviour Research and Therapy, 3,* 113-124.

Walder, L.O., Breiter, D.E., Cohen, S.I., Datson, P.G., Forbes, J.A., & McIntire, R.W. (1966). *Teaching parents to modify the behaviors of their autistic child.* Paper presented at the meeting of the American Psychological Association, New York, September 4, 1966.

Walder, L.O., Cohen S.I., Breiter, D.E.,

Datson, P.G., Hirsch, I.S., & Leibowitz, J.M. (1967). *Teaching behavioral principles to parents of disturbed children.* Paper presented at the meeting of the Eastern Psychological Association, Boston, April 6, 1967.

Walker, H.M., Colvin, G., & Ramsey, E. (1995). *Antisocial behavior in school: Strategies and best practices.* Pacific Grove, CA: Brooks/Cole.

Waterhouse, L., Wing, L., & Fein, D. (1989). Re-evaluating the syndrome of autism in the light of empirical research. In G. Dawson (Ed.), *Autism: Nature, diagnosis, and treatment* (pp. 263-281). New York: Guilford Press.

Watson, L., Lord, C., Schaffer, B., & Schopler, E. (1989). *Teaching spontaneous communication to autistic and developmentally handicapped children.* Austin, TX: Pro-Ed.

Weingarten, K., & Mechner, F. (1966). The contingency as an independent variable of social interaction. In T. Verhave (Ed.), *The experimental analysis of behavior* (pp. 447-459). New York: Appleton-Century-Crofts.

Weiss, B., Dodge, K.A., Bates, J.E., & Pettit, G.S. (1992). Some consequences of early harsh discipline: Child aggression and a maladaptive social information processing style. *Child Development, 63*(6), 1321-1335.

Weiss, S.J. (1991). Stressors experienced by family caregivers of children with pervasive developmental disorders. *Child Psychiatry and Human Development, 21*(3), 203-216.

Wener, C., Ruttenberg, B.A., Dratman, M.L., & Wolf, E.G. (1967). Changing autistic behavior: The effectiveness of three milieus. *Archives of General Psychiatry, 17*(1), 26-35.

Wilder, D.A., Draper, R., Williams, W.L., & Higbee, T.S. (1997). A comparison of noncontingent reinforcement, other competing stimulation, and liquid rescheduling for the treatment of rumination. *Behavioral Interventions, 12,* 55-64.

Williams, C.D. (1965). The elimination of tantrum behavior by extinction procedures. In L.P. Ullmann & L. Krasner (Eds.), *Case studies in behavior modification* (pp. 295-297). New York: Holt, Rinehart and Winston.

Wilton, K., & Renaut, J. (1986). Stress levels in families with intellectually handicapped preschool children and families with nonhandicapped preschool children. *Journal of Mental Deficiency Research, 30,* 163-169.

Wing, J.K. (1966). *Early childhood autism.* Oxford: Pergamon Press.

Wing, L., & Gould, L. (1979). Severe impairments of social interaction and associated abnormalities in children: Epidemiology and classification. *Journal of Autism and Developmental Disorders, 9,* 11-29.

White, O.R., & Haring, N.G. (1980). *Exceptional teaching.* Columbus, OH: Charles Merrill.

Wolery, M., Ault, M.J., Gast, D.L., Doyle, P.M., & Griffin, A.K. (1990). Comparison of constant time delay and the system of least prompts in teaching chained tasks. *Education and Training in Mental Retardation, 25*(3), 243-257.

Wolery, M., Bailey, D.B., Jr., & Sugai, G.M. (1988). *Effective teaching: Principles and procedures of applied behavior analysis with exceptional students.* Boston: Allyn and Bacon.

Wolf, M.M., Risley, T.R., & Mees, H. (1966). Application of operant conditioning procedures to the behavior problems of an autistic child. In R. Ulrich, T. Stachnik, & J. Mabry (Eds.), *Control of human behavior* (pp. 187-193). Glenview, IL: Scott, Foresman and Co.

Yates, A.J. (1958). The application of learning theory to the treatment of tics. *Journal of Abnormal and Social Psychology, 56,* 175-182.

Zeilberger, J., Sampen, S.E., & Sloane, H.N., Jr. (1968). Modification of a child's problem behavior in the home with the mother as the therapist. *Journal of Applied Behavior Analysis, 1,* 47-53.

Author
Index

About the Author

Martin A. Kozloff received his Ph.D. in Sociology (1969) from Washington University in St. Louis, Missouri. From 1967 to 1971, he was a teacher, researcher, and Director of the Autism Program—one of the first schools for children with autism that provided a comprehensive, multi-level curriculum coupled with applied behavior analysis. He continues to develop and test educational programs for children with autism and other developmental disorders, and programs for training and supporting families and teachers. His publications include *Improving educational outcomes for children with disabilities: Principles for assessment, program planning, and evaluation* (1994); *Improving educational outcomes for children with disabilities: Guidelines and protocols for practice* (1994); *Productive interaction with students, children, and clients* (1988); *A program for families of children with learning and behavior problems* (1979); and *Educating children with learning and behavior problems* (1974). He served in the Sociology Department at Boston University from 1971 to 1996. He currently teaches at the University of North Carolina at Wilmington, where, in 1997, he was awarded the Donald R. Watson Distinguished Professorship in Education.